W0230373

Pro Windows Embedded Compact 7

Producing Device Drivers

Abraham Kcholi

Pro Windows Embedded Compact 7

Copyright © 2011 by Abraham Kcholi

All rights reserved. No part of this work may be reproduced or transmitted in any form or by any means, electronic or mechanical, including photocopying, recording, or by any information storage or retrieval system, without the prior written permission of the copyright owner and the publisher.

ISBN 978-1-4302-4179-9

ISBN 978-1-4302-4180-5 (eBook)

Trademarked names, logos, and images may appear in this book. Rather than use a trademark symbol with every occurrence of a trademarked name, logo, or image we use the names, logos, and images only in an editorial fashion and to the benefit of the trademark owner, with no intention of infringement of the trademark.

The use in this publication of trade names, trademarks, service marks, and similar terms, even if they are not identified as such, is not to be taken as an expression of opinion as to whether or not they are subject to proprietary rights.

President and Publisher: Paul Manning
Lead Editor: Ewan Buckingham
Technical Reviewer: Valter Minute
Editorial Board: Steve Anglin, Mark Beckner, Ewan Buckingham, Gary Cornell, Morgan Ertel,
    Jonathan Gennick, Jonathan Hassell, Robert Hutchinson, Michelle Lowman, James Markham,
    Matthew Moodie, Jeff Olson, Jeffrey Pepper, Douglas Pundick, Ben Renow-Clarke,
    Dominic Shakeshaft, Gwenan Spearing, Matt Wade, Tom Welsh
Coordinating Editor: Jessica Belanger
Copy Editor: Lori Cavanaugh
Production Support: Patrick Cunningham
Artist: SPi Global
Indexer: BIM Indexing & Proofreading Services
Cover Designer: Anna Ishchenko

Distributed to the book trade worldwide by Springer Science+Business Media, LLC., 233 Spring Street, 6th Floor, New York, NY 10013. Phone 1-800-SPRINGER, fax (201) 348-4505, e-mail orders-ny@springer-sbm.com, or visit www.springeronline.com.

For information on translations, please e-mail rights@apress.com, or visit www.apress.com.

Apress and friends of ED books may be purchased in bulk for academic, corporate, or promotional use. eBook versions and licenses are also available for most titles. For more information, reference our Special Bulk Sales–eBook Licensing web page at www.apress.com/bulk-sales.

The information in this book is distributed on an "as is" basis, without warranty. Although every precaution has been taken in the preparation of this work, neither the author(s) nor Apress shall have any liability to any person or entity with respect to any loss or damage caused or alleged to be caused directly or indirectly by the information contained in this work.

Any source code or other supplementary materials referenced by the author in this text is available to readers at www.apress.com. For detailed information about how to locate your book's source code, go to http://www.apress.com/source-code/.

Contents at a Glance

Contents

About the Author

Abraham (Avi) Kcholi holds a B.Sc. degree in Pure Mathematics from London School of Economics. He has developed time critical systems, GIS infrastructure components, and command and control systems for military and industrial automation based on Windows CE technologies since 1998 and Windows XP Embedded technologies since 2004. Some of his projects include designing medical and GIS systems for military usage and creating the 2008 classroom materials for the SPARK initiative. Authored the preparation kit for MCTS examination 70-577 "Windows Embedded Standard 2009."

About the Technical Reviewer

Valter Minute has been working on Windows CE since 1999 (version 2.12) and spends most of his time developing drivers and BSPs. He is a trainer for Windows CE 5, 6 and 7. He also participated in the development of the official Windows Embedded Compact 7 training materials.

Valter is a Windows Embedded MVP since 2009 and has a blog about embedded computing and Italian cooking at http://geekswithblogs.net/WindowsEmbeddedCookbook.

Acknowledgments

This book is dedicated to embedded developers, especially Windows Embedded Compact developers. I had so many developers asking me for recommended reading on this subject of development for Windows CE (Windows Embedded Compact) since I started developing for the system back in 1999. Having developed BSPs and device drivers for so long and developed my own tool to help me with the development process I set out to write this book about the development process of Windows Embedded Compact device drivers, it is finally ready with much inspiration, patience, and help from my family, friends, and colleagues.

First and foremost I have to thank my wife for putting up with me while I was in the process of writing this book.

Without Sondra Weber's encouragement this might not have happened. Many thanks to Ewan Buckingham of Apress, without whom this book would not have been published. Jessica Belanger who coordinated everything and Nancy Wright, Jonathan Hassel, Lori Cavanaugh, and last but definitely not least my friend Valter Minute who reviewed the book and provided invaluable insight. A special thank you to Kay Unkroth of Microsoft, for unloading on me his know-how with regard to authoring a technical book.

Many, many thanks to Stephan Lauterbach who loaned me the TRACE 32 ICD for the chapter on debugging, and Rudi Dienstback who helped me out so kindly to understand the nuances of working with it. Special thanks to Yannick Chammings and Nicolass Besson of Adeneo for their help in migrating the Adeneo BSP for the TI OMAP 3530 to Windows Embedded Compact 7 for the development board I had on loan from Variscite. When I went through the effort of understanding the Variscite board, Ohad Yaniv and Oren Rokach of Variscite provided me with the development platform and helped me to work with it on Windows Embedded Compact 7. To anyone I've forgotten to list: my apologies. Thanks to everyone who made it possible!

Introduction

Windows Embedded Compact 7 is really the latest version of Windows CE. Books dedicated to this operating system are relatively scarce. Windows CE turned into a proper RTOS when Windows CE 3.0 was launched. A few books were published, most notably by Douglas Boling and James Wilson. The first book concentrated on application programming and was updated for new versions of the system as these appeared. The second book was a comprehensive tutorial on the creation of Windows CE based systems. Recently, books by Samuel Phung and others continue with this trend of introducing developers of embedded systems to Windows CE. However authoring a book that is dedicated to one aspect of the system wasn't challenged. Device drivers are at the core of embedded system development. Every computer system, be it a general purpose computer or an embedded computer system time critical or not, has to address three phases: data input, data manipulation, and data output. Embedded systems commonly go through all three phases without human intervention. Data input and data output have to be handled via peripheral I/O devices.

This book endeavors to usher the reader into the development process of stream interface device driver model used in Windows Embedded Compact 7 and previous versions of Windows CE. The stream interface device driver model is the most commonly used in the Windows Embedded Compact (Windows CE) operating system. There are native device drivers for user interface input and display device drivers but most device driver developers use the stream interface driver model for their development needs.

If Windows Embedded Compact operating system would have been another general purpose operating system, this book would be of interest only to device driver developers. However Windows Embedded Compact is anything but a general purpose OS. It is an embedded hard real-time operating system and therefore application developers of time critical software have to understand how to access I/O hardware. Understanding kernel mode device drivers and developing user mode interaction with these should benefit the application developers as much.

Understanding the new filter driver model of Windows Embedded Compact 7 can help application developers move code of input data filtering algorithms such as Finite Impulse Response to Fast Fourier Transformations from the user mode process to the kernel for better performance and modularity.

This book is not an introduction to Windows Embedded Compact and how to create Windows Embedded Compact 7 based operating system images. It assumes the reader already knows how to perform these tasks. Therefore it skims the surface when discussing Platform Builder and kernel debugger techniques.

At the end of the book there is a bibliography list, divided by topics to help the reader find out more about topics that may need more clarification, such as JTAG and the related "scan chains."

Who This Book Is For

This book is devoted to the development of device drivers, and as such is for experienced developers of Windows Embedded Compact 7 and previous versions of Windows CE. This book is not an introduction to Windows Embedded Compact and how to create Windows Embedded Compact 7 based operating system images. It assumes the reader already knows how to perform these tasks. Therefore it skims the surface when discussing Platform Builder and kernel debugger techniques.

CHAPTER 1

The Foundation of Device Driver Development for Windows Embedded Compact

Any discussion about device drivers should provide some perspective of what device drivers are and why we need them. Practically, a device driver is an executable piece of software dedicated to access a specific peripheral hardware device in order to control it and to perform input/output (I/O) operations. Figuratively, you can think of a device driver as a negotiator between the operating system software and the hardware it uses. To understand this analogy we need to look at how multitasking operating systems, such as Windows Embedded Compact, handle peripheral hardware devices to provide a unified generic access method for their higher-level applications and processes.

In this chapter:

- Embedded Operating System Architectures
- Windows CE System Architecture and I/O Handling

Embedded Operating System Architectures

The evolution of embedded operating systems architectures brought about the need for device drivers. This becomes clearer if you look back 30-40 years when 4-bit microprocessors appeared. At that time, embedded operating systems were simple control loops that did not include any device drivers, yet Central Processing Units (CPUs) steadily advanced to the 32-bit and even 64-bit CPUs of today. With advanced processors came multitasking capabilities, and with multitasking came the need for centralized hardware control to avoid data conflicts and chaos. Without centralized control it is difficult to synchronize hardware access between the various concurrent tasks on a multitasking operating system.

Essentially, there are two ways to implement centralized hardware control: Either the operating system provides exclusive hardware access to only one application at a time or facilitates hardware access for all its applications and processes. Both approaches can rely on device drivers to establish a single point of hardware control, but exactly how these device drivers are implemented and how the hardware is accessed depends to a large degree on the operating system architecture itself and its device driver model.

For embedded device driver developers, the two most relevant commercial operating system architectures are:

- **Microkernel Architecture** – In this architecture device drivers run in user mode, so it is possible to embed I/O handling routines directly into user-mode applications. However, this means that sharing the same peripheral I/O device with other user mode applications needs a complicated mechanism of synchronizing access to this hardware.

- **Monolithic Kernel Architecture** – In this architecture device drivers that directly access I/O hardware run in kernel mode, so user-mode applications must use device drivers to access the hardware devices. A device driver implementation can allow multiple user mode processes use the same device driver to share access to the I/O hardware.

Microkernel Architecture

In the microkernel architecture, the kernel process is the only process executing at the most privileged level provided by a CPU with multiple privilege levels. At this privileged level, usually referred to as kernel mode, code has access to the kernel address space and implements low-level address space management, thread management, and inter-process communication. All other operating system services, such as file systems, device drivers, protocol stacks, and user interface code run in user mode. User mode means that only user mode address space is available to user mode threads. User mode threads cannot perform any kernel mode calls or access kernel mode addresses. The system services must communicate with the kernel via inter-process communication mechanisms.

Microkernel Architecture and Windows CE

Windows CE up to and including version 5.0 was based on the microkernel architecture. Figure 1-1 shows Windows CE 5.0 Microkernel architecture. What's particularly important to note in this figure is that the device driver hosts (that is, GWES.exe and Device.exe) are user mode processes. Hence, all device drivers run in user mode.

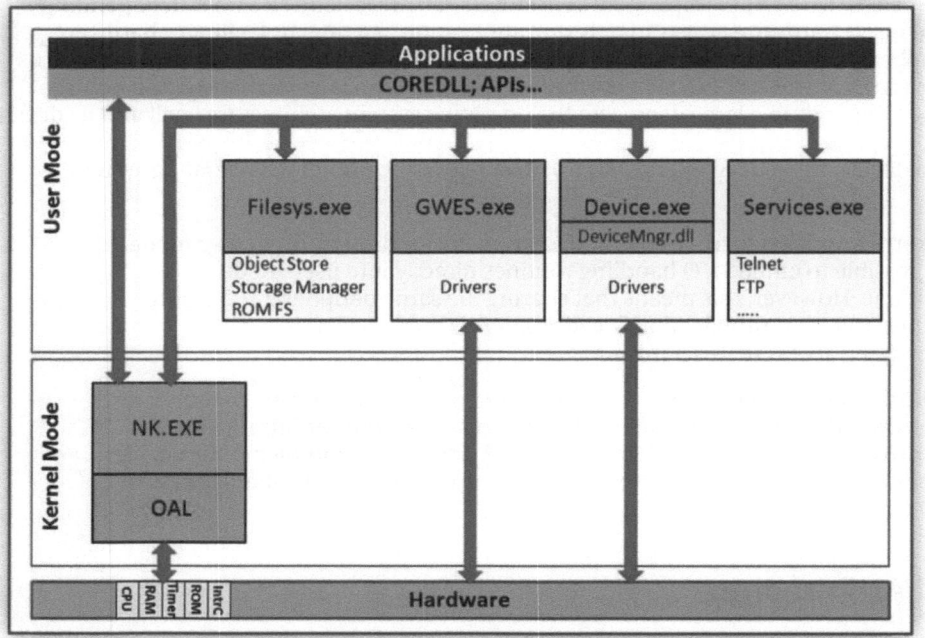

Figure 1-1. *Microkernel architecture of Windows CE 5.0*

Microkernel Architecture and Time-Critical Systems

In time-critical systems, it is sometimes worth implementing the code that accesses a peripheral device directly into the application. This method provides performance enhancements for time critical systems because I/O is handled directly by the application process. However this practice should be limited to I/O peripheral devices that are exclusively accessed by a one process and not shared with other processes. It is also important to point out that this technique is no longer valid for Windows CE developers because latest versions do not rely on the Microkernel architecture anymore.

Monolithic Architecture

In the monolithic architecture, the kernel is still the only process executing at the most privileged level provided by a CPU with multiple privilege levels. However, the system services that used to be implemented as user mode processes in the microkernel architecture now moved as dynamically linked libraries (DLLs) into the monolithic kernel. In other words, the system services now run within the kernel process, which means that most device drivers now run in kernel mode as the device driver server is now part of the kernel.

Monolithic Architecture and Windows CE

Windows Embedded CE 6.0 (henceforth Windows CE 6.0 for brevity) and later versions are based on the monolithic kernel architecture. Figure 1-2 shows the Windows CE 6.0 architecture and Windows Embedded Compact 7. What's particularly important to note in this figure is that the device driver hosts (that is, GWES.dll and DevMgr.dll) are dynamically linked libraries themselves. Componentization is still available to the designer who may add or remove system services as needed.

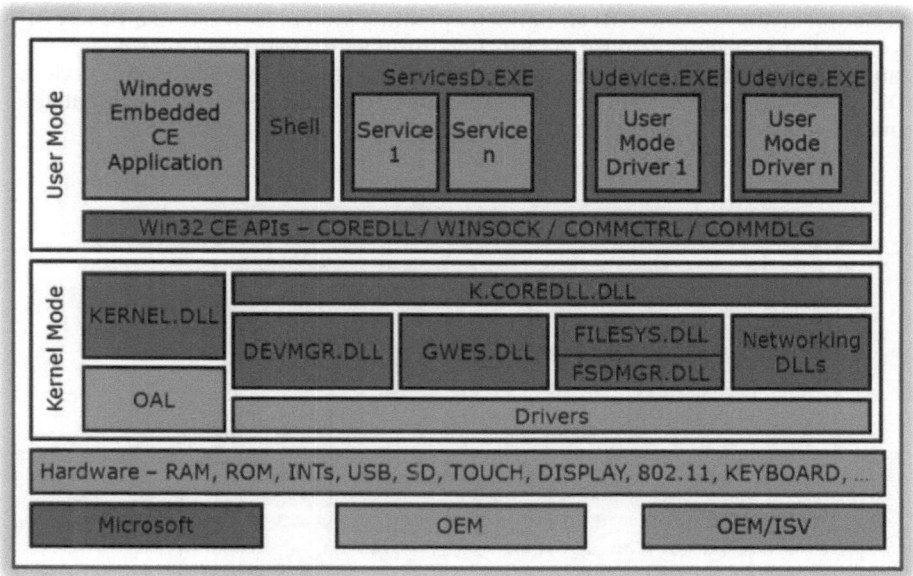

Figure 1-2. *Windows CE 6.0 and Windows Embedded Compact 7 System Architecture*

User-Mode versus Kernel-Mode Drivers in the Monolithic Architecture

Running in kernel mode implies that a malfunctioning device driver can jeopardize the entire system. In order to provide robustness installable device drivers can run in user mode hosted by the Udevice.exe process, thus protecting the kernel from rogue device drivers. The main disadvantage is a slower performance. From experience it seems that kernel mode device drivers in a monolithic kernel provide better performance then user mode device drivers in the microkernel architecture, while user mode device drivers in a monolithic kernel take a nose dive in performance. For more information, refer to the section "*Windows CE Device Drivers in Kernel or User Mode*" later in this chapter.

Windows CE System Architecture and I/O Handling

Windows Embedded Compact 7, as its predecessors Windows CE 6.0, is a commercial embedded Real Time Operating System (RTOS) based on a monolithic kernel. The specific device driver model adopted by the operating system is simple and provides for uncomplicated device driver implementation.

Device Driver-Related System Components

Windows Embedded Compact, like any modern embedded operating system, consists of a variety of system components each with a specific purpose to form a platform with a wide-ranging set of functionality and features. The kernel provides the core operating system services additional services, such as GWES and Device Manager, provide further functionality and interfaces. Figure 1-3 highlights those system components that are particularly important for device driver developers.

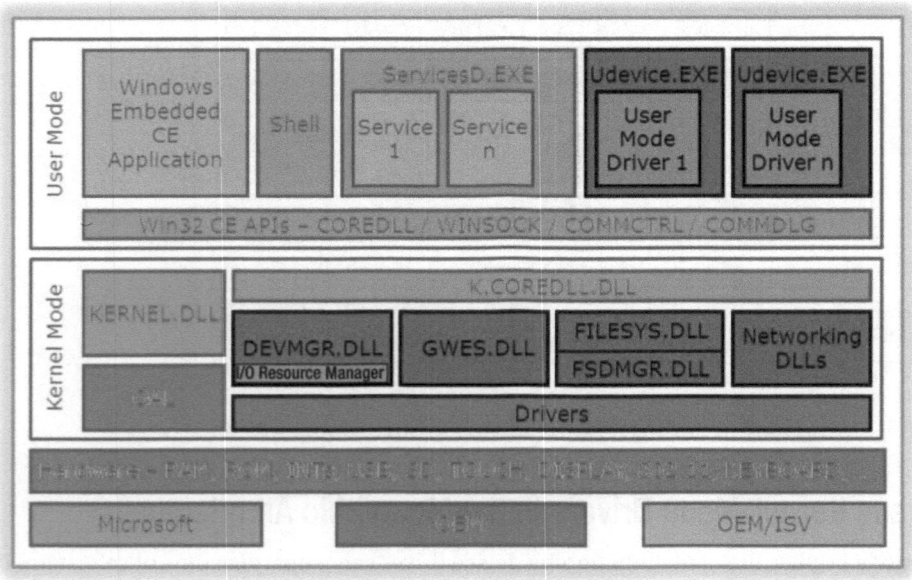

Figure 1-3. *Device Driver-Related Windows CE System Components*

Windows CE relies on the following system components to implement a flexible device driver model:

- **GWES.DLL** – This is the Graphic Windowing and Events Subsystem, which loads native device drivers and manages them and their interfaces while loaded. The section "*Windows Embedded Compact Device Driver Model*" later in this chapter introduces GWES in more detail.

- **DEVMGR.DLL** – This is the Device Manager, which loads kernel mode stream interface device drivers. In addition Device Manager tracks interfaces advertised by drivers and supports searches for drivers based on a globally unique identifier (GUID). For details, see the section "*Windows Embedded Compact Device Driver Model*" later in this chapter.

- **I/O Resource Manager** – Device Manager includes an I/O Resource Manager to enumerate a list of available resources from the registry.

- **FILESYS.DLL and FSDMGR.DLL** – These are the Windows Embedded Compact file system manager and file system driver manager, which load partition drivers and file system drivers into the Windows CE Storage Manager. You learn more about these types of drivers in Chapter 6 "Understanding Device Driver Types."

- **Networking DLLs** – These DLLs enable networking functionality, such as TCP/IP. Chapter 10 "Network Driver Interface Specification" provides more details about network communication in Windows CE.

- **UDEVICE.EXE** – This is a user mode process to run device drivers in user mode. The section "*Windows Embedded Compact Device Drivers in Kernel or User Mode*" later in this chapter discusses the advantages and disadvantages of running device drivers in user mode in more detail.

Windows Embedded Compact 7 Memory Architecture

Windows CE 6.0 and Windows Embedded Compact 7 use a Virtual Memory model that divides the address space into separate regions for kernel and user-mode processes (see Figure 1-4). This Virtual Memory model predominantly provides protection to the kernel and for one process from other processes. This is no different than a general purpose OS. However, unlike general purpose OSs, the Virtual Memory model of Windows CE 6 0 and Windows Embedded Compact 7 does not provide a backing store to swap out memory pages.

Figure 1-4 provides a broad view of the two separate virtual memory regions for the kernel and applications with their starting addresses.

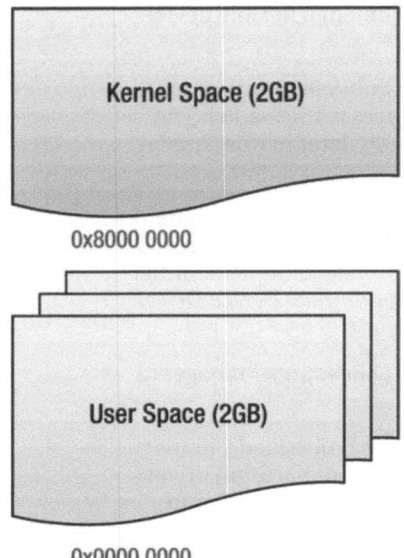

Figure 1-4. *Virtual Memory Model of Windows CE 6.0 and Windows Embedded Compact 7*

Kernel Space Virtual Memory

Windows CE separates the kernel virtual memory space into separate regions. Figure 1-5 shows how the kernel virtual memory space is structured. New in Windows Embedded Compact 7 is the ability to address physical RAM larger than 512 MBs, up to 3 GBs. However this has to be enabled by the OEM by implementing this support within the OAL. The OEM must describe the extended RAM region within the OEMRamTable structure which defines the additional physical RAM available for any hardware platform. The OEM needs to provide the OEMRamTable function to access the OEMRamTable structure. To make OEMRamTable available to the kernel and kernel independent transport layer (KITL), the OEM must set the pfnGetOEMRamTable member of OEMGLOBAL to point to the OEMGetOEMRamTable function.

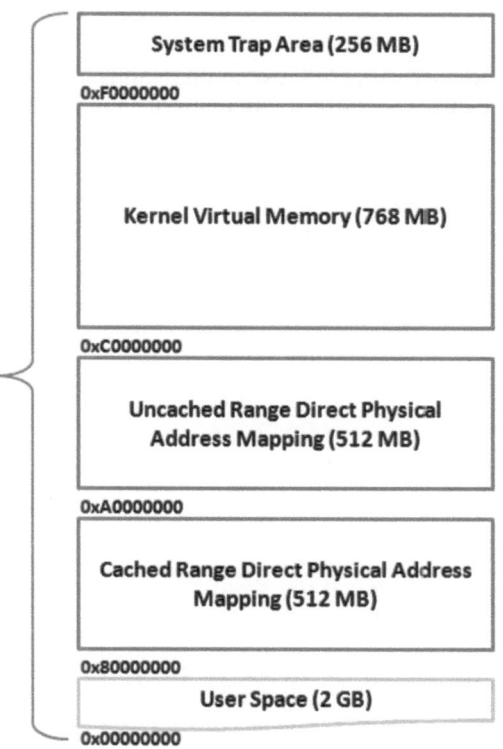

Figure 1-5. *Kernel Space Virtual Memory Structure*

Table 1-1 summarizes the regions in kernel-space virtual memory and describes their purpose.

Table 1-1. *Kernel-Space Virtual Memory Regions*

Start Address	End Address	Name	Description
xF000 0000	xFFFF FFFF	System Trap Area	CPU specific VM System call trap area
xC000 0000	xEFFF FFFF	Kernel VM	Virtual memory for the kernel, CPU-specific. To allow Address Space Layout Randomization
xA000 0000	xBFFF FFFF	Static Mapped Uncached Address Space	For access to physical memory bypassing the CPU cache.
x8000 0000	x9FFF FFFF	Static Mapped Cached Address Space	For access to physical memory through the CPU cache.

User Space Virtual Memory

Windows Embedded Compact separates the user virtual memory space into two main regions for the user process and shared DLLs and memory mapped files. Figure 1-6 shows a schematic structure of the user virtual memory address space.

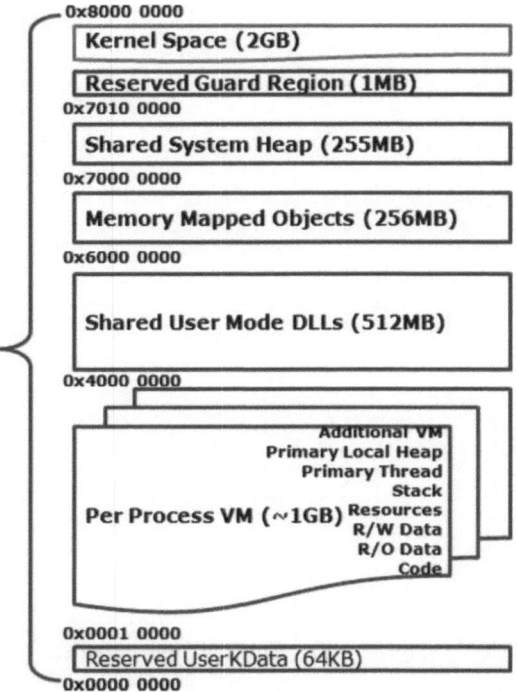

Figure 1-6. *User Space Virtual Memory Structure*

Table 1-2 summarizes the regions in user-space virtual memory and describes their purpose.

Table 1-2. User-Space Virtual Memory Regions

Start Address	End Address	Name	Description
x7FF0 0000	x7FFF FFFF	Reserved guard region	Buffer between user and kernel spaces.
x7000 0000	x7FEF FFFF	Shared system heap	Shared heap between the kernel and processes.
x60000000	x6FFFFFFF	Memory mapped objects	RAM-backed map files for cross-process communication, expecting all processes to map views at the same virtual address. This is Windows CE shared memory space.
x4000 0000	x5FFF FFFF	Shared user-mode DLLs	DLLs are loaded starting at the bottom of the stack and moving up.
x0001 0000	x3FFF FFFF	Per-process VM	Executable code and data.
x0000 0000	x0001 0000	Reserved user data	Allocated block for user data

Input/Output Handling

Windows Embedded Compact 7 as well as Windows CE 6.0 provides nested interrupts to provide low interrupt latencies and assure minimal latencies for top priority hardware device interrupts. The interrupt model is based on three elements:

- **Kernel Interrupt Service Handler** – Can handle up to 64 separate hardware IRQ sources. It determines interrupt priority level and calls an ISR hooked to it and then sets event that is associated with the related Interrupt ID to schedule the associated IST.

- **Interrupt Service Routines (ISRs)** – The ISR is hooked to a hardware interrupt request (IRQ) in kernel mode. it acknowledges hardware and determines Interrupt ID. The ISR can be static, that is, built into NK.EXE, or installable (chained in) via kernel call.

- **Interrupt Service Threads (ISTs)** – The IST performs device-specific servicing for the specified Interrupt ID and must signal completion of interrupt processing to the hardware.

Interrupt Processing

Figure 1-7 shows how Windows Embedded Compact handles interrupts.

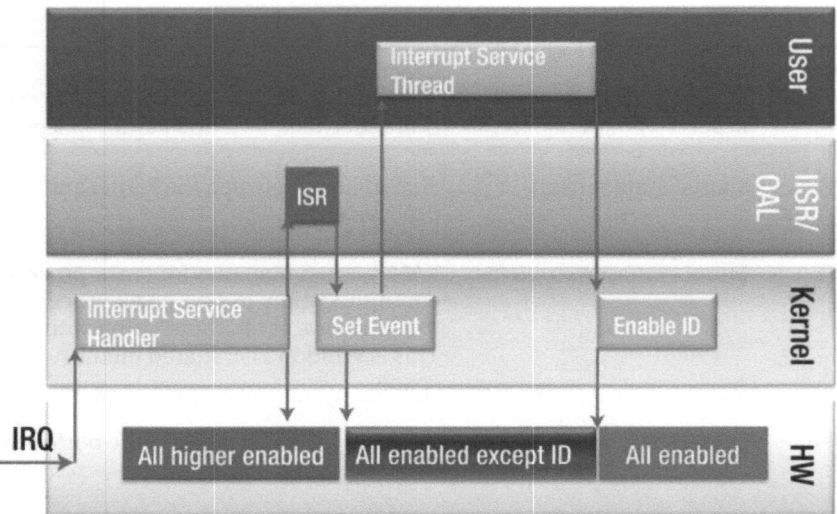

Figure 1-7. *Interrupt Processing in Windows CE*

As visualized in Figure 1-7, the process of handling an interrupt is handled in five steps:

1. Device raises registered hardware interrupt

2. Kernel gets exception, calls associated Interrupt Service Routine (ISR)

3. ISR quickly deals with pending interrupt

4. IST in driver is signaled to process interrupt

5. IST completes processing

ISRs and ISTs

ISRs and ISTs work together to perform the necessary Input/Output operations with minimal impact on other processing tasks and to prevent the loss and delay of high-priority interrupts. This interaction is mainly a task of coordinating thread execution between ISR and IST. ISRs and ISTs always work in pairs - the ISR identifies and masks interrupt quickly while the IST handles the bulk of the work and re-enables interrupts as soon as possible.

The interaction between ISR and IST involves the following steps:

1. The IST creates an Event Object mapped to the related SYSINTR ID. The Event Object is a kernel resource on which a WaitForSingleObject function call can wait and exit after the Event Object becomes signaled. The SYSINTR ID identifies the Event Object.

2. The ISR returns the SYSINTR ID to the Kernel Interrupt Service Handler so that it can signal the Event Object when ready.

3. The IST blocks on the event with a WaitForSingleObject function call until the Kernel Interrupt Service Handler sets the related event, thus unblocking the IST.

4. When unblocking the IST, if the IST is the highest priority runnable thread, it will be scheduled to run immediately.

Installable ISRs and Interrupt Sharing

Installable ISRs allow multiple devices to share interrupts and to share a single hardware platform interrupt request (IRQ). Essentially, shared interrupts trigger one interrupt line that is shared by more than one IRQ. For the operating system to handle these IRQs, there must be multiple ISRs chained to handle the shared interrupt. Each ISR, in turn, determines if it owns the interrupt and if so returns the related SYSINTR ID to unblock its associated IST.

Figure 1-8 illustrates how Installable ISRs can share an interrupt to support multiple peripheral devices.

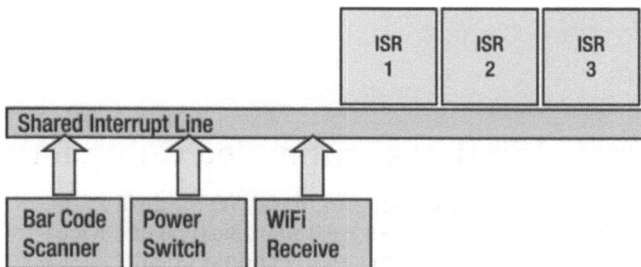

Figure 1-8. *Shared Interrupts Using Chaining*

An Installable ISR is implemented in a DLL. A device driver can load the ISR into the kernel at runtime by using the LoadIntChainHandler function. The interrupt handler is unloaded by using the FreeIntChainHandler function. Chapter 8 "*Device Driver I/O and Interrupts*" provides more details about the use of LoadIntChainHandler and FreeIntChainHandler in a device driver.

Windows Embedded Compact Device Driver Model

Windows Embedded Compact 7 implements a simple device driver model that distinguishes between native and stream interface device drivers.

Native Windows CE Device Drivers

Native drivers correspond to user input device drivers and display device drivers that are loaded into the Graphic, Windowing and Event System (GWES). Stream interface device drivers on the other hand adhere to the stream interface so that Device Manager, another kernel server, can manage these drivers. Figure 1-9 shows the Native Device Driver Model Interface.

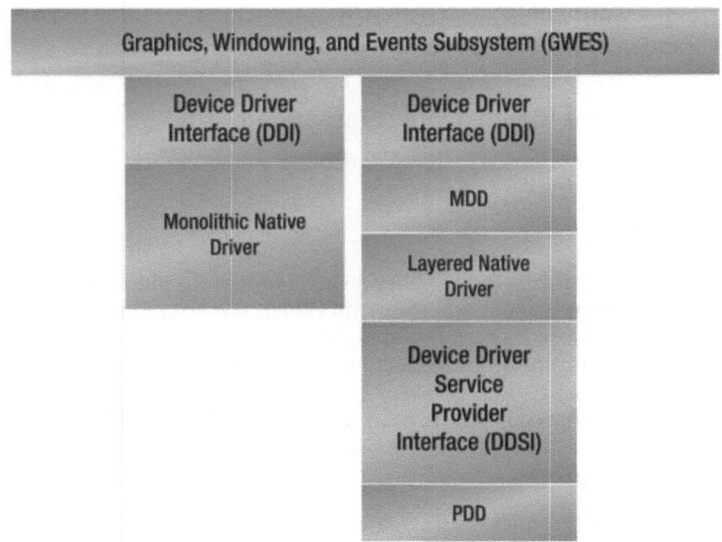

Figure 1-9. *Native Device Driver Model Interface*

Stream Interface Device Drivers in Windows Embedded Compact

The term *Stream Device Driver* can be misleading as it is often used for peripheral I/O hardware that processes a stream of data such as serial port device drivers. It might suggest that this type of device driver is not the right choice for block devices that refer to hardware managing chunks of data such as storage disks. However, stream interface device drivers in Windows Embedded Compact handle stream devices as well as block devices. For this reason, I strongly recommend using the term *stream interface* device driver, which means that the device driver has to expose a defined set of functions that allows applications to communicate with the device driver via the file system API.

Figure 1-10 shows the Stream Interface Device Driver Model Interface.

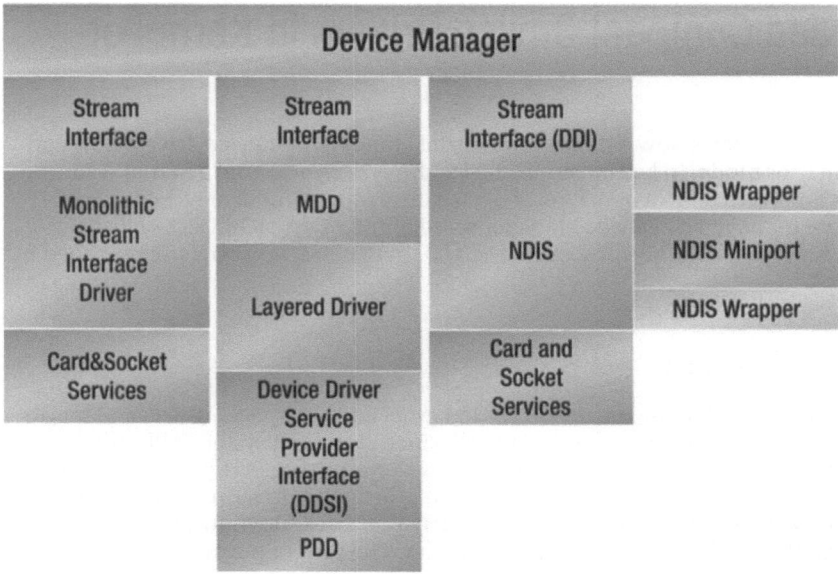

Figure 1-10. *Stream Interface Device Driver Model Interface*

Device Manager loads kernel mode stream device drivers and manages them and their interfaces while loaded. When the Device Manager loads, it initially loads the I/O Resource Manager to enumerate a list of available resources from the registry. In addition Device Manager tracks interfaces advertised by drivers and supports searches for drivers based on a globally unique identifier (GUID). The section "Loading and Unloading Device Drivers" later in this chapter provides more details about the load process for stream interface device drivers.

Monolithic and Layered Device Drivers

Both native and stream drivers can use either the monolithic or layered driver design as illustrated in Figures 1-9 and 1-10 in the previous sections. A monolithic driver relies on a single DLL to implement both the interface to the operating system and applications, and the logic to the hardware, while the layered driver architecture is based on model device driver (MDD) and platform device driver (PDD).

Monolithic and layered device drivers have the following advantages and disadvantages:

- **Monolithic device drivers** – Monolithic drivers might be the right choice if you want to avoid the additional function calls between MDD and PDD for performance reasons.

- **Layered device drivers** – The layered architecture based on MDD and PDD is advantageous because it facilitates code reuse and the development of driver updates. It is therefore the preferred choice for many device driver developers.

Windows Embedded Compact Device Drivers in Kernel or User Mode

Because Windows Embedded Compact is now a monolithic kernel architecture device drivers now can either be in kernel mode or in user mode. In kernel mode, device drivers have access to kernel resources. This presented security risks and has lead to a new type of device driver – user mode device drivers. Kernel mode device drivers are managed by Device Manager server library DEVMGR.DLL while user mode device drivers reside each in a user mode process named UDEVICE.EXE however still managed by Device Manager.

Kernel Mode Device Drivers

In Windows Embedded Compact kernel mode means access to kernel address space. However it has to be noted that when a user mode thread makes a system API call, since almost all system APIs are implemented in server libraries running in kernel mode thus the user mode thread runs in kernel mode. This has some bearing on kernel mode device drivers. If a kernel mode device driver receives a pointer to a user mode callback function, without the proper precaution such a callback function can access kernel mode calls and addresses even though it runs in a user mode thread. The proper precautions will be discussed later on in the book.

Kernel mode device drivers are practically the same implementation wise as they were in previous versions of the OS, however the user mode device drivers do not have access to kernel data structures and resources and are hosted in special user mode processes that are created and communicate with a kernel reflector service to provide a secure method for the user mode device driver to perform their tasks.

Kernel mode device driver are loaded into the kernel by either Device Manager or GWES, depending on their interface. Stream device drivers are loaded by Device Manager, DEVMGR.DLL and are managed by it. Native device drivers load into Graphic Windowing and Events subsystem, GWES.DLL. Kernel mode device drivers have full access to kernel data structures and kernel memory. Kernel mode device drivers link to KCOREDLL which is the kernel version of COREDLL to provide access to APIs.

User Mode Device Drivers

User mode means, that only user mode address space is available to the device driver, and this means that the device driver cannot directly perform any kernel mode calls or access kernel mode memory. User mode device drivers are managed by Device Manager however hosted in special user mode processes - udevice.exe. User mode device drivers have no kernel privileges and have no access to kernel structures or memory and cannot call kernel only APIs such as VirtualCopyEx. User mode device drivers improve stability because user mode device drivers are isolated from each other and have no access privileges to the kernel. User mode device drivers provide increased security because compromised user mode device drivers cannot crash the system because user mode privileges restrain a compromised driver. User mode device drivers offer better recoverability so the OS can recover after a driver crash and the driver can be restarted without rebooting.

Loading and Unloading Device Drivers

Native and stream drivers only differ in terms of the APIs they expose. You can load both types of drivers during system startup or on demand. However, exactly how Windows Embedded Compact loads a device driver depends on the driver type.

Loading Stream Interface Device Drivers

Device Manager loads kernel mode stream device drivers and manages them and their interfaces while loaded. The Device Manager is a system server dynamically linked library named (DEVMGR.DLL) and is loaded by the kernel at boot time. Once loaded it runs continuously and it loads kernel mode stream device drivers and manages them and their interfaces while loaded. When the Device Manager loads, it initially loads the I/O Resource Manager to enumerate a list of available resources from the registry. In addition Device Manager tracks interfaces advertised by drivers and supports searches for drivers based on a globally unique identifier (GUID). The IClass interface can associate an interface GUID with the driver's legacy name, its $device name, or its $bus name. For example, COM1:, $device\com1, or $bus\pci_0_3_0.

Device Manager Architecture

Device Manager searches the HKLM\Drivers\ Drivers\BuiltIn registry key to determine the key to begin the driver loading process. Device Manager calls ActivateDeviceEx API to load the driver specified by the Dll subkey value found in the key specified by the Drivers\BuiltIn value. The Dll subkey value is by default BusEnum.dll, also referred to as the bus enumerator. Loading BusEnum.dll causes all device drivers to load. A device loaded by ActivateDeviceEx can read its activation handle from its Active registry key. Device Manager controls the Active key in the registry. Only Device Manager should access the Active key for read or write access. Device Manager uses the Active and BuiltIn subkeys of the HKLM\Drivers registry key. Device drivers should never modify programmatically the values placed in this part of the registry by Device Manager. Figure 1-11 depicts initializing a device driver at boot time.

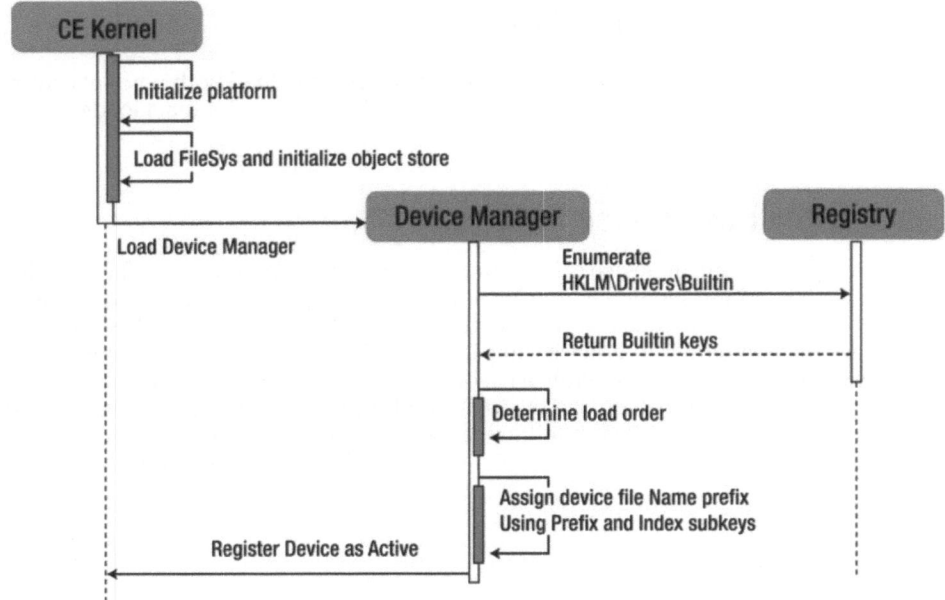

Figure 1-11. Device Driver initialization during system boot

Device Manager Registry Keys

The HKLM\Drivers\Active registry key contains currently active device drivers that Device Manager loaded. Device driver routines should not modify the **Active** key nor rely on any specific values within the **Active** key. When a driver is loaded, Device Manager passes the path to the driver's **Active** key with the dwContext parameter to the initialization routine. The initialization routine may read and create new values in the **Active** key; however, it is not allowed to access the key after the initialization function returns.

Device File Names

Applications can access device drivers through file system functions, for example CreateFile to get a handle to a device driver, and using this handle to perform I/O requests such as read, write or perform more elaborate I/O operations via I/O control requests. When calling a file system API such as CreateFile the first parameter it requests is a file name. A device driver's namespace is used instead of a file name as such. A device driver's name space can be one of the following formats:

- Three-letter prefix, followed by a number between 0 and 9, followed by a colon. For example "TST0:"

- $bus mount point, followed by the bus name, bus number, device number, and function number. For example "\$bus\PCMCIA_0_0_0"

- $device mount point, followed by a three-letter prefix representing the device, followed by a number, this allows for more than 10 device instances for the same device prefix. For example "\$device\TST0"

Device File Name Prefixes

The prefix consists of three uppercase letters that identify the device file name corresponding to a particular stream interface. The prefix is stored in a registry value called **Prefix**. When implementing the stream interface, typically the three-letter prefix is designated. Chapter 3 provides an incisive discussion on this subject.

First, the prefix identifies all possible device file names that can access the stream interface driver. Second, the prefix tells the operating system what entry-point file names to expect in the stream interface DLL. For example, to implement a device driver for a PC Card pager, the PGR indicating PAGER as the three-letter prefix, which in turn would dictate entry-point names, such as PGR_Init, PGR_IOControl, and so on.

Device File Name Indexes

The index differentiates devices with the same prefix that the stream interface manages. The index is the digit that follows the prefix. By default, Device Manager indexes logically from 1 through 9, with 1 corresponding to the first device file name. If a tenth device file name is required, the index 0 is used.

If device file names starting index need to be other than 1, a starting index in a registry value called **Index** within the registry key is specified. This is often necessary if a stream interface driver serves a device that uses a common prefix, such as COM. For example, "COM1:", "COM2:", and "COM3:" usually correspond to built-in serial port hardware. However if a driver is for a serial device, such as a packet-radio modem, it should appear as a COM port because modem software often assumes that modems are connected to COM ports. Thus an Index value of 4 is specified to differentiate this packet-radio modem device from the built-in serial devices.

Device Manager can register only one device file name, so if the **Index** value is specified, rather than letting Device Manager assign indexes, this device driver will support only one device.

I/O Resource Manager

When the OS boots, the bus enumerator enumerates the registry and loads all the built-in devices based on registry information. The I/O Resource Manager then tracks the current state of resources available in the system and manages all further I/O resource requests and allocations by bus drivers. Therefore, bus drivers should request I/O resources from the I/O Resource Manager when they load a client driver for installable devices or other types of devices.

The I/O Resource Manager is an intrinsic part of Device Manager. The I/O Resource Manager tracks the available system resources initialized from the registry before any devices are loaded. Tracking these resources prevents accidental collisions when more than one device driver attempts to employ the same resources.

The OAL and the registry are used to pre-allocate IRQ and I/O space resources that bus drivers request. However, the I/O Resource Manager is not limited to managing I/O and IRQ spaces. Bus drivers, such as the PCI bus driver, request IRQ and I/O space resources from the I/O Resource Manager as it loads device drivers for the devices found in the registry. The same is true for the PC Card bus driver and I/O resources required by PC Card client drivers. When users remove PC Cards from the system PC Card bus driver releases these resources.

Every hardware platform has unique IRQs and I/O space available. IRQs for built-in and fixed devices are mapped to interrupt identifiers (SYSINTRs) in the OAL. The IRQs for built-in and fixed devices should be excluded from the available resources. IRQs used with the PCI bus are usually shared.

IRQs and I/O space resources are predefined in `HKLM\Drivers\Resources\IRQ` and `HKLM\Drivers\Resources\IO` registry keys which provide the initial state of the I/O Resource Manager.

Chapter Summary

Understanding the operating system architecture is cardinal to writing robust device drivers. The memory architecture governs how memory is allocated and passed between kernel mode components, which kernel mode device drivers actually are, and user mode processes. Understanding the virtual memory scheme employed by Windows Embedded Compact 7 helps in designing well-behaved device drivers. Device Manager is the operating system's component that loads, tracks, and interacts with stream device drivers, which are the main topic of this book.

CHAPTER 2

The Tools of the Trade

"Tools of trade" is a term utilized in bankruptcy law to establish what assets a person would commonly use for the purpose of making a living. To make a living as device driver developers, our "Tools of trade" are VS2008, Platform Builder (PB), and third-party tools.

Visual Studio with Smart Device support only allows you to develop applications for devices. For Windows Embedded Compact 7 (and previous versions) device driver development, Platform Builder is an absolute must. Platform Builder provides you with the device driver development kit (DDK) and the ability to build an operating system image for testing the device driver. Moreover Platform Builder provides you with the build tools necessary to build device drivers for Windows Embedded Compact 7 (CE), such as setting the build environment variables and debugging and testing tools such as kernel debugger tool and an extensive set of remote tools.

Visual Studio and Platform Builder provide a solid foundation for development, still third-party tools are available to speed up the process of creating a device driver. Two tools that device driver developers should find particularly useful are TRACE32 JTAG debugger, and the Windows CE Device Driver Wizard. This chapter provides an overview of these tools and later chapters will provide in-depth discussion and examples how to use these tools.

In this chapter:

- Visual Studio 2008
- Platform Builder
- Windows CE Build System
- The Device Driver Development Kit
- TRACE32
- The Windows CE Device Driver Wizard

Visual Studio 2008

Visual Studio 2008 is in actual fact the host of Platform Builder 2008 IDE which is a Visual Studio 2008 plugin wizard, which means that you have to install Visual Studio 2008 prior to installing Platform Builder 2008. Visual Studio 2008 together with Platform Builder 2008 provides you with a comprehensive environment for developing OS images, subprojects, downloading the OS images to the target device and debugging capabilities all in one development tool. What is of interest to Windows Embedded Compact developers and device driver developers for this OS is the integration of Platform Builder into Visual Studio 2008 and less Visual Studio as a general developer tool.

Visual Studio 2008 and Platform Builder IDE

Platform Builder for Windows Embedded Compact 7 IDE is integrated into Visual Studio 2008. It provides the user a graphical user interface to create OS designs, connect and download OS images to target devices, a graphical interface to the kernel debugger, edit source code build subprojects, BSP components, and many more capabilities. The build results are the same results as if using command line tools to perform all development efforts, moreover results are interchangeable, meaning that you can interchange command line development and IDE development.

After installing Platform Builder, Visual Studio has specific Windows Embedded Compact related UI components, including a specific device-related menu called the "Target" menu; OS design-specific "Build" menu options; and three new "Tools" sub menus "Platform Builder," "Windows Embedded Silverlight Tools," and "Remote Tools." The main feature however is the Platform Builder wizard and under the "Other Languages ➤ Visual C#" project types the "Remote Tools Framework" wizard. Figure 2-1 shows the Platform Builder Wizard in the "Project Types" tree.

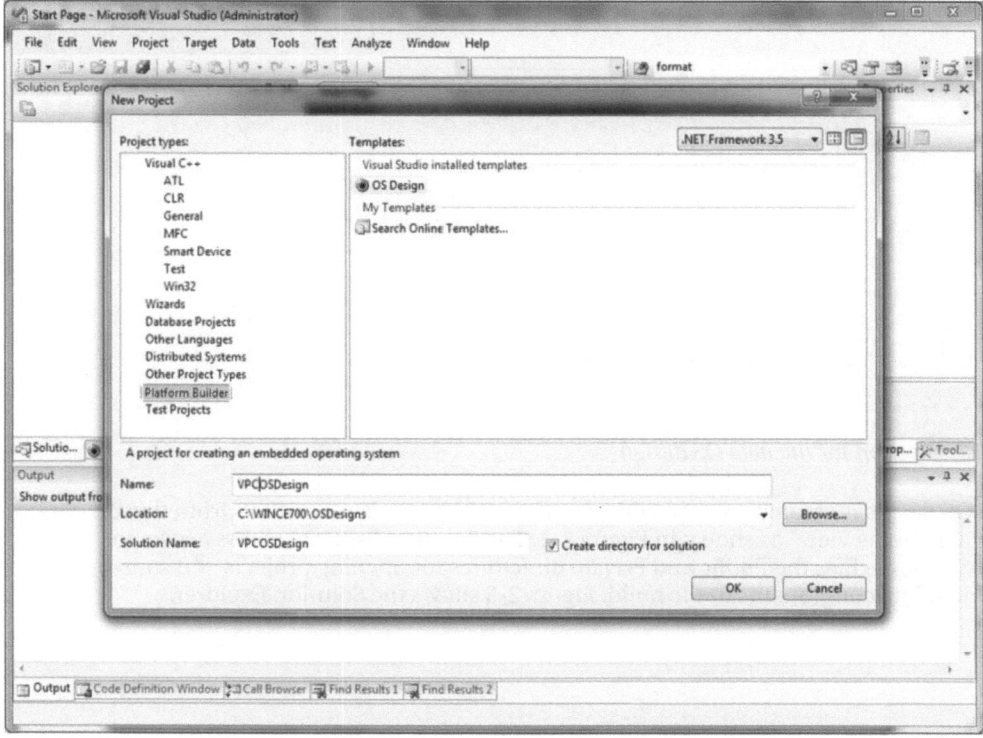

Figure 2-1. *Creating an OS design using Platform Builder IDE wizard*

At the same time the new window called "Catalog Items View" is added and can be found under the "View ➤ Other Windows" menu. The OS design wizard will ask for a BSP on which the OS design is built, and offer a set of jumpstart OS design templates from which to choose. Figures 2-2 and 2-3 describe these steps. Selecting a Board Support Package (BSP) is of the utmost importance when creating a new OS design; however, it is not difficult to add another BSP to the newly created OS design later if the need arises to run the exact same operating system image on another device using a different architecture.

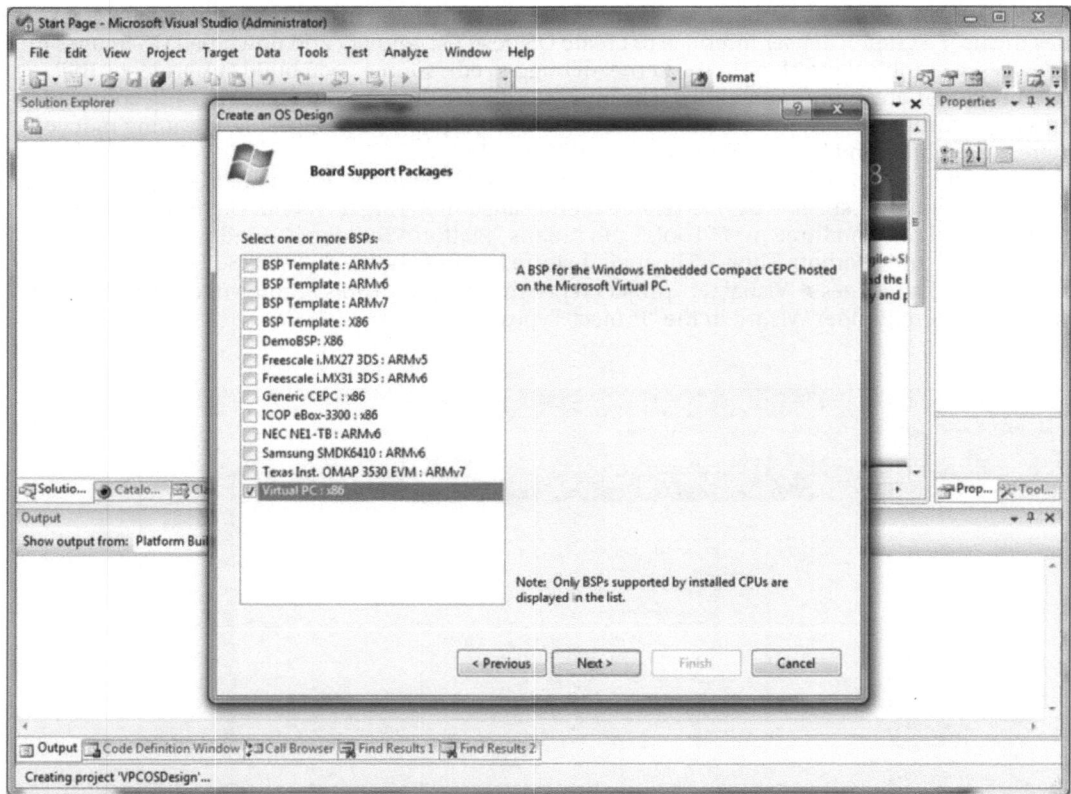

Figure 2-2. *BSP selection for the new OS design*

Once the OS design is created you can add or remove OS components or BSPs from this OS design using the "Catalog Items View" as shown in Figure 2-4. The Solution Explorer allows access to subprojects. BSP source files the Public and Private directories for opening projects and source files, and excluding or including components in the build. Figure 2-5 shows the Solution Explorer.

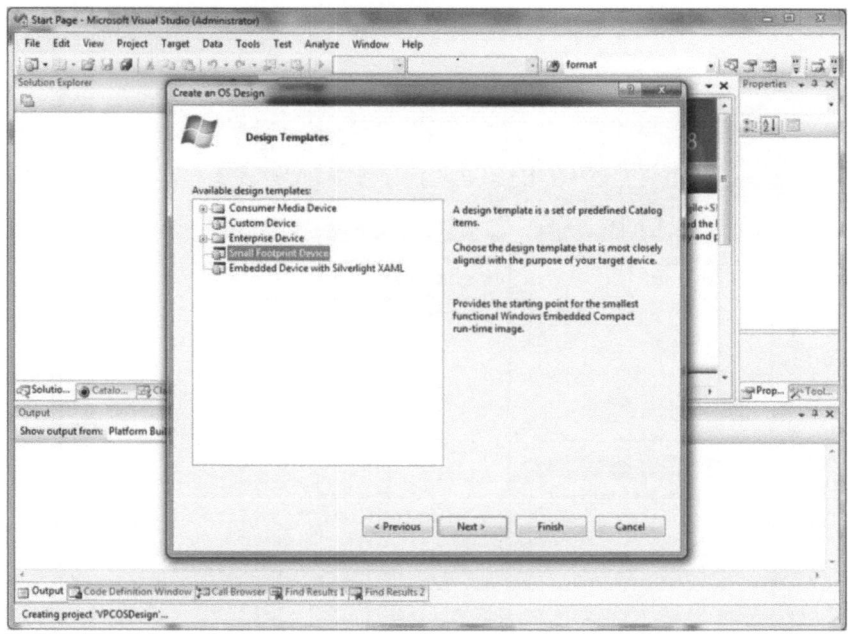

Figure 2-3. *Selecting a jumpstart design template*

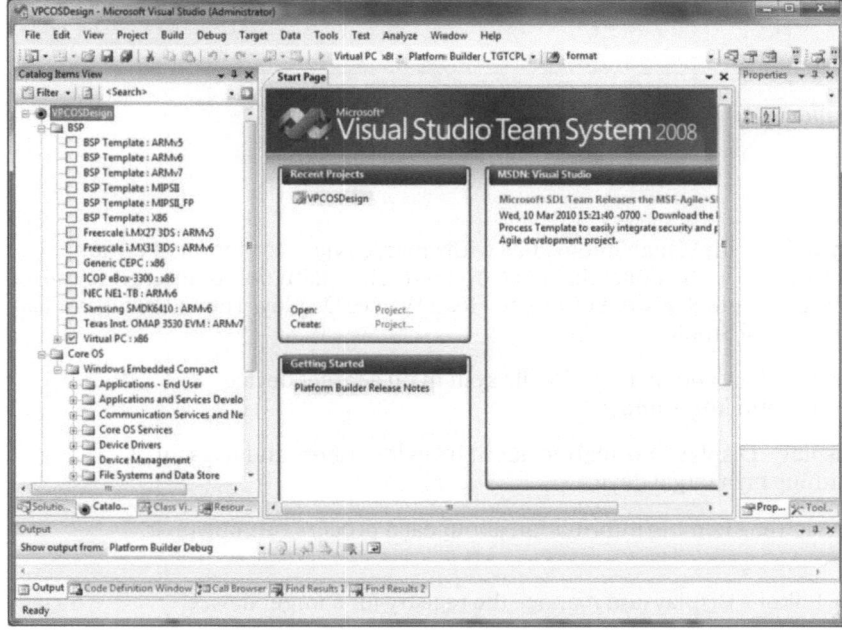

Figure 2-4. *The Catalog Items View*

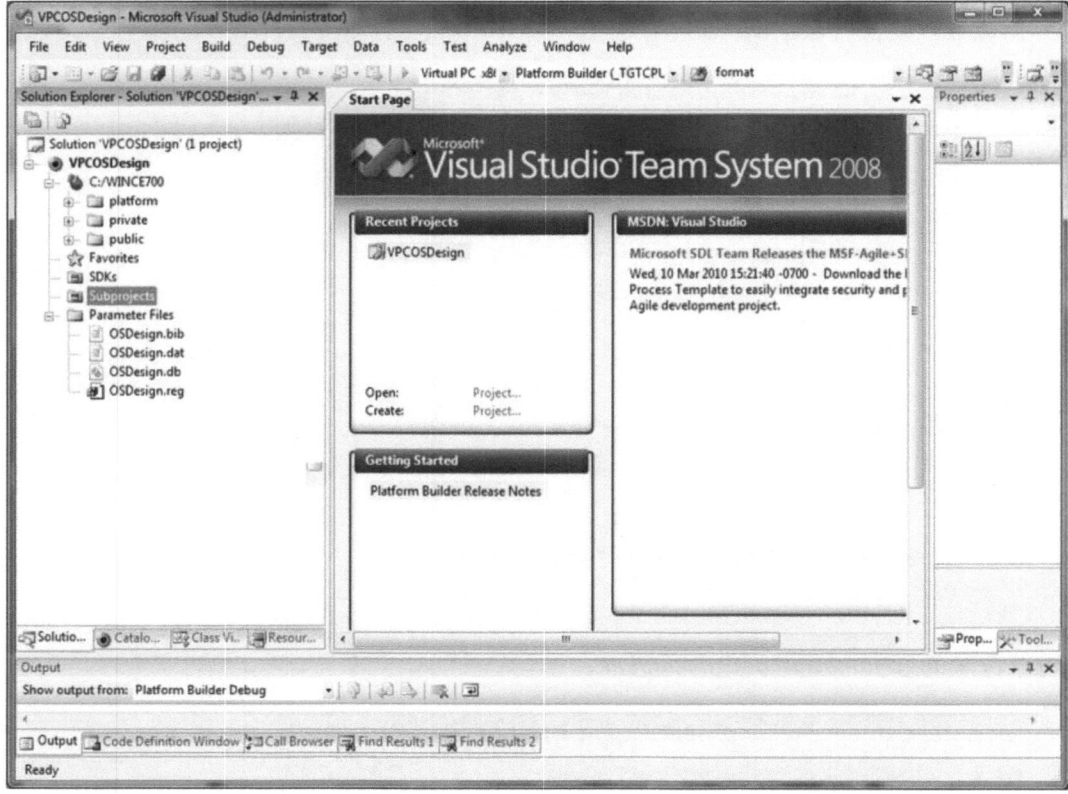

Figure 2-5. *The Solution Explorer*

Remote Tools

The remote tools that are installed with Visual Studio 2008 with smart device development option selected are designed mainly to help with application development. The main tools of interest to the device driver developer are the Remote Registry Editor and Heap Walker Display. The following is a list of remote tools available with Visual Studio.

- Remote File Viewer - View and manage the file system on a target device (including exporting and importing)

- Heap Walker Display - Display information about heap identifiers and flags for each process running on a target device

- Remote Process Viewer - Remote information about each process running on a target device

- Remote Registry Editor - Display and manage the registry for a target device

- Remote Spy - Display messages received by windows associated with applications running on a target device

- Remote Zoom-in - Capture a screen image in bitmap (.bmp) file format from a target device

Remote Tools Framework

The remote tools framework is installed with Platform Builder 2008 and is a development SDK that spans both device side and development workstation plug-in libraries to create a custom remote tool and a remote tool shell to host the custom plug-in. Developing a remote tool involves creating a device side console application that can either push data or respond to requests from the custom remote tool on the development workstation, and of course developing the custom remote tool plug-in. You have a choice to develop the device side application either using a native API, or a .NET compact framework managed API. Although a native client side remote tool application will serve well a device that needs real-time determinism and thus does not support the .NET compact framework, a managed device side application has the advantage of rapid development. The plug-in side is developed using the .NET framework and installs into Visual Studio a remote tools frame wizard to ease the development. An example of such a custom remote tool will be discussed later in the chapter dealing with debugging and testing.

■ **Note**   Previous versions of Windows CE: In the case of Windows CE 6.0 you have to install Visual Studio 2005 and then install platform Builder 6.0. Prior to Windows CE 6.0 Platform Builder IDE was a standalone tool and did not require Visual Studio.

Platform Builder

Platform Builder is the tool you use to develop and build operating system designs based on your choice of hardware. An operating system design is composed of all the systems components that the developer chooses out of the catalog to incorporate in his/her operating system. To allow this, Platform Builder has all the operating systems components within Platform Builder's directory structure.

Platform Builder Directory Tree

All the necessary files and tools that are needed to create a Windows CE operating system image are collected under a directory hierarchy located on the installation disk. For Windows CE 7.0 the OS installation root directory is WINCE700, this directory is referred to by the build environment variable %_WINCEROOT%. For example, it would typically be set to C:\WINCE700 where 'C:' is the installation disk. Under this folder you should find the following five folders:

- Platform Directory
- Public Directory

- SDK Directory

- Others Directory

- Private Directory

When a new OS design is created for the first time a new folder will be created: **OSDesigns**. See Figure 2-6.

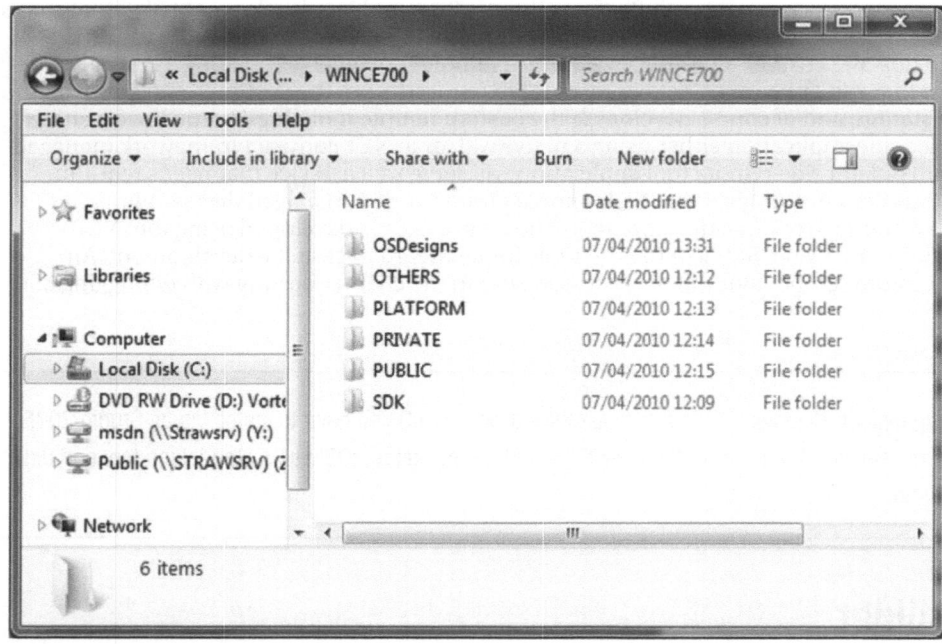

Figure 2-6. *Platform Builder Folder Hierarchy*

Platform Builder subdirectories that are most relevant to device driver developers are PLATFORM and PUBLIC subdirectories, because these contain device driver source code which is separated into specific board dependent drivers, system-on-chip (SOC) drivers, and common drivers.

- Specific board (BSP) dependent device driver source code is located under %_WINCEROOT%\PLATFORM\%_TGTPLAT%\SRC\DRIVERS directory

- System on Chip device driver source code is located under %_WINCEROOT%\PLATFORM\COMMON\SRC\SOC

  - SoC device drivers handle peripheral I/O devices that are integrated on the CPU chip to form the SoC.

- Common source code for device drivers that is supplied by Microsoft is located under %_WINCEROOT%\PLATFORM\COMMON\SRC\

- Source code for common drivers for non-native peripheral devices. The source code for these device drivers is platform-independent code and is not specific to a hardware platform or CPU architecture and is located under %_WINCEROOT%\PUBLIC\COMMON\OAK\DRIVERS

PLATFORM Directory

This directory is the root directory for the board support packages (BSPs) that were installed with Platform Builder. Each such BSP is located in its own directory hierarchy with the top folder named to reflect the hardware it supports. Another extremely important subdirectory within the PLATFORM directory tree is the COMMON subdirectory which contains OEM adaptation layer source code, including routines that are generic to all BSPs and routines that are specific to certain architecture.

PUBLIC Directory

This directory contains a platform-independent set of components and configurations. The subdirectories in the PUBLIC directory that contain modules and components have the same name as Windows CE 7.0 modules. It contains three types of subdirectories:

- Module and component subdirectories

- Reference configuration subdirectories

- Custom configuration subdirectories

Platform Builder IDE

Platform Builder Integrated Development Environment (IDE) is a graphical user interface contained within Visual Studio 2008 and consists of an integrated set of tools, context-sensitive menus, toolbars, and shortcut keys, that enable you to create, test, and refine OS designs and Catalog items.

Platform Builder Wizards

Platform Builder provides a set of wizards in the IDE that enable you to create OS designs and subprojects.

Windows CE OS Design Wizard

The Windows CE OS Design Wizard is an add-in wizard within Visual Studio 2008. It provides a set of templates that you can use to jumpstart creating and configuring an OS design. The OS Design Wizard guides you to select first a BSP for your OS design, then asks you to select a design template and completes the process by stepping through a set of components you can add or remove a selection of Catalog items, including various communication components.

> ■ **Note** Design Templates: Design templates provide examples of how to develop an OS for a specific device category and can help reduce your overall OS development time. These are XML files that include the basic building blocks of the operating system with a variety of components that make up a device category, including an industrial controller.

Windows CE Subproject Wizard

The Windows CE Subproject Wizard will conduct you throughout the process of creating a subproject that you can use to develop items based on your OS design, including applications, dynamic-link libraries (DLLs), static libraries, and a TUX test harness. The resulting subproject is added to the currently active OS design. Because subprojects depend on the specific OS design that contains them, they are built only in the context of that specific OS design.

Platform Builder Remote Tools

The remote tools that are installed with Platform Builder are an invaluable set of software tools that help you as a device driver developer connect and remotely monitor information and test your creation. These tools are divided into two groups: tools for debugging and testing, and tools for information management. In the second group, the most relevant tool is the Remote Registry Editor. Checking the active device driver node in the registry is the surest way to ascertain that your device driver was loaded by Device Manager. In the first group the most helpful tools are the Remote Kernel Tracker and Remote Call Profiler. The first helps to track interrupts, and synchronizes object triggering and thread execution for your device and the second helps you create efficient code by detecting coding bottlenecks.

Platform Builder Registry Editor

The registry editor is valuable to you as a device driver developer because of its RegEdit view as well as the source view. The RegEdit view provides a precise visual view where the device driver registry entry is located, with the ability to edit single key values or add new keys. Figure 2-7 shows the RegEdit view of registry editor within Visual Studio 2008.

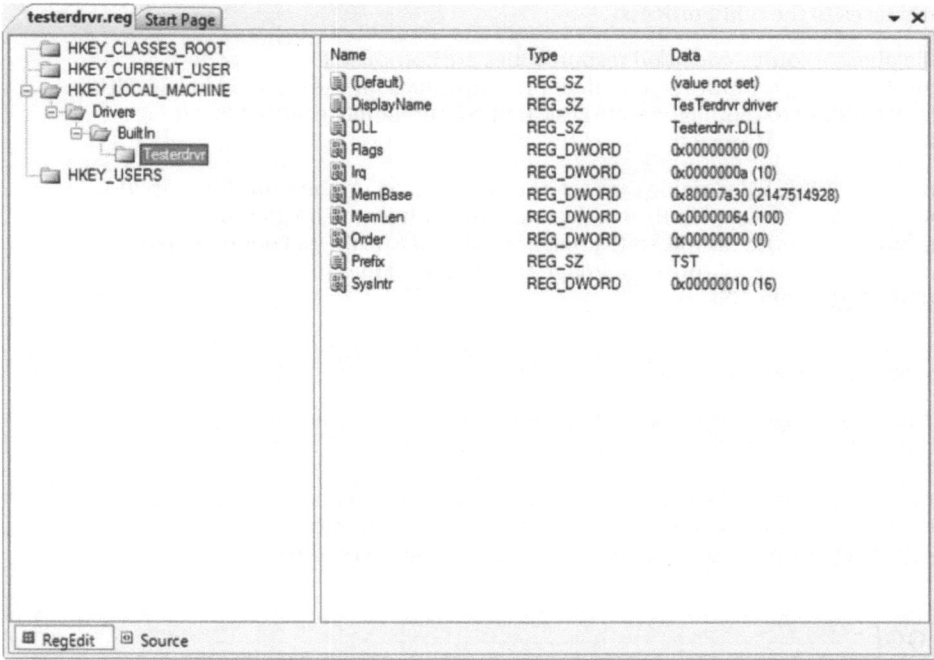

Figure 2-7. An example of a device driver registry entry in registry editor RegEdit view

The Build System

Building software amounts to the process of going from source code to a binary executable so that this executable runs and performs its functionality. To accomplish these tasks a set of tools, executables, and scripts are provided to perform an automated build using one command. Understanding the build process is detrimental to the development of device drivers for Windows CE.

Overview

In Windows CE the build system process involves building operating system components, device drivers, applications, libraries, and configuration files such as registry entries and more into a single operating system image. The Windows CE build system is composed of a set of tools, such as specific architecture compilers, the make tool, and other command line executables and batch files to automate the build process.

There are four phases to the build process:

- Compile phase – source code and resource files are compiled and linked to generate executables, libraries, and binary resource files for the selected locales. It is seldom required to rebuild operating system components because binaries are already provided by Microsoft.

- Sysgen phase - SYSGEN variables are set or cleared based on the catalog items and dependency trees included in the OS design. It then filters the header files and creates import libraries for the Software Development Kits (SDKs) defined in the OS design, creates a set of run-time image configuration files for the OS design, and builds the specific BSP.

- Release copy phase - all files required to create the run-time image are copied to the OS design's release directory.

- Make run-time image phase - project-specific files such as Project.bib and Project.reg are copied to the release directory and based on environment variables specified in .reg and .bib files creates the final run-time image in the release directory. Configuration files are merged for example registry configuration files are merged into reginit.ini to be compiled into the image registry file. OS image localization is performed during this final phase of image creation.

The Build Tools

The launch of Windows CE 5.0 introduced the Platform Builder IDE as a mere graphical user interface thin layer on top of the command line tools that compose the build system, this means that the command line build and IDE build are therefore interchangeable. The build tools are a bundle of command line executables and batch files that work together to build an OS image. Refer to Figure 2-8 that shows how the build tools are represented for each of the four phases. A color scheme is introduced in order to distinguish between the executable tools which are colored in blue and the batch tools which are colored in olive. Understanding the build tools goes a long way to ease the process of developing device drivers for Windows CE.

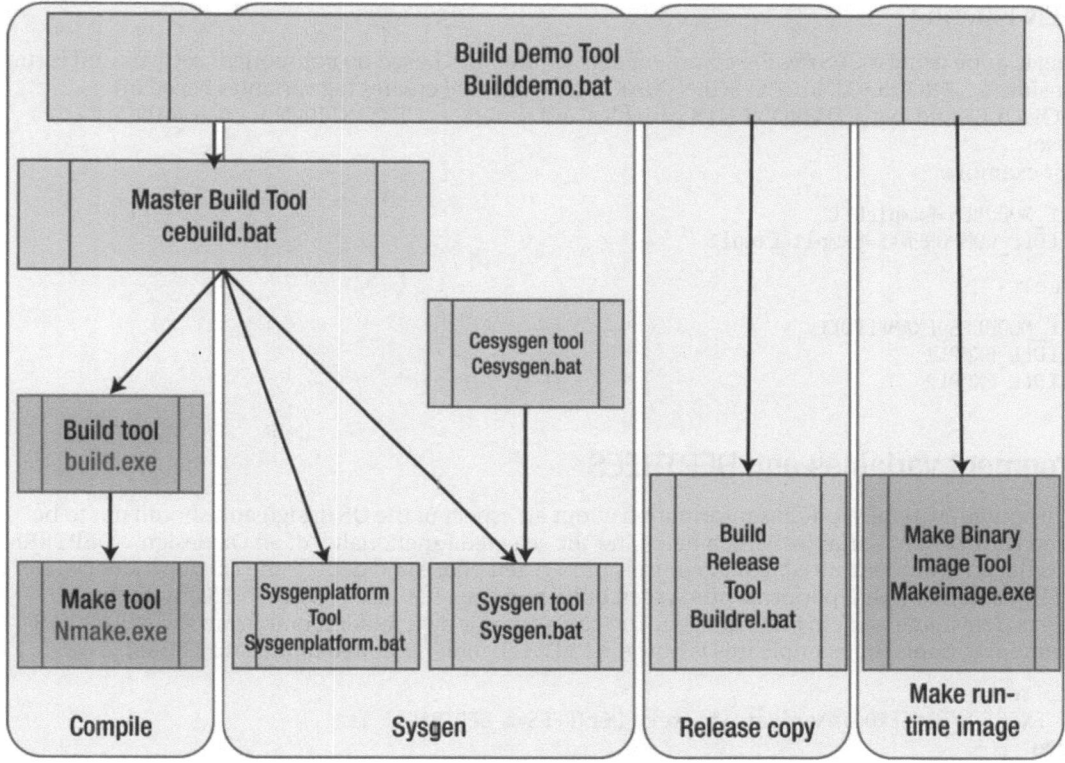

Figure 2-8. *OS image build phases and corresponding build tools*

Command line build

The command line build uses the build demo tool to jumpstart the whole build process. Build demo tool is a batch file that calls the master build tool cebuild.bat and when the first two phases are done it calls buildrel.bat and makeimage.exe to complete the build. You should be aware that Platform Builder IDE calls builddemo.bat with arguments as designated by the menu items that are selected by the user. Platform Builder documentation does a good job detailing all the possible options. You should review builddemo.bat as it is self-documented with good comments.

Understanding the SYSGEN process

SYSGEN phase is, as its name suggests, a system generation process where components are filtered and some are built to form the collection of components that will comprise the image of the selected OS design. SYSGEN.BAT is the tool that is effectively an extensible component dependency database in BAT file "code". It sets xxx_MODULES and yyy_COMPONENTS variables for filtering. Runs NMAKE.EXE on MAKEFILE in CESYSGEN folder in each _DEPTREES folder, where the components are linked to the targets.

SYSGEN Filtering

Filtering is done using @CESYSGEN comment tags to filter files based on component settings and is run from inside %__PROJROOT%\CESYSGEN\MAKEFILE. Filtering creates tag variables based on xxx_MODULES and yyy_COMPONENTS variables and generates CECONFIG.H for use with C pre-processor.

For example:

```
EXAMPLE_MODULES=ExmpleDLL
EXAMPLEDLL_COMPONENTS=Exmpl1 Exmpl2
```

generates:

```
EXAMPLE_MODULES_EXAMPLEDLL
EXAMPLEDLL_EXMPL1
EXAMPLEDLL_EXMPL2
```

Environment variables and DEPTREES

An environment variable contains information about an aspect of the OS design and should not to be confused with System Variables, which help filter the selected functionality of an OS design. _DEPTREES which is the environment variable that controls pre-sysgen phase and depicts the OS dependency tree. It is used by cebuild.bat that performs pre-sysgen build and sysgen. It uses _DEPTREES environment variable to determine what to build/sysgen. You can add your own folder hierarchy to the DEPTREES environment variable for example this is how the PRIVATE folder is added to the DEPTREES:

```
:AddDepTree
    if EXIST %_WINCEROOT%\private\%1 set _DEPTREES=%_DEPTREES% %1
    goto :EOF
```

There are four groupings of environment variables

- BSP Environment Variables - define the level of optional support available with a board support package.

- BSP_NO Environment Variables - define the level of optional support available with a hardware platform.

- IMG Environment Variables - remove modules from your OS design, but leave the associated registry entries in your design intact.

- Miscellaneous Environment Variables

The Master Build Tool

The Master Build Tool (Cebuild.bat) builds the modules and functionality and generates the source code for an entire OS design. Cebuild.bat performs the following steps to create a run-time image:

For each project specified by the _DEPTREES environment variable, Cebuild.bat runs Build.exe in the %_WINCEROOT%\Public\Tree directory, where Tree is a project specified by _DEPTREES. Build.exe compiles the source code in the project's directories.

For each project specified by the _DEPTREES environment variable, Cebuild.bat runs Sysgen.bat –p Tree, where Tree is a project specified by _DEPTREES. Sysgen.bat builds the project's modules, which are selected in Cesysgen.bat. Sysgen.bat builds the modules in the %_PROJECTROOT%\Oak\Misc directory.

Cebuild.bat runs Build.exe in the %_PLATFORMROOT%\%_TGTPLAT% directory to compile the code for the hardware platform.

How to Prepare Your Development Environment

Windows Embedded Compact Build Environment tool WINCE.BAT is the tool that prepares the build environment. It uses three input parameters to set environment variables. The first parameter indicates the CPU architecture for the build and sets the %_TGTCPU% environment variable; the second parameter indicates the OSDesign directory name for the build and sets the %_TGTPROJ% environment variable and last parameter indicates the BSP being used for the build to set the %_TGTPLAT% environment variable. Once you have prepared the build environment, you are ready to build your device driver. You will use the build tool, Build.exe for the actual build.

Build.exe

For device driver developers the most significant procedure of the build process is building the source code of the device driver. Build.exe is the tool that performs this task. Build.exe activity is described in the diagram in Figure 2-9 and the following steps:

1. Build.exe looks for a DIRS file in the current directory; then, if the DIRS file exists, the file directs Build.exe to additional subdirectories that contain source code or additional DIRS files.

2. If there is no DIRS file in the current directory, Build.exe searches for a SOURCES file.

3. If Build.exe finds a SOURCES file in the current directory, it calls the Microsoft make utility -Nmake.exe, to compile the specified C/C++ or assembly source files or link an object module.

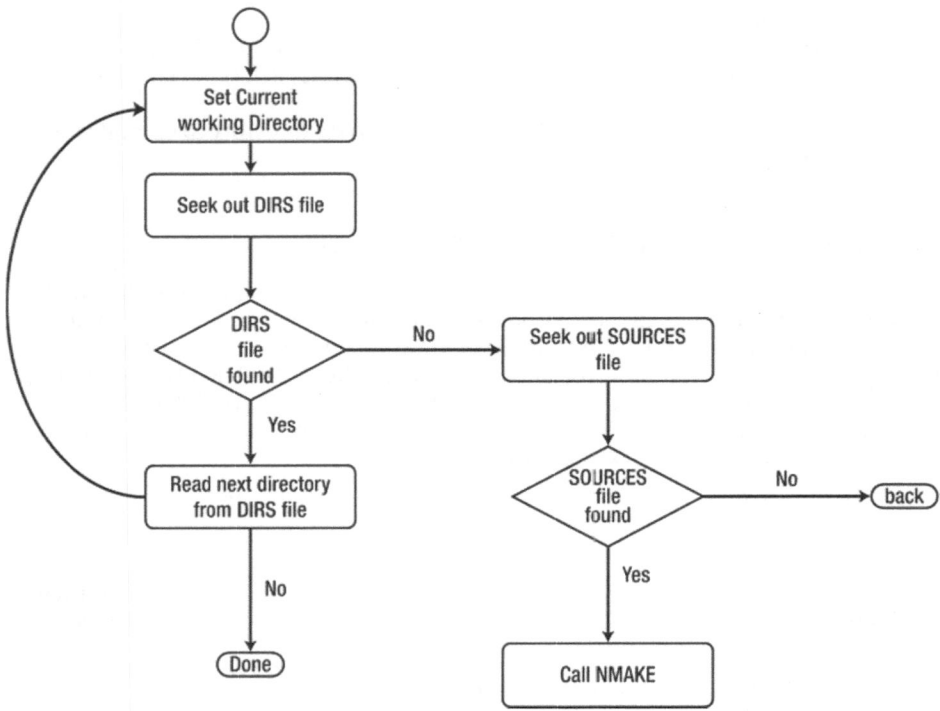

Figure 2-9. *Build.exe activity flow*

DIRS Files

A DIRS file is a text file that lists subdirectories containing other DIRS or SOURCES files. The following example shows a DIRS file that lists the device drivers to be built for to the VirtualPC BSP. When build.exe evaluates this file, it will traverse the ISR_VPCMOUSE, KEYBD, NDIS_DC21X4, and WAVEDEV2_SB16 directories looking for SOURCES file or another DIRS file. The DIRS directive orders the build sequence, so in the following example the build.exe will traverse the directory three starting with wavedev2_sb16 and so on. It is possible to use the wild card sign * in a DIRS file to traverse the entire set of subdirectories but this would not be an ordered sequence.

```
DIRS= \
    wavedev2_sb16 \
    ndis_dc21x4 \
    keybd \
    isr_vpcmouse \
```

SOURCES Files

The SOURCES file is a text file that contains the component specific directives needed by build.exe and NMAKE utility. The SOURCES file is included by the shared system wide makefile named makefile.def.

This allows the component makefile to remain relatively simple. The shared system makefile is included by a simple one line makefile in the component subdirectory.

```
!INCLUDE $(_MAKEENVROOT)\makefile.def
```

Makefile.def provides default MAKE rules for most aspects of the build and provides standard rules for various types of targets thus reduces amount of MAKEFILE script needed for each project. Located in %_WINCEROOT%\public\common\OAK\misc. An example of a SOURCES file for the VirtualPC mouse ISR is a non-complicated example of the makefile macro definition directives involved. For example TARGETLIBS macro definition directive specifies additional library files that should be linked into the target executable. Platform Builder documentation is a good reference for the various macro definition directives that are used by NMAKE utility.

```
TARGETNAME=isr_vpcmouse
RELEASETYPE=PLATFORM
TARGETTYPE=DYNLINK
DLLENTRY=DllEntry
TARGETLIBS= \
    $(_COMMONSDKROOT)\lib\$(_CPUINDPATH)\coredll.lib \
SOURCES=isr_vpcmouse.c
```

Figure 2-10 describes how the complete project makefile is composed using SOURCES file and the makefile.def file. The makefile is then processed by the NMAKE utility to compile and link the project's source code files and dependent libraries into a target executable.

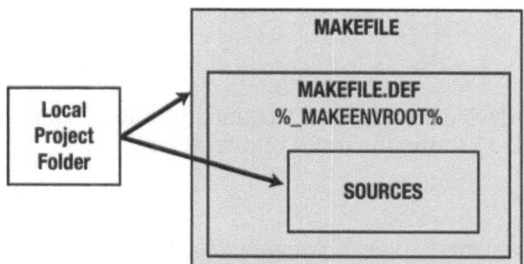

Figure 2-10. *Inserting the project SOURCES file directives into a makefile*

SOURCES.CMN

Sources.cmn is a text file that provides a place to store common settings that apply to the entire source tree. It is located at the topmost directory of the sources directory tree where the topmost DIRS file is located. The following example is of the Sources.cmn file for the VirtualPC BSP.

```
WINCEOEM=1
IMGNODFLTDDK=1
WARNISERROR=1
RELEASETYPE=PLATFORM
_COMMONPUBROOT=$(SG_OUTPUT_ROOT)
__PROJROOT=$(_PROJECTROOT)
```

```
_PLATCOMMONLIB=$(_COMMONPUBROOT)\platcomm\$(_TGTPLAT)\lib
_PLATLIB=$(_COMMONPUBROOT)\platform\$(_TGTPLAT)\lib

_OEMINCPATH=$(_WINCEROOT)\public\common\sdk\inc
_OEMINCPATH=$(_OEMINCPATH);$(_WINCEROOT)\public\common\oak\inc
_OEMINCPATH=$(_OEMINCPATH);$(_WINCEROOT)\public\common\ddk\inc

_ISVINCPATH=$(_WINCEROOT)\public\common\sdk\inc

INCLUDES=$(_TARGETPLATROOT)\src\inc
INCLUDES=$(INCLUDES);$(_WINCEROOT)\platform\common\src\soc\x86_ms_v1\inc
INCLUDES=$(INCLUDES);$(_PLATFORMROOT)\common\src\x86\inc
INCLUDES=$(INCLUDES);$(_PLATFORMROOT)\common\src\inc
```

Creating Command Line Build Batch Files

When developing device drivers, using command line build is extremely quick and efficient. It is very easy to prepare batch files to set up the command line build environment and run the build from a command line prompt window. First you have to setup your environment, the following example sets up the build environment for building projects for x86 architecture, using the VirtualPC BSP. Because I may create various environment batch files, I would name this file VPCENV.BAT.

```
echo on
set _WINCEROOT=C:\wince700
cd %_WINCEROOT%\public\common\oak\misc
call Wince.bat x86 CEBASE VirtualPC
set WINCEDEBUG=debug
```

This batch file sets up everything we need to build a device driver that will be incorporated on an operating system running on a virtual PC device. Figure 2-11 shows the result of running this environment batch file.

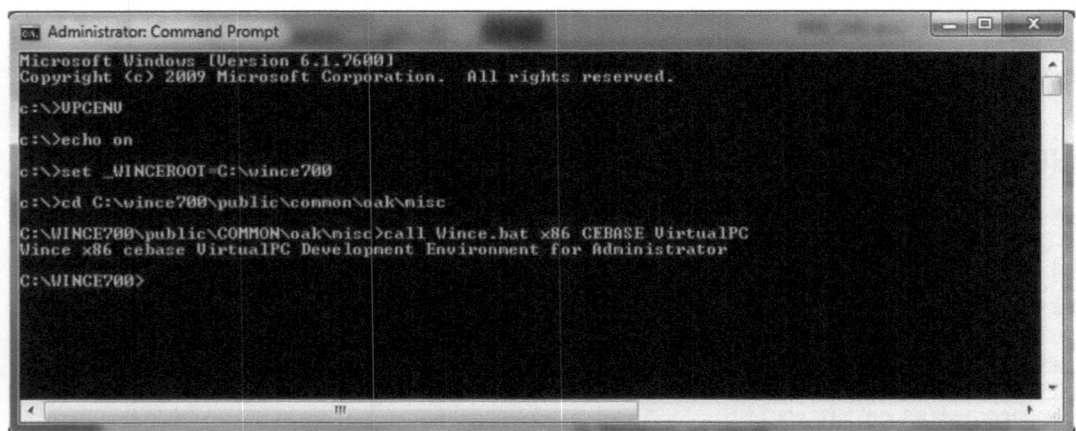

Figure 2-11. *Running VPCENV.BAT in a command line prompt*

The next step would be to create a batch file to perform the actual build. The following example shows a batch script to build the demo driver for the VirtualPC BSP.

```
REM DEMODRIVER build
echo on
call VPCENV.bat
REM build the DEMO DRIVER
cd %_WINCEROOT%\platform\VirtualPC\src\drivers\DEMODRIVER
%_WINCEROOT%\PUBLIC\COMMON\OAK\BIN\I386\build -c
```

As before, you would be advised to give the file a meaningful name for example demodriver_bld.bat. Figure 2-12 shows the result of running this device driver build batch file.

Figure 2-12. Running DEMODRIVER_BLD.BAT in a command line prompt

Device Driver Development Kit

The Device Driver Development Kit or DDK for Windows CE amounts to two major helper libraries and a set of headers that provide definitions for structures and helper functions available in the helper libraries, the CEDDK library and the Registry Helper library. The main directories that contain the DDK files are under the PUBLIC tree:

- `%PUBLICROOT%\COMMON\oak\drivers\ceddk`

- `%PUBLICROOT%\COMMON\ddk\inc`

CEDDK Dynamic-Link Library

CEDDK library provides functions, structures, and IO Control codes used by drivers for handling bus address translations and bus access, allocating and mapping device memory, setting up direct memory access (DMA) buffers, performing I/O, power management functionality, and stall counter.

Registry Helper Library

The registry helper functions and structures provide device driver developers a consistent method to read resource configurations from the registry.

TRACE32-ICD

TRACE32-ICD is offered by Lauterbach Datentechnik GmbH is an extremely powerful debugging tool that is used on chip debugging capabilities. It is by no means the only third-party tool that is available, but it is a tool I have used for debugging device drivers, boot loaders, and OAL code.

Overview

An In Circuit Debugger is a tool that uses debug and trace logic integrated on the microprocessor chip. Most microprocessors implement on chip debug systems. For example the JTAG interface for the ARM microprocessor families. The debug interface requires some microprocessor pins that are used for communication between the on-chip debug system and a third-party development tool. An on chip debug system provides the following basic features:

- Read/write memory

- Read/write CPU registers

- Single step and real time execution

- Hardware breakpoints and trigger features (this may not be supported by all microprocessors)

TRACE32-ICD uses these features of the on chip debug system capabilities to provide a powerful debug tool that offers:

- Easy high-level and assembler debugging

- Display of internal and external peripherals on a logical level

- On chip break and trigger support

- RTOS awareness

- Flash programming

- Powerful script language
- Multiprocessor debugging

TRACE32-ICD supports a wide range of on-chip debug interfaces. The hardware for the debugger is universal and allows interfacing to different target processors by simply changing a debug cable and the software. The debugger hardware comes in three versions that differ only in the way they communicate with the development workstation.

- Power Debug USB 2 communicates via a USB 2 port
- Power Debug Ethernet communicates via USB 2 and 100 MB Ethernet Interface
- Power Debug II communicates via USB or Gigabit Ethernet Interface

Figure 2-13 is of the Power Debug USB 2. Of course there is a marked cost differential between the three. Otherwise all three provide the same capabilities:

- Support for a wide range of on-chip debug interfaces
- Easy high-level and assembler debugging
- Interface to all compilers
- Fast download
- RTOS awareness
- Interface to all hosts
- Display of internal and external peripherals at a logical level
- Flash programming
- Hardware breakpoints and trigger (if supported by chip)
- Trace extension available
- Multiprocessor/multicore debugging
- Software trace
- Virtual analyzer

The TRACE32 System includes a configurable multitask debugger to provide symbolic debugging in real-time operating systems. It contains a ready-to-run configuration for the Windows CE Real Time Kernel provided by Microsoft. The following are capabilities specific to Windows CE.

- Real Time, non-intrusive Display of Windows CE System Resources
- Debugging Windows CE Kernel
- Debugging Windows CE Device Drivers
- Debugging Several Windows CE Applications at Once
- Dynamic Thread Performance Measurement
- Windows CE Specific Evaluation of Real Time Trace Listing

- PRACTICE Functions for OS Data

- Windows CE related Pull-Down Menu

Figure 2-13. *Power Debug USB 2*

How to Prepare your Trace Tools

Preparing your environment for TRACE32-ICD means that you have to connect you target device hardware and install and prepare your TRACE32 PowerView software tools. Figure 2-14 shows how to connect the target device to the development station with the In Circuit Debugger module in-between. The Debug Cable is microprocessor specific thus not interchangeable.

Install the ICD – In Circuit Debugger software using the setup program. Once you have it installed you need to create your specific command batch file, because it will save you configuring the session each time from scratch. TRACE32 uses its own command language for batch jobs. All the commands of TRACE32 development tools, such as commands for program flow, conditional commands and I/O commands are allowed. The default extension for batch files is ".cmm".

We shall discuss this tool in-depth combined with hands-on experience in Chapter 15. We will create a specific batch file to load and run kernel device drivers, measure performance, and debug a device driver.

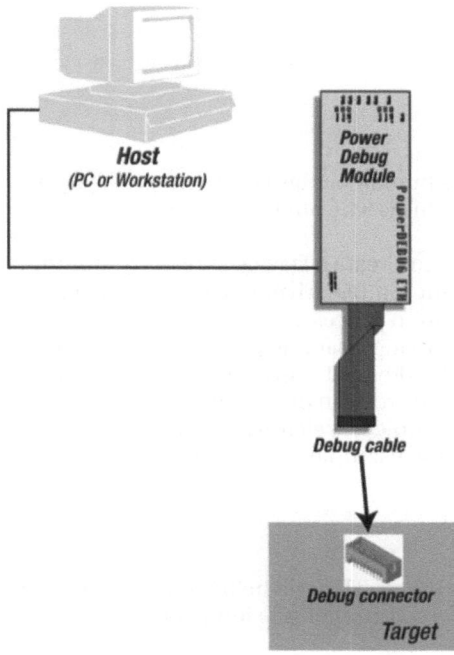

Figure 2-14. *Hardware setup for TRACE32 assisted debugging*

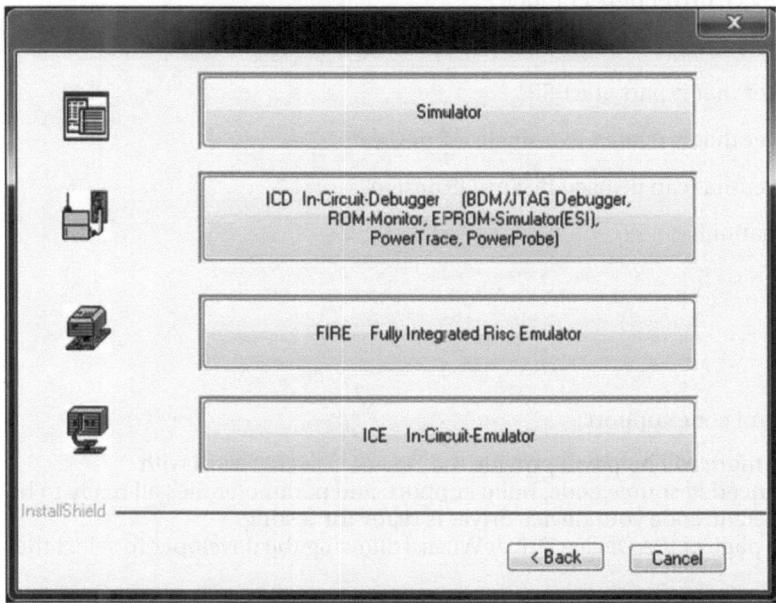

Figure 2-15. *Installing TRACE32 software*

Device Driver Wizard

Overview

Developers learn by example. As much as we learn theory, still as human beings we learn by analyzing examples. This is how we learn as children how to do things and this is why books are littered with examples; this book is no exception.

The Windows CE documentation offers a topic named "How to Create a Device Driver." In this topic in step 4 it tells you to "Copy the power management development sample driver to your OS design." It then goes on to instruct you what to do during the rest of the creation process.

Wizards are designed to take out the cumbersome work of copying a sample project, renaming it, and adapting it to create a new project. This is exactly what the Windows CE Device Driver Wizard is all about. It is designed to help device driver developers jump start the creation of stream device drivers for Windows CE of versions 5.0, 6.0, and 7. It helps create a buildable project skeleton and takes away a mountain of tedious work that is associated with copying a skeleton example and renaming it.

Best Practice

Before you start it you should consider the design of your device driver. This will help going through the creation steps the Device Driver Wizard provides to end up with a comprehensive jumpstart device driver project. You should plan for the following information:

- A meaningful name for the device driver

- If it is a kernel mode device driver or user mode

- The location for the device driver

  - Is it a device driver that is part of a BSP?

  - Is it a device driver that is related to a single OS design?

  - Is it a device driver that can be used by any OS design?

- Registry-related information

- CPU architecture

- DMA support

- Interrupt support

- Device specific IO control code support

Planning for all the above and more will help you provide the Device Driver Wizard with information that will create all the needed source code, build support, and parameter files all ready to be built. Once you add your device specific code your device driver is ready for testing.

Figure 2-16 shows the starting page of the Device Driver Wizard allowing the developer to select the location for the device driver.

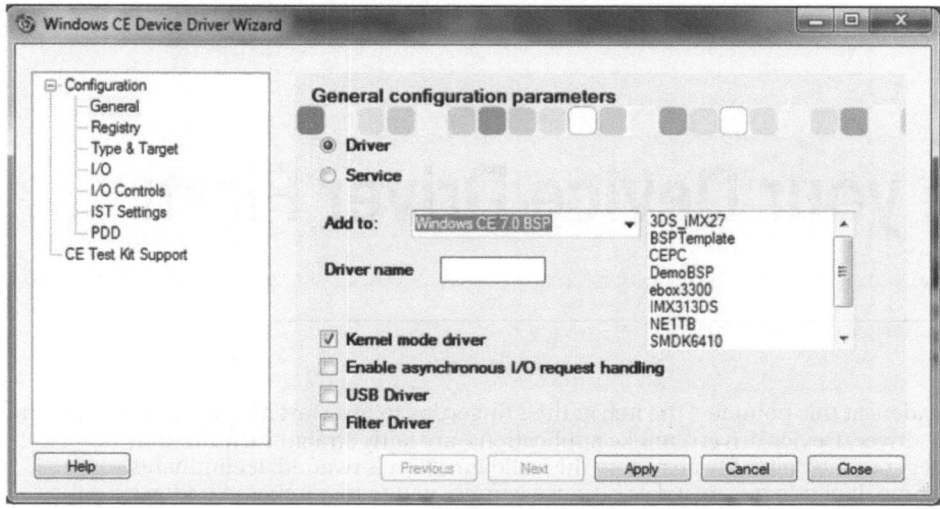

Figure 2-16. *Device Driver Wizard General Configuration Parameters Page*

Chapter Summary

Visual Studio 2008 provides the foundation for the Platform Builder IDE, which enables you to create, build, and debug device drivers. Platform builder includes troubleshooting tools, wizards, and build tools to guide you through the build process. Windows Embedded Compact comes with a defined build system that uses four phases: compile, sysgen, release copy, and make run-time image, and the Platform Builder tools help you at each phase to create a working driver. To troubleshoot and debug issues, and simplify device driver development, you can use the tools included in Platform Builder, such as the Device Driver Wizard, as well as third-party tools such as TRACE32-ICD. Next on our agenda is designing our device driver, considering its location, mode, kernel mode, or user mode and many more considerations that have to be decided upon before diving into actual development.

CHAPTER 3

Design your Device Driver First!

I know that most readers at this point feel the itch at their fingertips to just start hitting the keyboard and implement a device driver. Device drivers, unlike applications, are fairly straightforward units of software so why not get to the point. My answer to this valid question is twofold; it eliminates costly mistakes and saves time. It eliminates mistakes because it forces you to research and understand the hardware. Select the right model for your design. Plan the device driver structure; think through how the device driver will access memory. Think through and plan the device driver interrupt handling. You save time by avoiding ad hoc development and the information you gather for the design helps even if using a third-party tool like the device driver wizard to generate a jumpstart device driver skeleton more efficient. This chapter is designed to highlight the points you should *consider* when planning and designing your device driver.

In this chapter

- Device driver location considerations
- Considering between kernel mode and user mode
- Considering registry settings
- Considering device driver type
- Considering memory access methods
- Considering interrupt Support
- Considering Power Management Support
- Considering IO Control Codes
- Designing Physical Device Driver (PDD)
- Designing for Testing

The Device Driver Location

In Chapter 2 when we discussed the Platform Directory tree, it was noted that the two most relevant directories are PLATFORM and PUBLIC directories. Under the PLATFORM directory are BSP specific device drivers and under the PUBLIC directory are located all the platform-independent device drivers. When we develop a device driver we have to consider to what this device driver belongs. Is it a device driver that is specific to your OS image? Is it a device driver that is part of a BSP? Or maybe I am creating a device driver that is architecture agnostic and I want to market it with my OEM hardware. Figure 3-1 shows how to create and add a device driver to a BSP.

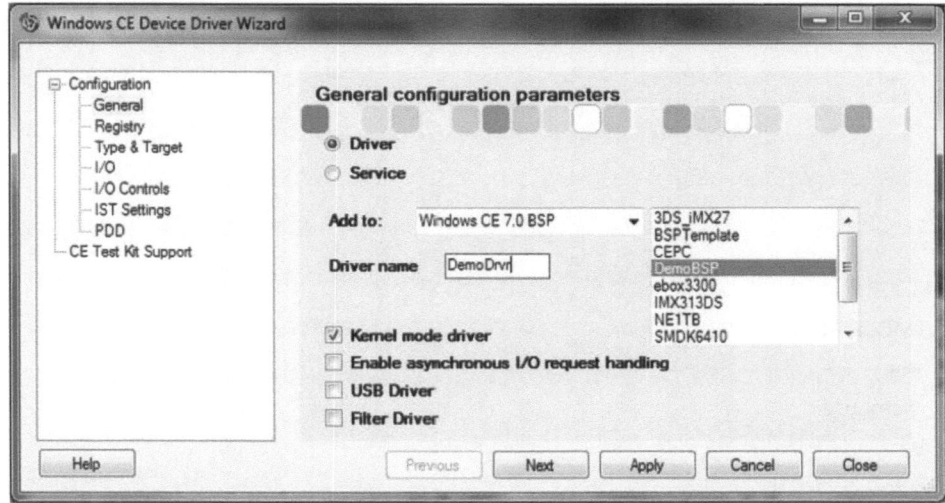

Figure 3-1. *Adding a device driver to a BSP*

The resulting device driver location can be viewed in Figure 3-2; here you can see the folder hierarchy for the DemoDrvr device driver located in the DemoBSP device drivers' folder.

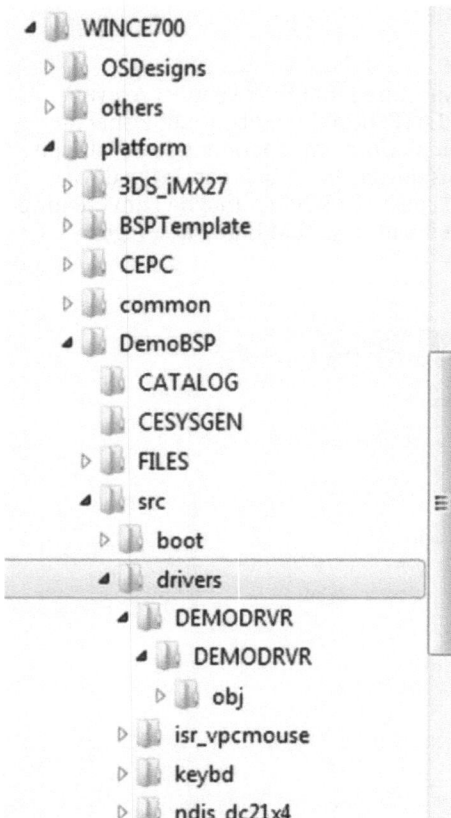

Figure 3-2. *A BSP driver location*

BSP

If the planed device driver is supposed to be handling a peripheral IO device that is a built-in part of your target board, then it should be located in the boards BSP directory. This will ensure that any OS design based on the BSP will be able to access the peripheral IO device. The Production Quality OAL initiative calls for board-specific device drivers to be located under $(PLATFORMROOT)\<BSPName>\src\drivers folder in the platform directory hierarchy. This location will ensure that your device driver will be part of your BSP build.

Specific OS Design

This location allows the developer to create a one of device driver that is placed within the OS design and is built into the image. Previous versions' device driver development documentation suggested you take this path and implement and test your device driver within a test bed OS design and when test and when debugging and testing is done move the device driver to the final location. This version however provides a template stream device driver within a template BSP, in a location similar to the location described above.

It is useful however to locate a device driver in the OS design if this device driver is not needed in any other target device.

PUBLIC Tree

The PUBLIC tree location provides for all agnostic device drivers including out of box device drivers supplied by Microsoft under $(PUBLICROOT) \COMMON\oak\drivers folder. However this is not the location you want to locate your device driver but rather under a third-party folder such as $(PUBLICROOT) \ThirdParty\catalog\<CompanyName>\<DriverName>. This will not corrupt the integrity of the PUBLIC tree and will allow smooth integration of the device driver in the catalog.

Deciding the Mode

Windows CE 6.0 brought about a change in the architecture of the Windows CE operating system. While before that all device drivers were user mode device drivers from this point onwards device driver can either reside in the kernel or in user mode. We have already touched on this subject in Chapter 1 and discuss it further and delve into it deeply in later chapters it is still important to us as developers to decide ahead of implementation if the device driver that we are going to develop will reside in the kernel that is a kernel mode device driver or it will be a user mode device driver.

Kernel Mode

Kernel mode device drivers reside and run in the context of the kernel thus have all the privileges that any other kernel mode code has. It can access kernel mode memory space; it can read and write to kernel structures and use kernel specific APIs. Kernel mode device driver can therefore access hardware without any restrictions. These privileges make a device driver very dangerous and risky to the operating system.

Choosing to develop a kernel mode device driver puts a burden on the developer to produce safe and robust code. This further emphasizes the importance of planning and designing a well-behaved and riskless device driver.

- How the device driver will access memory

- How user mode processes will access the retrieved data

- How user mode processes will send data out

- How the device driver will notify a user mode process that an interrupt has occurred and retrieved data is ready

All through the book these subjects will be discussed in depth.

User Mode

A user mode device driver executes in a user mode process designed to host it and communicate with Device Manager. Device Manager you may recall executes in kernel mode and verifies requests made by a user mode device driver and acts as a go-between the physical hardware and the user mode device driver. This means that a user mode device driver has no kernel mode privileges and kernel mode API access is very restricted. User mode device drivers take a marked performance hit because of the multiple transitions occurring between user mode and kernel mode.

It is appropriate for installable device drivers that handle devices attached to extension buses such as USB and Secure Digital buses.

The Registry

The registry plays a major role in loading and initializing a device driver because a device driver is a dynamically linked library. As such it has to be hosted by a host process. The host process needs to know where to find the executable file in order to load it. There are two main kernel components that host and handle device drivers:

- Graphics, Windowing and Events System (GWES)
- Device Manager.

During the planning and design phase of the development the decision which component hosts the device driver will determine the registry settings for it. For stream device drivers it is a registry node under HKEY_LOCAL_MACHINE\Drivers\BuiltIn.

The registry entries one should plan for are load flags, memory configuration, and interrupt settings. This is not to say that these values are required or more important than others, but it is useful to plan ahead for these if needed. In Chapter 5 a comprehensive discussion of the registry and should provide all the tools to design for registry entries for a stream device driver.

Device Driver Type

Device drivers fall under a few device driver classes distinguished by the component that loads them. Native device drivers are loaded by GWES, stream device drivers are loaded by Device Manager and File System Drivers (FSDs) are loaded by FSD Manager (FSDMGR.DLL). Apart from user interface device drivers such as display and user input drivers such as keyboard, or file system drivers most of the device drivers you are going to develop are stream device drivers. So choosing the class should be straight forward. However stream device drivers can be either built-in drivers such as an I2C device that is an integral part of the SoC or bus drivers or even bus agnostic drivers such PC cards device drivers.

Device Driver Features

Very important points to consider when planning your device driver are memory management, how to handle interrupts, and power management support. It is important because the performance of the device driver is influenced by how data is stored by the device driver and how it handles interrupts. Power management is extremely important for battery-operated devices.

Direct Memory Access

When considering how your device driver stores incoming data performance is of the utmost importance. A device that handles large data input needs to move it with the least delay. Considering direct memory access (DMA) is advisable as it moves data without involving the processor. However you should be acquainted with the DMA capabilities of your peripheral device. A thorough discussion on memory handling is presented in Chapter 10.

Interrupt Support

Planning interrupt support means that you know the hardware interrupt request level that your IO peripheral device is mapped to. Next you have to map a logical system interrupt ID that will correlate your ISR to the IST. Another consideration is the ISR itself, it very much depends on the SoCs architecture and whether you are planning an installable device driver where the ISR will be chained.

Power Management Support

Besides the consideration of whether to provide power management or not, you may want to design what specific power management support the device driver needs to implement. For example should the device driver provide wake up capabilities or not?

IO Control Codes

IO Control codes (IOCTLs) are used to specify device specific system calls that are handled through a single system API - **DeviceIoControl**. This allows an application to request of the driver to perform functions that the regular file system APIs do not offer. For example, suppose the device driver needs some event that it would set to notify some IO completion. The device driver can provide a name for a named event that an application can retrieve calling a specific IOCTL. The application would then create a named event that the device driver would set to trigger waking an application's thread. Chapter 9 is dedicated to this subject. However, it is a good idea to plan for device specific IOCTLs to enhance your device driver's functional capabilities. Figure 3-3 shows how to add IOCTLs to a device driver created by the device driver wizard.

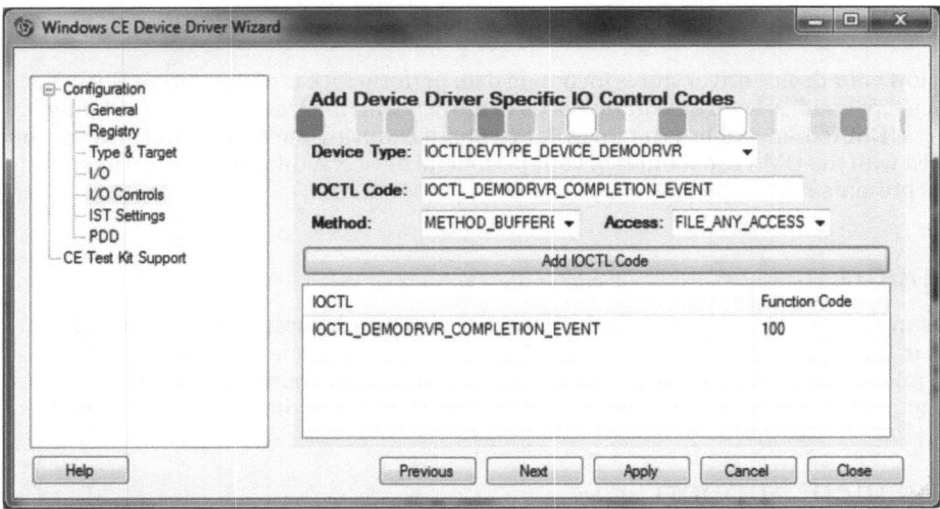

Figure 3-3. *Adding an IOCTL to a device driver*

Designing Physical Device Driver (PDD)

The Physical Device Driver (PDD) is a set of hardware interface functions that allow isolating hardware-specific code. For example when you initialize a device driver and call into its **XXX_Init** function (for a stream device driver) you may need to initialize the devices hardware, sending some command words to it command register, reset interrupts, and so on. You could add this code to the **XXX_Init** function but you could implement a specific **PDD_Init** function specific to the hardware. This would allow for better code maintenance code quality. Part of planning and designing the device driver could be designing the PDD function that can do the hardware interface. The device driver wizard offers adding PDD functions to the device driver code, which means that if you plan ahead you can save a lot of time by adding the designed functions. Figure 3-4 shows how to PDD functions using the device driver wizard.

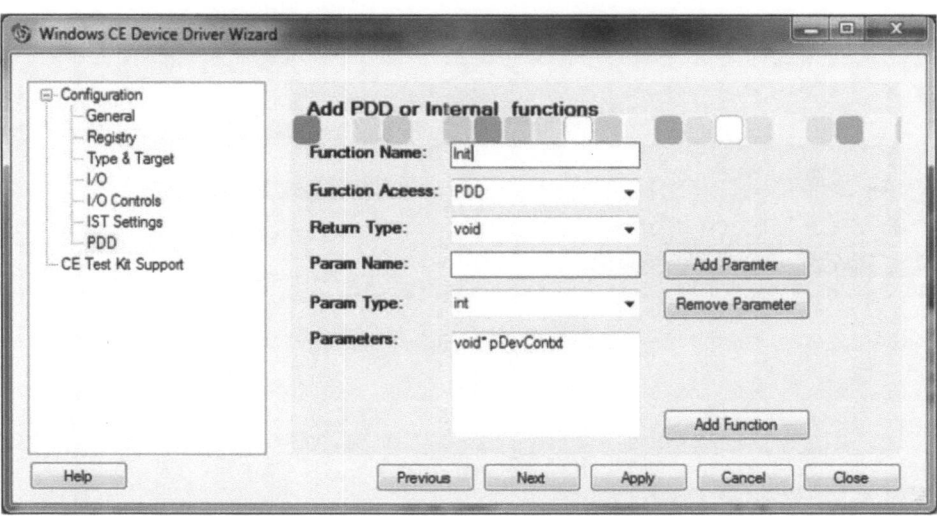

Figure 3-4. *Adding PDD functions to the device driver*

Designing for Testing

Habitually this is the most neglected area of development. Developers debug their code to eliminate errors and when it seems that no more failures befall our development we seem to be happy and supply our device driver only to have our clients frustrated. There may be more to making sure that our device driver works as it is supposed to work than just the obvious bugs. It may not stand up to timing performance needs, thus dropping invaluable data, it may be inconsistent, and it may encounter a bug that only happens in some sporadic combination of specific data and timing. To test for such shortcomings, it is the person with the utmost knowledge of the device driver who has to design a testing scenario for testing the device driver. Microsoft provides a very nice tool for implementing test case suites for device drivers, the Windows Embedded Compact Test Kit (CTK). This tool as an improved version of the Windows CE Test Kit (CETK) tool however uses the same Tux test harness. Chapter 15 is dedicated to developing TUX test modules for testing device drivers. Figure 3-5 shows the latest CTK IDE. The device driver wizard offers a skeleton test module implementation ready for customization and build. CTK provides a set of predefined tests for various drivers implementing common device drivers such as USB host controllers.

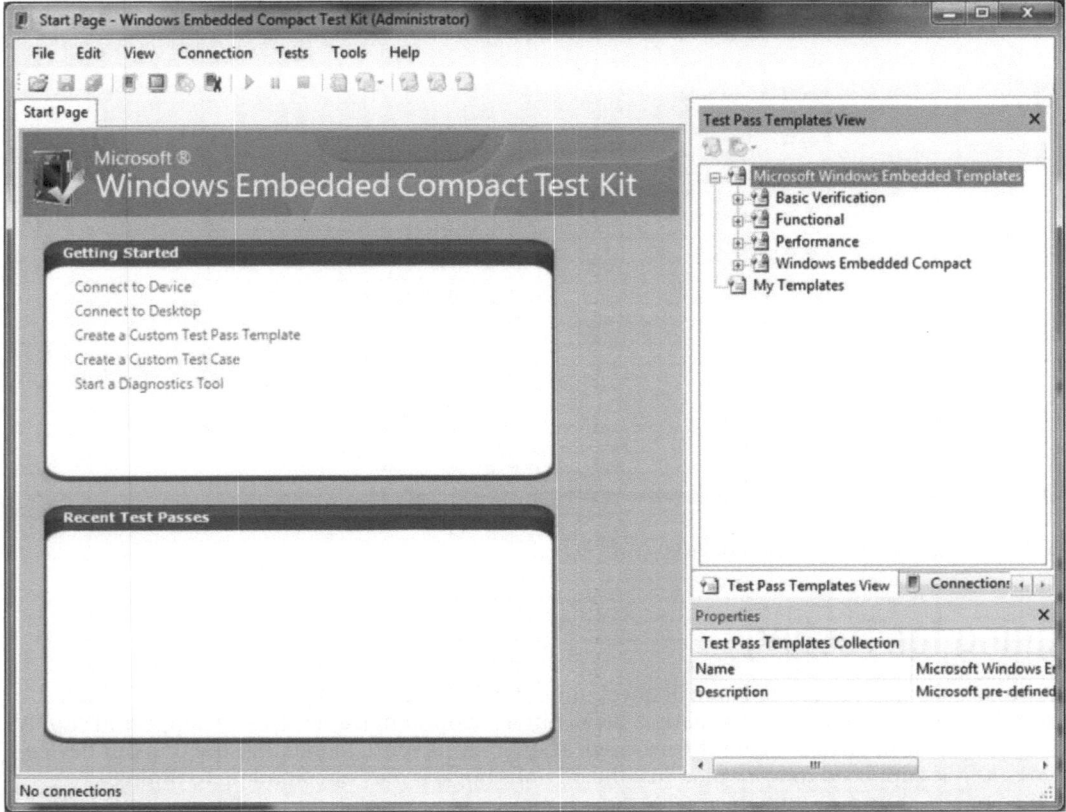

Figure 3-5. *The Windows Embedded Compact Test Kit IDE*

Chapter Summary

This chapter has discussed what you should consider before you start implementing device driver code. Later chapters in the book will discuss how to determine using the alternatives between these considerations. However taking all aspects of the device driver implementation into consideration ahead of the implementation phase should shorten the development period of time and most likely even cut on possible errors and bugs.

CHAPTER 4

Mastering the Hardware Environment

The device driver developer community is a mixed bag of either hardware-predominant developers or software-predominant developers. If you belong to the latter you need to keep it in mind that it is impossible to write device driver interface code for the hardware, without understanding the hardware. This chapter is beneficial to developers of both backgrounds as the former will find useful programming tips and the later useful hardware specification tips.

In this chapter:

- Understand I/O Device Registers

- Understand I/O Device Interrupts

- Understand I/O Device Memory

- Understand DMA – Direct Memory Access

Introduction

As many experienced device driver developers know from their hard-earned experience, the first step of developing a device driver is to understand the underlying hardware. The device driver developer does not need to be a hardware developer, however understanding the functionality of the hardware and how to interface with it programmatically is of the utmost importance. Without a deep understanding of how the hardware works its magic, there is no hope for the device driver developer to achieve his or her goal of ever developing a solid device driver. To put it simply, I/O hardware peripherals are the lifeline to the world for an embedded device or for that matter, for any computer system, I/O devices are analogous to a human being's eyes, ears, nose, or mouth to name but a few. Without the functional operation of I/O devices, a computer system would be rendered useless, unable to communicate with the surrounding world. The I/O peripheral is connected to some source or sink of data; it accepts data coming in or pushes data out. For example, suppose that you need to create a device driver for an analog input device that accepts data coming from some machine in a manufacturing plant. In order to develop your device driver you need to know of the range of analog signals that the device accepts from the machine, how it converts it, and how it is calibrated to have meaningful data that the device driver will pass on to the application that will process the data. Your hardware accepts some data in the form of an electric current, which is otherwise meaningless to the system, to have your device driver pass on meaningless information is really not what you want.

As a programmer you surely know that such a peripheral device is a piece of microelectronics hardware that presents to the system a set of data ports and a way to control it, or retrieve status information. It is your responsibility as a device driver developer to write the unit of execution that will allow this peripheral device to connect with the operating system and offer applications the ability to get meaningful data from the machine on the shop floor. The device driver you develop has to map itself to the data ports and retrieve or write data to and from these ports, to perform this task, your code must setup the peripheral device for correct operation by sending specific commands to the device command ports, this is why it is so important for a device driver developer to understand the underlying hardware. You need to add code to recover status information so that the control code logic you design is coherent with the various states the device may be in.

I/O Device Registers

The mechanism by which a peripheral device passes data to the system is a set of data ports, however data ports are not the only registers a peripheral device presents to the platform. It becomes clear to the device driver developer that device driver code must manage the device so that the data has some coherent meaning to the applications that need the input data. Moreover, the developer needs to consider the state of the hardware, in order to manage the device appropriately, which means that any such device has to report its status to the system as well as allow the system to control it. For this reason any such hardware provides three basic groups of ports or registers:

- Status registers – The combination of bits set or not in the status registers indicate the current state of the device.

- Control registers – Setting or clearing bits in a control register create a command that the device will act upon.

- Data registers – Depending on the direction in which these registers are configured to move data these will either transmit or receive bits of data.

The best way to follow the discussion would be to look at a relatively simple peripheral device such as Two Wire Serial Interface bus (TWSI, formerly known as I2C). It is used for example, by power management ADC controllers, built-in cameras, and more. Imagine that you have the task of managing the battery of a mobile device and the design provides for example a single chip power management unit that provides a TWSI communication interface. The way to communicate with this chip that will provide information about the state of the battery is developing a device driver for a TWSI controller that resides on your target device SoC (System on Chip).

The following example describes the TWSI device of the PXA3xx SoC which I was working on at the time of writing this chapter, and is found in Chapter 10 of *Serial Controller Configuration Developers Manual* which is the fourth volume in the Marvell PXA3xx Processor Family developer's documentation. Although this is a specific example it serves the purpose of describing how to access hardware peripherals in general.

As a device driver developer you must get acquainted with the Two Wire Serial Interface which is a serial communications I/O device to be able to develop the required code. You have to be intimately acquainted with the TWSI interface on your device's SoC. You have to know how to address it, understand the timing of its signals, and control it. Table 2-1 describes the limited number of registers that TWSI uses to interface to the system.

Table 4-1. *Standard Two-Wire Serial Interface Register Addresses*

Address Offset	Description
0x4030_1680	Two-Wire Serial Interface Bus Monitor Register (IBMR)
0x4030_1688	Two-Wire Serial Interface Data Buffer Register (IDBR)
0x4030_1690	Two-Wire Serial Interface Control Register (ICR)
0x4030_1698	Two-Wire Serial Interface Status Register (ISR)
0x4030_16A0	Two-Wire Serial Interface Slave Address Register (ISAR)

Looking at this table notice that the first column gives you an address offset from the base address of this device. When I stated that you need to map your device driver to the peripheral device's ports (or registers) this is exactly what I was referring to. The first register is the IBMR register and is at offset 0. Because all registers are 32 bits wide you have to define the base address of the device as the address at offset 0. You do this by defining a base address in your device driver code. This will help you refer to the entire device as a structure of 32-bit registers.

```
#define BASE_TWSI_REGS    0x40301680
```

Later in this chapter we will be discussing accessing registers using structures.

■ **Note** Device driver coding: It is very likely that most of your coding will be done using the 'C' language (sometimes C++) which is syntactically identical; the structures referred to in the text are 'C' language structures.

Status Registers

At this point you see the importance of getting familiar with your hardware to be able to develop a device driver for this specific hardware. We shell stay consistent and further look at the example we started in the previous section. In this example the status register is named ISR. TWSI interrupts are signaled to the processor interrupt controller by the TWSI Interrupt Status register. Device drivers use the ISR bits to check the status of the TWSI unit and bus. ISR bits (bits 9-5) are updated after the ACK/NAK bit (bit 1) has been received on the Two-Wire Serial Interface bus. Table 2-2 describes ISR status bits visually.

Table 4-2. TWSI status register (ISR) Register bits

31	30	29	28	27	26	25	24	23	22	21	20	19	18	17	16	15	14	13	12	11	10	9	8	7	6	5	4	3	2	1	0
Reserve																					BAD	SAD	GCAD	IRF	ITE	ALD	SSD	IBB	UB	ACKNAK	RWM
																					0	0	0	0	0	0	0	0	0	0	0

- RWM – Read/Write Mode status bit where 0 indicates TWSI interface is in master-transmit or Slave-Receive mode, while 1 indicates TWSI interface is in master-receive or Slave-Transmit mode. This is a read-only access bit and is cleared automatically by hardware after a Stop state.

- ACKNAK - ACK/NACK Status bit, where 0 indicates TWSI interface received or sent an ACK on the bus, while 1 indicates TWSI interface received or sent a NAK on the bus. This bit is used in Slave-Transmit mode to determine when the byte transferred is the last one. This is a read-only access bit and is updated after each byte and ACK/NAK information is received.

- UB - Unit Busy status bit, where 0 indicates TWSI interface not busy, and 1 indicates TWSI interface is busy. This is a read-only access bit. This is a good example of where you need to know the state of the device before you can even send a command to the device.

- IBB - TWSI Bus Busy status bit, where 0 indicates TWSI bus is idle or the TWSI interface is using the bus (that is, unit busy), and 1 indicates the TWSI bus is busy but the processor TWSI interface is not involved in the transaction. This is read-only access bit.

- SSD - Slave Stop Detected status bit, where 0 indicates No Stop detected, and 1 indicates when the TWSI interface detects a Stop while in slave-receive or Slave-Transmit mode. This is a read bit for getting status, and write bit setting 1 to clear.

- ALD - Arbitration Loss Detected status bit, used during multi-master operation where 0 indicates arbitration is won or never took place and 1 indicates TWSI interface loses arbitration. This is a read bit for getting status, and write bit setting 1 to clear.

- ITE - IDBR Transmit Empty status bit, where 0 indicates the data byte is still being transmitted and 1 indicates TWSI interface has finished transmitting a data byte on the TWSI bus. An interrupt is signaled when enabled in the ICR. This is a read bit for getting status, and write bit setting 1 to clear.

- IRF -IDBR Receive Full status bit, where 0 indicates IDBR has not received a new data byte or the TWSI interface is idle and 1 indicates IDBR register received a new data byte from the bus. An interrupt is signaled when enabled in the ICR. This is a read bit for getting status, and write bit setting 1 to clear.

- GCAD - General Call Address Detected status bit, where 0 indicates no general call address received and 1 indicates TWSI interface received a general call address. This is a read bit for getting status, and write bit setting 1 to clear.

- SAD - Slave Address Detected status bit, where 0 indicates no slave address was detected, and 1 indicates TWSI interface detected a seven-bit address that matches the general call address or ISAR. An interrupt is signaled when enabled in the ICR. This is a read bit for getting status, and write bit setting 1 to clear.

- BAD – Bus Error Detected status bit, where 0 indicates no error detected and 1 indicates TWSI interface sets this bit when it detects one of the following error conditions:

  - As a master transmitter, no ACK was detected on the interface after a byte was sent.

  - As a slave receiver, the TWSI interface generates a NAK pulse.

- All other bits in this register have no meaning.

Another status register for the same device is the TWSI Bus Monitor register (IBMR) which tracks the status of the SCL and SDA pins.

Control registers

Control registers determine how the peripheral hardware device functions. The device driver developer provides code that sets and clears bits of a command word that is then written to the control register to configure the device's functionality. A device may have more than one control register if it needs more bits than a single register can offer. In the following example we look at the ICR which is the TWSI control register. The processor uses the bits in the TWSI Control register (ICR) to control the TWSI unit; all are read/write bits. Reserved bits are ignored. Table 2-3 describes ICR register bits.

Table 4-3. *TWSI control register (ICR) Bit Definitions*

31	30	29	28	27	26	25	24	23	22	21	20	19	18	17	16	15	14	13	12	11	10	9	8	7	6	5	4	3	2	1	0
Reserved																MODE	UR	SADIE	ALDIE	SSDIE	BEIE	BRFIE	ITEIE	GCD	IUE	SCLE	MA	TB	ACKNAK	STOP	START
																0	0	0	0	0	0	0	0	0	0	0	0	0	0	0	0

Each bit description can be found in Chapter 10 of *Serial Controller Configuration Developers Manual*. A sample of such command bit definition is the following:

- START - Start control bit, is used to initiate a START condition to the TWSI unit when in master mode, where 0 setting means do not send a Start pulse and a 1 means send a Start pulse.

You can learn the bit definitions of this control register in the documentation. However this demonstrates what a control register provides, bit 0 of this control register tells the device how to initiate a start condition on the TWSI device.

Data Registers

In the example there are two data registers. One is the Slave Address Register (ISAR) which defines the TWSI interface's seven-bit slave address. In Slave-Receive mode, the processor responds when the seven-bit address matches the value in this register. The processor writes this register before it enables TWSI operations. The other data register is the TWSI Data Buffer Register (IDBR). The processor uses the TWSI Data Buffer register to transmit and receive data from the TWSI bus. The IDBR is accessed by the device driver on one side and by the TWSI Shift register on the other. The IDBR receives data coming into the TWSI unit after a full byte is received and acknowledged. The processor core writes data going out of the TWSI interface to the IDBR and sends it to the serial bus.

Only the low byte of this register is used as the data sent and received is byte size. This means that only bits 0-7 are bytes to read from and write to.

I/O Port Registers

Depending on the system's CPU architecture, the peripheral device registers can be specific I/O space addresses. These addresses are not part of the memory space that the CPU can address. These addresses can only be accessed by special machine instructions. For example Intel's x86 architecture provides an I/O address space that is separate and distinct from the physical-memory address space. The I/O address space consists of 2^{16} (64KB) individually addressable 8-bit I/O ports, numbered 0 through FFFFH. Any two consecutive 8-bit ports can be treated as a 16-bit port, and any four consecutive ports can be a 32-bit port. In this manner, the processor can transfer 8, 16, or 32 bits to or from a device in the I/O address space. However you should consult the Intel x86 developer's documentation on the differences between various versions.

Memory Mapped Registers

Memory mapped I/O on the other hand means that a peripheral device's registers are regarded as part of the physical memory of the system and are accessed as any other memory address. However you should note that caching of the address space mapped for I/O operations must be prevented. Preventing caching is CPU related and usually the BSP developers will see to provide the correct method. Furthermore, these registers become part of the virtual address space. Since Windows CE software, either user mode or kernel mode use virtual addresses in mapping I/O registers to memory it is preferred. Moreover performance of peripheral devices with large register sets is greatly improved by using memory mapping scheme even if the CPU architecture provides for specific I/O space. Typically I/O specific machine instructions are slower than using memory access instructions.

Accessing Registers

Whatever scheme of accessing I/O registers is employed, these must be accessed by the device driver in order to control the device, query its status and retrieve or dispatch data. To achieve this there are a few cardinal rules we have to follow when we embark on developing device drivers. The following is a list of the most important of these rules:

- Use the volatile qualifier for registers - The volatile type qualifier declares an item whose value can be changed outside the control of the program in which it appears. The compiler disregards optimization settings and generates code for each assignment to, or reference of a volatile variable even if it appears to have no effect.

- Use 'C' language structure overlays - This will enable access to all the device registers via a single pointer. This pointer is obtained by mapping the base physical address of the device to the virtual memory address space.

- Use OS-defined macros for PORT and REGISTER access. For example READ_PORT_UCHAR or READ_REGISTER_UCHAR. There are similar macros for 16- and 32-bit wide ports and registers.

To understand it better let's look at the TWSI example and use it. Table 2-1 tells us what registers TWSI employs and their system physical address offsets. As already mentioned I/O registers need to be mapped to the uncached memory. Because each architecture provides its own method to map uncached memory, Microsoft provides an architecture dependent OAL function for mapping physical address to uncached virtual memory; OALPAtoUA. To understand how it is implemented you can check the following files:

- C:\WINCE700\PLATFORM\COMMON\SRC\INC\oal_memory.h

- C:\WINCE700\PLATFORM\COMMON\SRC\ARM\COMMON\MEMORY\memory.c

- C:\WINCE700\PLATFORM\COMMON\SRC\X86\COMMON\MEMORY\memory.c

Having dealt with the technique of getting an uncached virtual pointer, let's figure out what this pointer is supposed to point to. Remember the first rule? It is good practice to define some volatile types and use these to define our structure to define TWSI's register set.

```
#define BASE_TWSI_REGS  0x40301680

typedef unsigned long    UINT32,  *PUINT32;
typedef volatile UINT32 VUINT32, *PVUINT32;

typedef struct
{
        VUINT32 IBMR;               /* Bus monitor register */
        VUINT32 IDBR;               /* Data buffer Register */
        VUINT32 ICR;                /* Global Control Register */
        VUINT32 ISR;                /* Status Register*/
        VUINT32 ISAR;               /* Slave address register */
} TWSI_REGS, *PTWSI_REGS;
```

Note that the base address offset of IBMR register, the first register of the TWSI device is 0x40301680 as indicated in Table 2-1. For example we can actually use it the following way:

```
PTWSI_REGS pTWSIRegs = (PTWSI_REGS)OALPAtoUA(BASE_TWSI_REGS);

// check if we are in read or write mode
UINT32 status = pTWSIRegs->ISR & 0x00000001;
......
```

There you have it, but wait, this is not right! We botched the address offset of ISR. Because as it stands ISR is the fourth register in a structure of long integers which means that it is offset by 12 bytes from IBMR (using for the sake of clarity the physical offsets) which is at 0x40301680 so it is pointed to 0x4030168C.

However if we look at Table 2-1 again we notice that for some reason the hardware maker tells us that ISR address offset is at 0x40301698. Let's look again at this table and fix the problem. The first thing we notice is that there is an offset of 8 bytes between each register of the TWSI device. So in order to create a structure that will allow us to overlay the memory mapped registers we need to add another long integer between each register. We add these and call them for clarity RESERVEx. Note however that because these are not really registers that we read from or write to, we need not qualify these as volatile. The following code example is now doing what it is supposed to do, and pTWSIRegs->ISR points to the ISR register correctly.

```
#define BASE_TWSI_REGS   0x40301680

typedef unsigned long   UINT32,  *PUINT32;
typedef volatile UINT32 VUINT32, *PVUINT32;

typedef struct
{
        VUINT32 IBMR;             // Bus monitor register
        UINT32  RESERVED1;        // addr. offset 0x84-0x88 no need for
                        // volatile type
        VUINT32 IDBR;             // Data buffer Register
        UINT32  RESERVED2;        // addr. offset 0x8C-0x90 no need for
                        // volatile type
        VUINT32 ICR;              // Global Control Register
        UINT32  RESERVED3;        // addr. offset 0x94-0x98 no need for
                        // volatile type
        VUINT32 ISR;              // Status Register
        UINT32  RESERVED4;        // addr. offset 0x9C-0xA0 no need for
                        // volatile type
        VUINT32 ISAR;             // Slave address register
} TWSI_REGS, *PTWSI_REGS;

. . . . . . . . . . . . . . .

PTWSI_REGS pTWSIRegs = (PTWSI_REGS)OALPAtoUA(BASE_TWSI_REGS);

// check if we are in read or write mode
UINT32 status = pTWSIRegs->ISR & 0x00000001;

. . . . . . . . . . . . . . .
```

We have learned two important lessons. First we need to carefully read the hardware specifications and understand these before we write the code to implement access to the device register. Second we should use the volatile qualifier for memory mapped registers as these are liable to change outside the control path of the code.

I/O Device Interrupts

The basic concept behind any computer, and embedded systems are no different, is that some input data comes in, the system (and by system we mean the entire package, the hardware operating system and applications) takes this incoming data and manipulate it the way the designer intended to manipulate it, and as a result it may send out some data as output. There are basically two ways to get incoming data input; either polling the I/O device input registers or ports and once data appears in these ports, retrieve it and clear these ports for the next data to come in, alternatively, wait for some signal from the I/O device telling the system that new data has arrived. Both ways have strengths and weaknesses however modern systems rely on the latter. The signal that the I/O device has triggered causes the system to stop what it's doing at that point, and retrieve the new input data, meaning the system was interrupted to accept new data input.

Interrupt Priorities

Various I/O peripheral devices have different importance to the system. Although the real-time clock of the system is of extreme importance to the operating system in order to time everything, other devices importance may be configured according to their function value for the entire system and possibly the device's needs. For example an I/O device that monitors a car engine is by far more important than an I/O device that plays multimedia.

A programmable interrupt controller is a chip that helps manage interrupt requests from peripheral devices, it determines which of the incoming requests is of the highest priority, ascertains whether the incoming request has a higher priority value than the level currently being serviced, and issues an interrupt to the CPU based on this examination.

One of the attributes that make Windows CE a real-time operating system is the use of nested interrupts. This allows a high-priority interrupt to interrupt the handling of a lower priority interrupt. The use of nested interrupts prevents the loss and delay of high-priority interrupts. The kernel handles the details of saving the ISR's state when a higher priority interrupt occurs and restoring it after the high priority ISR has completed. In most cases, the preempted ISR does not detect that it has been preempted.

Interrupt Vectors

An interrupt vector is a memory address of an interrupt handler, interrupt vectors are placed in an array called an interrupt vector table. In Windows CE a vectored function is called in the kernel which is controlled by hardware, so the implementation is CPU family dependent. The vector table is initialized by the kernel when it starts. When you install Platform Builder and accept the conditions for installing the source code for Windows CE, you may want to have a look at the code in C:\WINCE700\PRIVATE\WINCEOS\COREOS\CORE\DLL\exdsptch.c that implements the functions that dispatch the interrupt vectors.

Signaling Mechanisms

Hardware designers devised to schemes to generate interrupts. One is the change of state on the interrupt signal line from 0 to 1 or vice versa. This is termed rising edge detect or falling edge detect triggers. This scheme has a problem: it is sensitive to electrical noise. A random spike can trigger an interrupt even if there is no new data to merit it. The other scheme is level triggered where a device holds the interrupt line at a steady level until the interrupt service process dismisses the interrupt. This scheme is more robust against electrical noise.

In this section we just skimmed the surface of interrupt handling by the hardware and how it relates to Windows CE. In order to understand how interrupts are handled by the processor that you work with you need to read the documentation related to the interrupt controller, such as Chapter 9 of *System and Timer Configuration Developers Manual* which is the first volume in the Marvell PXA3xx Processor Family developer's documentation.

I/O Device Memory

Device drivers have to move data between the peripheral device and the system's memory. There are three mechanisms employed by hardware to perform memory transfers:

- Programmed I/O (PIO)
- Device Dedicated Memory
- Direct Memory Access – DMA

The memory transfer mechanism used by your device is dependent on the magnitude of data that it needs to move, the speed of the device and standard for the class of devices it may belong to.

Programmed I/O (PIO)

Programmed input/output is a method of transferring data between the CPU and a peripheral such as an ATA storage device. This mechanism basically uses the CPU to address memory and move it around. PIO devices typically generate an interrupt after each data transfer. Some PIO hardware devices have internal buffers or FIFO to reduce interrupts frequency. Even so, extensive transfers need a lot of CPU activity and still produce a torrent of interrupts which leads to reduced system performance.

■ **Note** Typical PIO: If your device uses I/O ports for example then it by default uses PIO. However if you read or write data from a memory mapped data register using memory manipulation instructions it is considered PIO just the same.

Device Dedicated Memory

There are devices that call for a dedicated range of addresses in physical memory. The reasons for this could be that the device uses a block of memory as a buffer for data transfers, such as video capture devices. Another reason is that the device may have an internal ROM that holds some startup code and for the CPU to run it, it has to be part of the memory address space.

Direct Memory Access – DMA

Direct Memory Access or DMA for short is a mechanism that moves data between an I/O device and memory without the intervention of the CPU. DMA comes in two modes: System DMA and the more modern, Bus Master DMA. DMA provides high performance data transfers. There are several DMA transfer types.

- **Common Buffer DMA** - In common-buffer DMA, the driver and the system share the same area of memory for data transfer. The driver is responsible for synchronizing access to the buffer. The memory is not cached, making this synchronization easier for the driver. After setting up a common buffer, both the driver and the hardware can write directly to the addresses in the buffer.

- **Packet DMA** - Performed when there is a single existing buffer that must be mapped for use by the hardware. For example, using packet DMA in the transfer of a file from memory to a disk. Using common-buffer DMA for this action would be wasteful, because the file would have to be transferred to the common buffer before the hardware could transfer it to the disk.

- **Scatter/gather DMA** - Scatter/gather DMA is a shortcut method that sets up several packet DMA transfers at once. If you are transferring a packet over the network, for example, each part of the network stack adds its own header (TCP, IP, Ethernet, and so forth). These headers are all allocated from different places in memory.

System DMA

System DMA is performed by programming the system DMA controller (DMAC) on the system board to perform the transfer directly. The DMAC acts as a very simple processor that is capable of moving a specified number of bytes between a peripheral device and main memory. At the start of an I/O operation the device driver will load into the DMAC a memory address and transfer count and the DMAC does the rest. When the DMAC has finished moving the data, it generates an interrupt to signal completion. While the DMAC transfers the data, the driver is suspended and the CPU is free to attend to other tasks. This was typical DMA operation for the ISA bus. Modern peripheral devices mostly use bus master DMA.

Bus Master DMA

An I/O device that has its own DMAC built in can take control of the data bus and initiate DMA operations. Full bus mastering implies that the I/O device is capable of performing more complex sequences of operations without CPU intervention. Drivers of bus-master DMA devices can use the following types of DMA support:

- Packet-based DMA if the bus-master adapter allows the driver to determine when a DMA transfer operation is done and/or when to begin another transfer operation. Packet-based DMA is the basis for Scatter/Gather DMA operations.

- Common-buffer DMA if the bus-master adapter does not provide a way for the driver to determine when a transfer operation will begin or complete, or if a single buffer area is used continuously or repeatedly for DMA transfers.

■ **Note** A DMAC example: Chapter 8 of *System and Timer Configuration Developers Manual* should give you a good idea about the DMA controller architecture and operation.

PCI Bus

PCI is the acronym for Peripheral Component Interconnect, which is a local bus *standard* developed by Intel. PCI is a 64-bit bus, though it is usually implemented as a 32-bit bus. It can run at clock speeds of 33 or 66 MHz. At 32 bits and 33 MHz, it yields a throughput rate of 133 MBps. PCI is a synchronous bus architecture with all data transfers being performed relative to the system clock (CLK). Although it was developed by Intel, PCI is not related to any particular family of microprocessors.

PCI implements a 32-bit multiplexed Address and Data bus. The multiplexed Address and Data bus allows a reduced pin count on the PCI connector that enables lower cost and smaller package size for PCI components. PCI bus cycles are initiated by driving an address onto the AD[31:0] signals during the first clock edge called the address phase. The address phase is signaled by the activation of the FRAME# signal. The next clock edge begins the first of one or more data phases in which data is transferred over the AD[31:0] signals.

In PCI terminology, data is transferred between an initiator which is the bus master, and a target which is the bus slave. The higher speed of PCI limits the number of expansion slots on a single bus to at most four. To permit expansion buses with more than 3 or 4 slots, the PCI SIG has defined a PCI-to-PCI Bridge mechanism. PCI-to-PCI Bridges are ASICs that electrically isolate two PCI buses while allowing bus transfers to be forwarded from one bus to another. Each bridge device has a "primary" PCI bus and a "secondary" PCI bus. Multiple bridge devices may be cascaded to create a system with many PCI buses.

■ **Note** PCI Specifications: A good source of understanding PCI is the PCI-SIG website

http://www.pcisig.com/home

Chapter Summary

Device drivers, by definition, are all about the hardware that they are responsible to interface to the system. In this chapter we looked at the hardware for which device drivers are designed. We used the Marvell PXA3xx Processor Family developer's documentation for examples, but it was just for convenience and by no means suggestive of anything.

Read the documentation for the hardware you are working on. Without understanding how the hardware works, there is no way to develop and implement robust device drivers. However it is not enough to read the data sheets and software developer documentation for the peripheral device that you develop a device driver for. You need to be totally familiar with the system processor or SoC it connects to.

In this chapter we discussed how to abstract and implement in device driver code:

- I/O Device Registers
- I/O Device Interrupts
- I/O Device Memory
- DMA – Direct Memory Access

CHAPTER 5

Device Driver Registry Settings

This chapter is all about the Windows Embedded Compact 7 registry and how it relates to device drivers. A general discussion about the registry and its role in the system is followed by a thorough discussion of all device driver related registry topics, including how the OS loads device drivers; naming conventions of device drivers, so that applications can interact with device drivers via the file system; which keys are required to set by the developer of a device driver and which keys are optional; and how to setup registry entries for user mode device drivers, and how to put it all together in practical terms.

In this chapter:

- Understand how Windows CE OS loads device drivers
- Understand the naming conventions for device drivers
- Create the necessary files for the registry entries for a specific device driver

Registry Overview

The Windows Embedded Compact 7 registry stores information about applications, drivers, user preferences, and other configuration settings. The registry is organized in a hierarchical system of keys and values. This hierarchy is similar to a folder hierarchy, and a key can contain values entries or other keys. Value entries are stored as name/value pairs. At the top of each folder tree hierarchy is the root, which is identified using a well-known constant value, or HKEY. Windows CE supports four root keys. The most relevant to the device driver developer is the HKEY_LOCAL_MACHINE root key where the hardware and driver configuration data is located. The structure of the Windows Embedded Compact 7 registry is similar to the registries in other versions of Windows, and previous versions of Windows CE.

Registry Types

Windows Embedded Compact 7 supports two different registry types: the RAM-based registry and the hive-based registry. OEMs can determine the registry type for their device, which will be transparent to either applications or users.

Windows Embedded Compact 7 implements the hive-based registry by default. The applications is unaware of registry type, however it affects persistence, boot sequence, speed, memory usage on a target device, and the behavior of user profiles. User profile support is present in all file system configurations.

The Object Store

The object store in Windows Embedded Compact 7 provides persistent storage for applications and related data even when the main power supply is lost, provided there is a backup power supply. One or more memory storage chips, which typically are nonvolatile RAM chips, compose the physical object store. The object store consists of three types of persistent storage:

- File systems
- Databases
- A system registry

The storage mechanism for data in the object store is transaction based. If power is interrupted while data is being written to the object store, Windows Embedded Compact 7 ensures that the store is not corrupted. It ensures this by either completing the operation when the system restarts or reverting to the last known good state before the interruption. For system files, including the registry settings, this can mean reloading the initial settings from ROM if a backup system for saving the current settings was not predefine.

RAM-Based Registry

The RAM-Based Registry stores all registry data within the object store. This is efficient in terms of speed and size in devices that have battery-backed RAM. Devices that do not power the RAM while turned off must back up the registry during power off and restore the registry when power is restored. The RAM-based registry is intended for use on devices that experience warm boot often, but rarely or never cold boot.

Hive-Based Registry

The Hive-Based Registry stores all registry data inside files, nicknamed hives, and these files can be stored on any file system. Consequently, the need for backup and restore operations on power off/on is removed, resulting in faster cold boot process. The hive-based registry is split into two hives: the system hive, which contains all system data, and the user hive, which contains all data pertinent to one particular user. A multi-user system will contain several user hives. A user's hive will be mounted on logon and dismounted on logoff. The hive-based registry is intended for use on devices that cold boots often, but has no impact on warm boot. It is also useful on devices that require support for multiple users.

A hive is treated as a single unit and is saved and restored as a single file. The system hive contains system settings that do not relate to any one user. The OEM selects the system hive file name and location. The system hive file is typically named System.hv, but location may vary.

Summary

The Windows Embedded Compact 7 registry is similar in its functional structure to the registry of the desktop and server Windows operating systems. However it is compact in comparison for obvious reasons. Unlike the registry implementation on other Windows OSs it supports two types; RAM-Based Registry and Hive-Based Registry.

Device Driver File Names

In order for user mode applications to interact with device drivers, an application uses file system functions. The first thing an application has to perform is to get a handle to an instance of the device driver. It does this by calling *CreateFile* and using the returned handle is then used by the application to call other functions such as *ReadFile* or *WriteFile* and Device Manager functions such as *DeviceIoControl*. *CreateFile* needs a file name for its first parameter, which means that a convention for device driver names is required. The naming convention falls under three device namespaces:

- Three-letter prefix, followed by a number between 0 and 9, followed by a colon.

- $device mount point, followed by a three-letter prefix representing the device, followed by a number.

- $bus mount point, followed by the bus name, bus number, device number, and function number.

Device File Namespace - Prefixes and Indexes

The prefix consists of three uppercase letters that identify which device file name corresponds to a particular stream interface. The prefix is stored in a registry value called Prefix, which is located within the key for the driver. First, the prefix identifies all possible device file names that can access the stream interface driver. Second, the prefix tells the operating system what entry-point file names to expect in the stream interface DLL. For example, *DMO_Ini*, *DMO_Read* or *DMO_IOControl* entry points where the designated prefix is DMO. An index is a digit that follows the prefix. The index distinguishes between similar devices that the stream interface manages. By default, Device Manager indexes logically from 1 through 9, with 1 corresponding to the first device file name. When a tenth device file name is required, 0 is used as the index. For example, the typical code to open a device driver by the device file name prefix should be:

```
CreateFile("DMO1:", ....
```

Device File Namespace – Mount points

There are two mount point namespaces; the $device mount point and the $bus mount point. These two namespaces support more than 10 instances of a device with the same three-letter prefix. Device Manager registers the file namespaces with the file system using *RegisterAFSEx*. This allows file system to return handles for the device driver. While the prefix namespace and the device namespace return the same handle, the bus namespace returns a handle to the bus, function, and device, which means that access may be handled differently by the OS.

Opening a device driver instance using the device namespace, calls for the device name being a path string, composed of a backslash the $device space identifier backslash, and the device prefix followed by an index. For example:

```
CreateFile(_T("\\$device\\DM01)", ....
```

Opening a device driver instance using the bus namespace, calls for the device name being a path string, composed of a backslash the $bus space identifier backslash, followed by bus type name, underscore bus number, underscore device number and underscore function number.

```
CreateFile(_T("\\$bus\\PCI_0_3_0)", ....
```

Load Sequence

Since device drivers actually help the operating system interact with the underlying hardware platform, it is of the utmost importance that they will be loaded as soon as possible during the system boot process. The operating component that is responsible for loading and managing stream device drivers is Device Manager. If GWES is part of the operating system, it is responsible for loading native device drivers such as the display device driver, keyboard drivers, and so on. It is possible that a system may be designed to be headless and thus dispose of the GWES component. However Device Manager is required in any meaningful OS design.

Loading Sequence of a Stream Device Driver

When the operating system is booted after the system hardware is initialized by the *OEMInit* function and the file system is up and running, Device Manager enumerates the registry entries under HKLM\Drivers\BuiltIn key by loading and executing BusEnum.dll that is located at the root of HKLM\Drivers\BuiltIn. The bus enumerator initializes the process of scanning the registry for additional buses and devices to be loaded for subkeys of HKLM\Drivers\BuiltIn. The bus enumerator examines the first level of keys just below the key passed to it, according to the Order registry subkey. It invokes *ActivateDeviceEx* on each subkey it finds. Each subkey can have any values interpreted by *ActivateDeviceEx* or by the loaded driver in its initialization routine. Additionally, driver can have an *Order* value between 0 and 255 which is not unique. The smallest *Order* value gets loaded first. If there is no *Order* value, the driver gets loaded after drivers with defined Order values. As the bus enumerator loads the device drivers, it traverses the first level keys of HKEY_LOCAL_MACHINE\Drivers\BuiltIn, one by one, initializing a device driver for each key. It loads the DLL indicated by the *DLL* value, and then creates a subkey for the driver under HKEY_LOCAL_MACHINE\Drivers\Active. Then, it calls the driver's *XXX_Init* entry point and passes in a string containing the registry path to the active key for the stream interface driver. Using the string it gets in return, the *XXX_Init* routine should call *RegOpenKeyEx* to get a handle for this key, and then call *RegQueryValueEx* to look up the key value, which contains the string corresponding to the registry key that Device Manager originally encountered under HKLM\Drivers\BuiltIn. Reading these values the device driver can initialize I/O resources, interrupt handlers, and so on. Figure 5-1 visualizes the load sequence of a stream device driver.

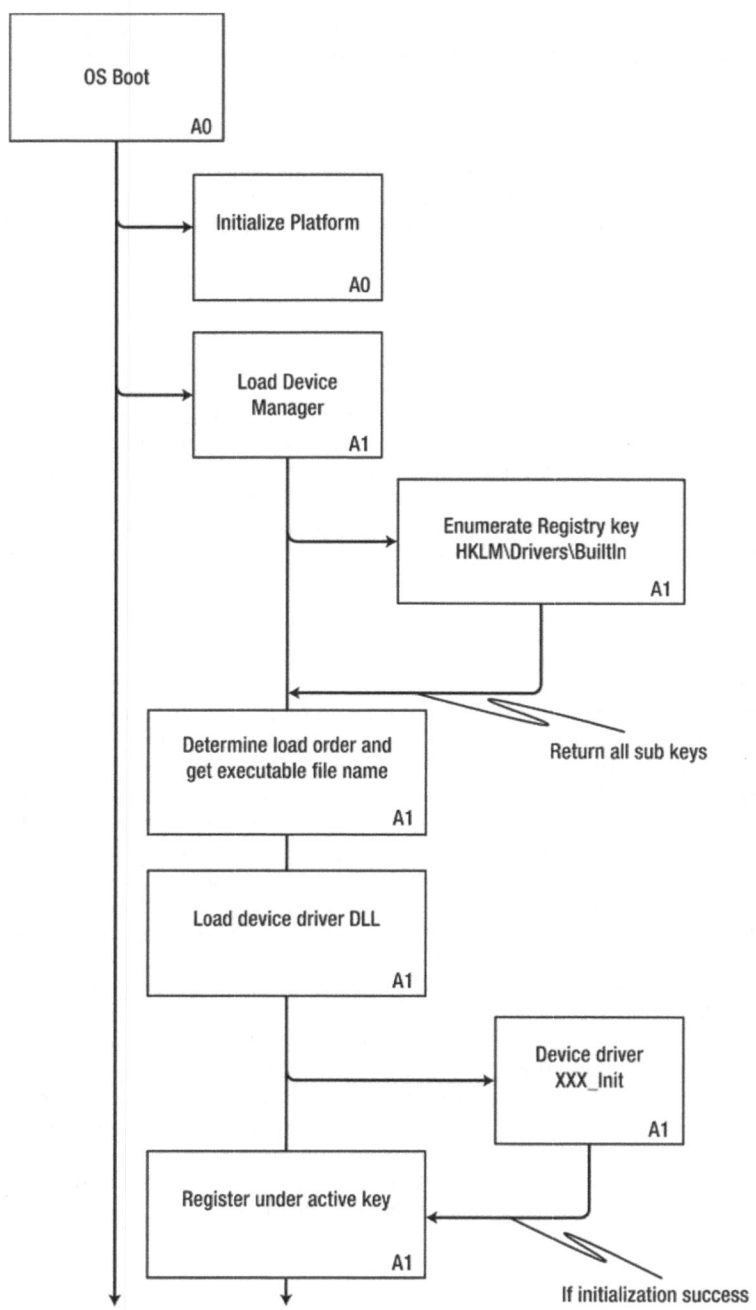

Figure 5-1. *Load sequence for stream device drivers*

Device Manager Registry Keys

Device Manager uses the **Active** and **BuiltIn** subkeys of the **HKLM\Drivers** registry key. The **HKLM\Drivers\Active** registry key contains subkeys that track currently active drivers that Device Manager loaded.

Active registry key

The following list shows the subkeys available in the Active registry key:

- **BusDriver** – Driver's bus name.
- **BusName** - Device's bus name.
    - The bus driver adds these subkeys for its subordinate devices.
- **DevID** - Unique device identifier added by Device Manager.
- **FullName** - Name added by Device Manager and used in conjunction with the \$device namespace.
- **Name** - Device driver's device file name. This subkey is only present for drivers that specify a prefix.
- **Order** - Bus enumerator examines keys according to the Order value.
- **Key** - Registry path to the device.
- **PnpId** - Plug and Play identifier string. Only present for PC Card drivers.
- **Sckt** - Current socket and function pair of the PC Card. Only present for PC Card drivers.

Registry Entries

The registry settings for a device driver are crucial in the development of a device driver. The registry settings govern how Device Manager loads the device driver, allowing the developer order the loading of the device driver if it depends on other device drivers to be loaded ahead of it. The registry settings can contain information that would help the initialization process, or even the creation of instances. For example a specific custom subkey indicating how many instances are allowed. Remember that the registry is an extremely important facet of the device driver package.

There is an array of registry settings that control how a driver loads. Most are optional, one is required. Several registry settings are used by the Device manager and may be used by all drivers. The device driver developer can create custom registry entries that will be referenced directly by the device driver after it has been loaded.

Required

The only required registry subkey value that is absolutely required is the `DLL` subkey. Without it Device Manager is not able to determine which DLL to load. This subkey holds the name of the device driver executable file within the file system.

`"DLL"="Demodriver.DLL"`

Even if, strictly speaking, the `Prefix` subkey is not a requirement it should be set. The `Prefix` is a three-character string that makes up the name of the driver. This value must be present in order to have a file handle based interface to the driver. The `Prefix` value is the same value that must be used in the stream driver entry points unless the `DEVFLAGS_NAKEDENTRIES` flag is set.

Optional

All other subkeys are optional, however some should nearly always be considered, especially the `Order` subkey. The `Order` subkey is a `DWORD` value that provides a mechanism supporting load order. Drivers will be loaded in the order specified by the `Order` subkey. If this subkey does not exist the driver will be loaded at the end. Listing 5-1 is an example of the registry entry generated by the device driver wizard for the demo device driver.

Listing 5-1. *Registry entries for a sample device driver*

```
; DemoDriver driver
[HKEY_LOCAL_MACHINE\Drivers\BuiltIn\Demodriver]
    "Prefix"="DMO"
    "DLL"="Demodriver.DLL"
    "SysIntr"=dword:1A
    "Irq"=dword:8
    "MemBase"=dword:90001000
    "MemLen"=dword:32
    "Order"=dword:0
    "DisplayName"="DemoDriver driver"
    "IsrHandler"="IsrHandler"
    "Flags"=dword:0
    "IClass"="{A32942B7-920C-486b-B0E6-92A702A99B35}"
```

Device Driver Registry Subkeys

A device driver developer can create device driver specific registry keys. For example, the registry entries for the RTL8139 Ethernet driver, has a subkey value for early transmission threshold which specifies the threshold level in the Tx FIFO to begin the transmission; `EarlyTxThreshold`. Listing 5-2 lists an example of the RTL8139 registry entries.

Listing 5-2. *Example of custom registry subkey entries*

```
"Transceiver"=dword:3
"DuplexMode"=dword:1
"EarlyTxThreshold"=dword:10000
"IsrDll"="giisr.dll"
"IsrHandler"="ISRHandler"
"PortIsIO"=dword:1
"PortOffset"=dword:3E
"PortSize"=dword:2
"PortMask"=dword:C07F
"UseMaskReg"=dword:1
"MaskOffset"=dword:3c
```

However most subkeys are preset common values as described by the following list:

- **Dll** - Specifies the name of the driver DLL

- **Prefix** - Specifies the file name for the device driver

- **Order** - Specifies order to load driver

- **Index** - Specifies the device index (x in COMx:)

- **IClass** - Specifies GUID(s) for device class(es) for use by PnP notification system

    - **For example** – a value of A32942B7-920C-486b-B0E6-92A702A99B35 for power managed device interface

- **Flags** - Specifies load flags for the driver

- **IoBase** - Specifies the base of an I/O mapped window used by the device. Port I/O must be supported by the architecture, i.e., special CPU instructions to access I/O ports.

- **IoLen** - Specifies the length of each I/O window needed by the device

- **MemBase** - Specifies the bus relative base of a memory mapped window used by the device. Memory mapped I/O maps the I/O registers to a region in the system memory.

- **MemLen** - Specifies the length of each memory mapped window needed by the device

- **IRQ** - Specifies the physical IRQ used by the device

- **SYSINTR** - Specifies the logical interrupt identifier.

- **IsrDll** - Specifies a DLL to containing an installable interrupt handler

- **IsrHandler** - Specifies the ISR handler in the ISR DLL

User Mode Driver Framework Registry Settings

A user mode device driver is not different in its implementation than kernel mode drivers. After all a user mode device driver needs to perform the same task as a kernel mode device driver. Still, user mode device drivers are restricted and have to be loaded into special user mode hosts, and perform their tasks with the help of a kernel mode reflector. To allow Device Manager to figure out if a device driver is a user mode driver before it loads it, specific registry entries must indicate to Device Manager that a device driver is a user mode device driver. Two subkeys make the difference; the subkey telling Device Manager the driver is a user mode driver is the **Flags** subkey, assigned the value 10. The other subkey indicates to Device Manager in which user mode host to load the device driver, **UserProcGroup**. If this subkey is set, Device Manager will load the driver's DLL into a user mode host that loads several drivers. Otherwise, Device Manager will launch the driver in a separate user mode host that it sole purpose is to load and manage this specific device driver. Listing 5-3 is an example of a user mode device driver that is loaded in a common user mode host.

Listing 5-3. *Example of a user mode device driver registry entry*

```
; SIP
[HKEY_LOCAL_MACHINE\Drivers\BuiltIn\SIP]
"Prefix"="SIP"
"Dll"="softkb.DLL"
"Order"=dword:1
"Index"=dword:0
;Flags==10 is DEVFLAGS_LOAD_AS_USERPROC
"Flags"=dword:10
"UserProcGroup"=dword:3 ; // default to group 3
```

Creating a Registry Entry for a Device Driver

Creating a registry settings entry for your device driver is not complicated, but needs some thought in advance. You must consider what is known in advance. For example information about I/O mapping and addresses, interrupt handling information, and so on. This knowledge assists in setting this information in the registry settings and saves code to set it up within the device driver code. This makes for robust and maintainable drivers, less code means less possible bugs, and having settings in an external file means easier maintenance for change or updating.

Creating the Registry Settings File

The registry files of the operating system are binary files that are created by the build system converting simple structured text files having the .REG file extension into OS registry files. The .REG files are structured to reflect the root key under which a key hierarchy is located. For example, [HKEY_LOCAL_MACHINE\Drivers\BuiltIn\DemoDriver] puts the DemoDriver registry settings under the HKEY_LOCAL_MACHINE root under built in device drivers.

To create a registry parameter file for example for a device driver named DemoDriver, you need to create a simple text file and name it "DEMODRIVER.REG". Next you can use any text editor to edit it and create your registry parameter file, or you can use the built in registry editor in Visual Studio. Figure 5-2 shows how the registry editor in Visual Studio looks after an empty text file named "DEMODRIVER.REG" is opened.

Using it is simple and you can add keys and values using the IDE. Just right-click on the root key, HKLM in this example and add the Drivers key go on to add the BuiltIn key and so on. Figure 5-3 shows the resulting DemoDriver registry settings and Listings 5-4 the resulting text file. One caveat with this editor is the resulting text file simply repeats the key hierarchy for each value so it may be "cleaned" for a streamlined look clarity of reading, and Listing 5-5 the end result.

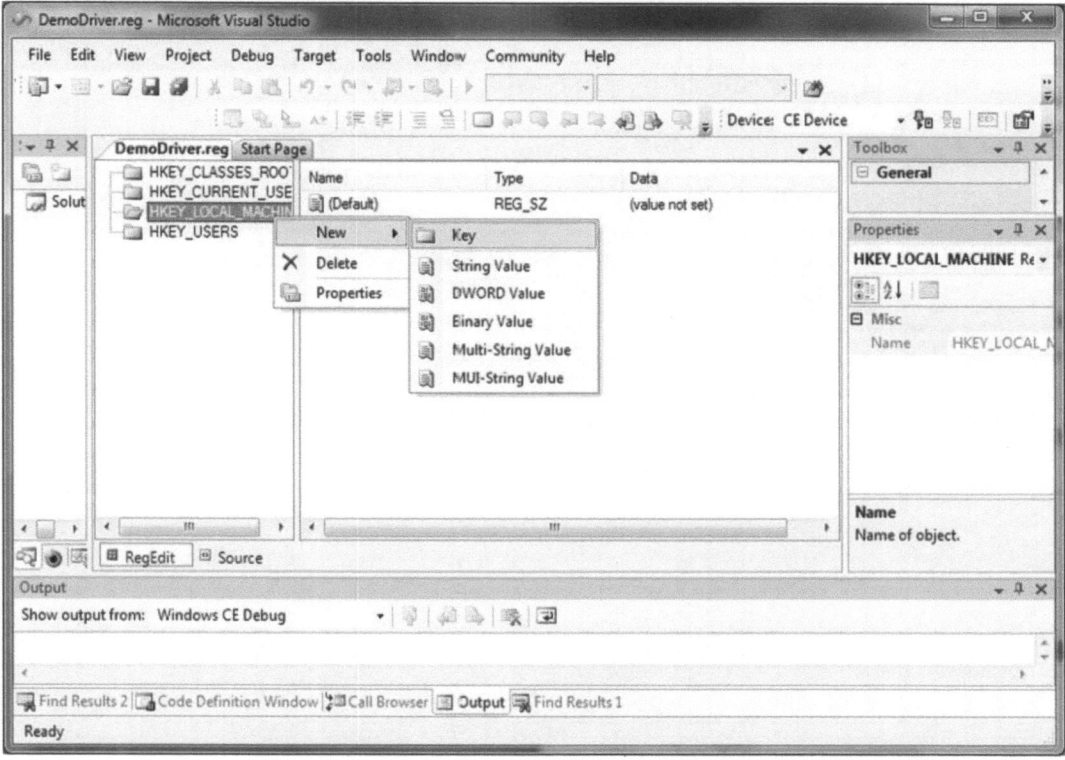

Figure 5-2. *Using registry editor in Visual Studio*

Listing 5-4. *Resulting source*

```
[HKEY_LOCAL_MACHINE\Drivers\BuiltIn\DemoDriver]
"Dll"="demodriver.dll"
[HKEY_LOCAL_MACHINE\Drivers\BuiltIn\DemoDriver]
"Prefix"="DMO"
[HKEY_LOCAL_MACHINE\Drivers\BuiltIn\DemoDriver]
"Order"=dword:0
```

Listing 5-5. *"Cleaned" source*

```
[HKEY_LOCAL_MACHINE\Drivers\BuiltIn\DemoDriver]
"Dll"="demodriver.dll"
"Prefix"="DMO"
"Order"=dword:0
```

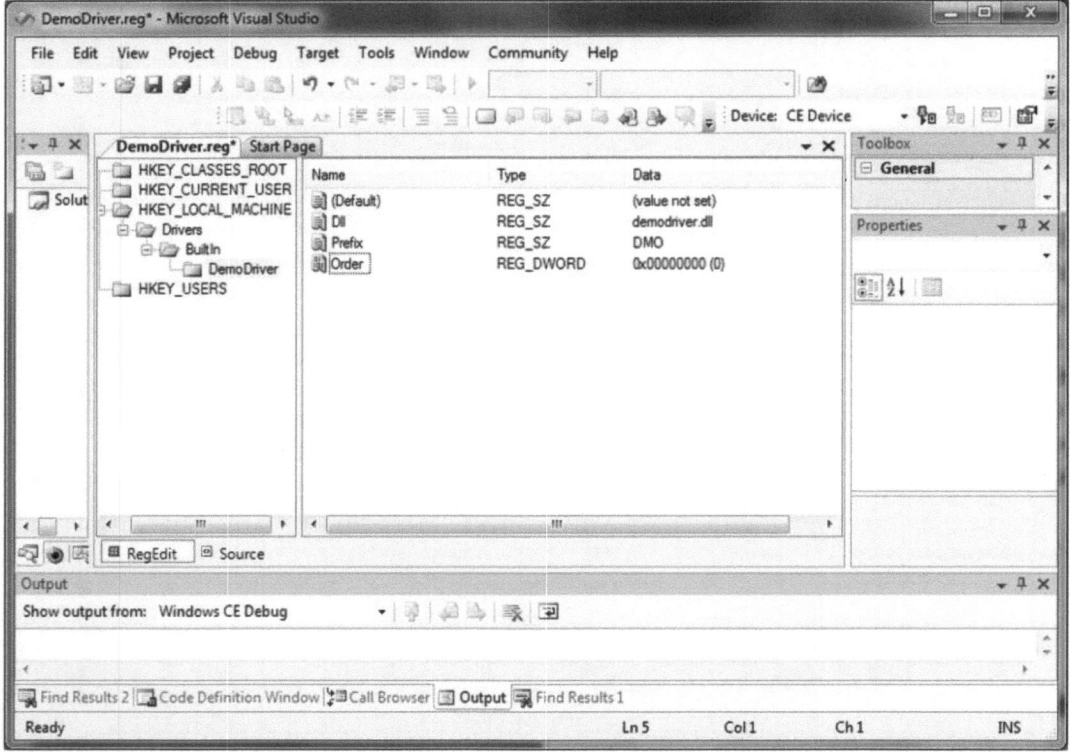

Figure 5-3. *Adding "DemoDriver" to the registry*

Chapter Summary

This chapter dealt with the registry settings of a device driver. The importance of creating the values so that there is no need to hard code device driver information such as base addresses for I/O registers or logical interrupt identifiers. Comprehensive registry settings allow for flexibility, maintainability and robustness. The capabilities of the Windows Device Driver Wizard help the developer jumpstart the creation not just of device driver code but also for a registry settings file. An example of basic entries can be viewed in Figure 5-4.

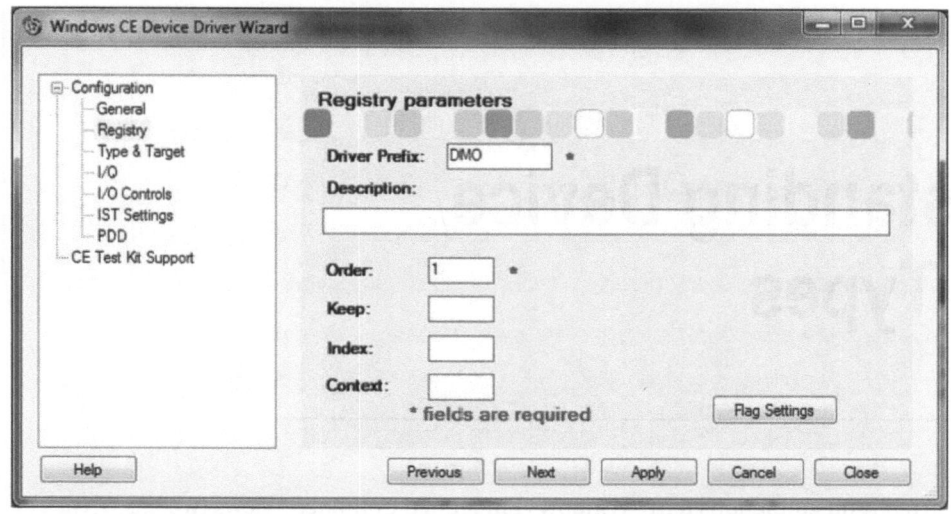

Figure 5-4. *The Registry parameters page of the Windows CE Device Driver Wizard*

In this chapter we discussed registry-related topics. Of specific importance are the following:

- Bus Enumerator
- Device Manager
- The Active registry key
- Device file names

CHAPTER 6

Understanding Device Driver Types

Device driver type is really an ambiguous term. Windows Embedded Compact 7 views two basic types of device drivers; Native and Stream device drivers. A third (which is really a combination of the two) is called a hybrid device driver. A native device driver is a built-in device driver that is loaded and called by GWES at boot time and exposes a custom API set that is unique to the device driver class. A device driver that manages an IO device built into the hardware platform and is managed by Device Manager and exposes a stream interface is regarded as a stream device driver. Hybrid device drivers expose both a custom-purpose interface and a stream interface to the rest of the system.

In this chapter:

- Native device drivers
- Stream device drivers
- Hybrid device drivers
- Monolithic vs. Layered
- Explain device interface class
- How to implement device interface notifications

Native Device Drivers

Native device drivers are typically device drivers that support user input and output peripheral devices such as keyboard, mouse, touch screen, and display peripherals. It seems reasonable to expect the Graphics Windowing and Events Subsystem (GWES) to handle these. GWES does indeed load and manage these device drivers directly. Native device drivers implement specific Device Driver Interface (DDI) functions relating to their functional purpose. Native device driver registry entries reside under HKEY_LOCAL_MACHINE\HARDWARE\DEVICEMAP\ or under HKEY_LOCAL_MACHINE\Drivers\Display\ registry nodes.

For example:

```
[HKEY_LOCAL_MACHINE\HARDWARE\DEVICEMAP\TOUCH]
    "DriverName"="touch.dll"
    "MaxCalError"=dword:10
```

Stream Device Drivers

Stream device drivers are loaded and managed by Device Manager. A stream device driver exposes a defined set of functions so Device Manager can interact with the device driver on behalf of the system or user mode applications. User mode applications access stream device drivers using the file system APIs to open an instance of the device driver and read and write device data. Extended operations are accessed by Device Manager API DeviceIoControl which can accommodate customized operations allowed by the device driver. Stream device driver registry entries reside under HKEY_LOCAL_MACHINE\Drivers\BuiltIn registry node.

■ **Note** Stream terminology: The term stream device driver implies that only stream content is handled by the stream device driver. This is not necessarily accurate since block device drivers such as device drivers for storage peripherals are stream device drivers. The term specifies device drivers loaded and managed by Device Manager and exposing the stream interface.

Hybrid Device Drivers

Hybrid device drivers expose both stream interface and a specific API. USB device drivers are a typical example exposing a partial stream interface and a USB specific API. For example:

```
LIBRARY          WAVEDEV

EXPORTS
    WAV_Init
    WAV_Deinit
    WAV_Open
    WAV_Close
    WAV_IOControl

    USBInstallDriver
    USBDeviceAttach
    USBUnInstallDriver
```

Monolithic vs. Layered Device Drivers

Windows Embedded Compact 7 device drivers can conform to either a monolithic or layered organizational model. A monolithic device driver is based on a single piece of code that exposes the hardware device's functionality directly to the operating system. A layered device driver consists of two layers:

- A model device driver (MDD) layer, which is the upper layer interfacing to the OS.

    - Accesses its devices through the PDD layer.

    - Implements a Device Driver Interface (DDI), a set of functions called by the operating system components such as GWES or Device Manager.

- A platform-dependent driver (PDD) layer, which is the lower layer interfacing to the underlying hardware.

    - Hardware dependent; typically must be customized to specific hardware.

    - Links the MDD to the hardware.

    - Implements a Device Driver Service Provider Interface (DDSI)

        - A set of functions called by the MDD layer.

Figure 6-1 shows a comparison between the layered device driver model and the monolithic model. Note however that monolithic device drivers can be either native or stream device drivers even though the figure only depicts a native monolithic device driver because of lack of space.

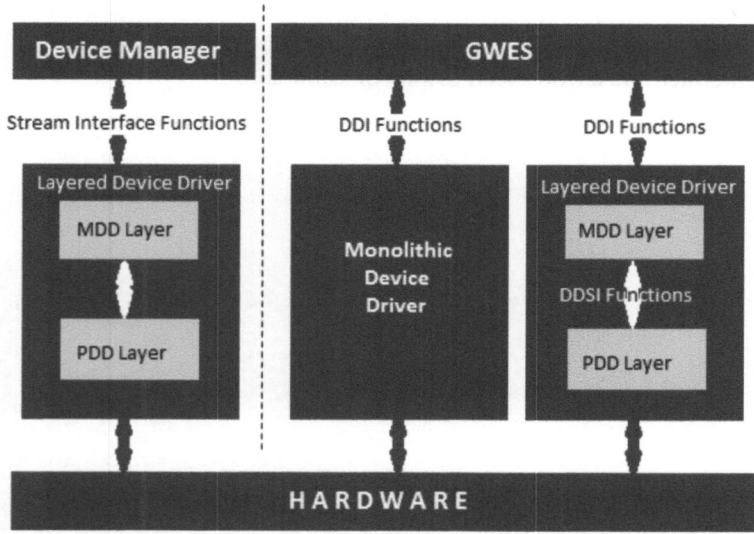

Figure 6-1. Monolithic vs. Layered device drivers

Device Interface Class

Device drivers are characterized by the device interface class they expose to operating system. A device driver may have multiple device interface classes, or it can have none. Question is, why do I care what interface class does a device driver belong to? Basically I don't. However, if for example a device driver supports power management, you want to characterize the driver as supporting the generic power management class interface, so that power manager can interface with the device driver.

Typically, however exposing an interface class by a device driver allows Device Manager to notify applications, services, or other device drivers the appearance and disappearance of the device interface. This is important for device drivers managing Plug and Play devices, USB devices, or other detachable media. It is also important for mountable storage device notifying an application of a volume being mounted or dismounted.

Applications, services, or device drivers that need to be notified of the appearance and disappearance of device interfaces need to register with Device Manager in order to be notified. The next section deals with device interface notifications.

Device Interface GUID

The header file that declares the interface typically defines the GUID and to be associated with the interface. An example extracted from Storemgr.h for a block storage device is listed in listing 6-1. Exposing the device interface is performed by publicizing the associated GUID by either setting the IClass subkey in the registry or by calling AdvertiseInterface during the device driver initialization.

Listing 6-1. Defining a block storage device interface and the associated GUID

```
#define STORAGE_DEVICE_CLASS_BLOCK          0x1
................
................
// {A4E7EDDA-E575-4252-9D6B-4195D48BB865}
static const GUID BLOCK_DRIVER_GUID = { 0xa4e7edda, 0xe575, 0x4252, { 0x9d, 0x6b, 0x41,
  0x95, 0xd4, 0x8b, 0xb8, 0x65 } };
................
................
#define BLOCK_DRIVER_GUID_STRING L"{A4E7EDDA-E575-4252-9D6B-4195D48BB865}"
```

IClass Registry Subkey

IClass registry subkeys reference device interfaces by their associated GUIDs. Listing 6-2 shows how to publicize the fact that DemoDriver supports the generic power management class interface - PMCLASS_GENERIC_DEVICE

Listing 6-2. Setting the IClass subkey value to PMCLASS_GENERIC_DEVICE GUID

```
; DemoDriver driver
[HKEY_LOCAL_MACHINE\Drivers\BuiltIn\Demodriver]
    "Prefix"="DMO"
    "DLL"="Demodriver.DLL"
    "SysIntr"=dword:1A
    "Irq"=dword:8
    "MemBase"=dword:90001000
    "MemLen"=dword:32
    "Order"=dword:0
    "DisplayName"="DemoDriver driver"
    "IsrHandler"="IsrHandler"
    "Flags"=dword:0
    "IClass"="{A32942B7-920C-486b-B0E6-92A702A99B35}"
```

Advertising the Interface

Another method to expose a device interface and publicize the associated GUID is to call during initialization the `AdvertiseInterface` API. This is a less desirable alternative to setting the `IClass` subkey, because the `IClass` value is passed into `ActivateDeviceEx` which allocates resources within the Device Manager. Calling `AdvertiseInterface` with the `fAdd` argument set to false, advertises the removal of the interface and should be called when de-initializing the device driver.

Device interface classes are essential for applications to access the capabilities of a device driver. They indicate to applications via notifications that a particular interface is present.

Device Interface Notifications

Device Manager's interface notification mechanism is Windows Embedded Compact 7 as well as previous versions, correspondent to the desktop Plug and Play event notification system. Device Manager notifies user mode applications and services, and device drivers to the appearance and disappearance of device interfaces. Device Manager uses message queues to deliver these notifications, either the GWES message queue or uses message queue point-to-point.

When Device Manager successfully loads and initializes a device driver it checks to see if there is an "IClass" value in the device key. If it finds a valid value it will start a thread that signals a device change via the application notification system and via a broadcast windows message. Figure 6-2 shows the registry "IClass" value set to stream interface class.

Message Queue Point to Point Notification

An application or even other device drivers can receive notifications by registering with Device manger. It involves setting up and creating a message queue point to point and providing the handle of this message queue to Device Manager by calling the function `RequestDeviceNotifications` API the implementation of which has been moved from Device Manager to File System. The following code is an example of how to implement the code to request and receive notifications from Device manager.

In the example in listing 6-3 the GUID is a generic stream interface GUID which is fine for stream device drivers; however you will be able to retrieve from the DEVDETAIL structure returned by the message queue only the first character of the interface name. This may provide an ambiguous result when compared in the application; therefore you may want to generate your own class interface GUID which will allow verifying the GUID value itself for consistency.

Listing 6-3. Sample code for receiving device notifications via message queue P2P

```
#include <pnp.h>
#include <msgqueue.h>
.......•
.......•
.......•
GUID guid = DEVCLASS_STREAM_GUID;     // or any relevant device interface GUID
HANDLE hMsgq = INVALID_HANDLE_VALUE;
HANDLE hNotfcn = INVALID_HANDLE_VALUE;
MSGQUEUEOPTIONS msgopts;
DEVDETAIL DeveDtls;
DWORD flags = MSGQUEUE_MSGALERT;
DWORD size = 0, dwLastError;
BOOL bReadMsg = FALSE;

memset(&DeveDtls, 0, sizeof(DeveDtls));
memset(&msgopts, 0, sizeof(msgopts));

msgopts.dwSize = sizeof(msgopts);
msgopts.dwFlags = 0;
msgopts.dwMaxMessages = 0;
msgopts.cbMaxMessage = sizeof(DeveDtls);
msgopts.bReadAccess = TRUE;
hMsgq = CreateMsgQueue(NULL, &msgopts);

if (hMsgq == INVALID_HANDLE_VALUE)
{
        printf("Failed to create message queue.\n");
        return 0;
}

hNotfcn = RequestDeviceNotifications(NULL, hMsgq, TRUE);
if (hNotfcn == INVALID_HANDLE_VALUE)
{
printf("Failed to register for TST notifications.\n");
return 0;
}
```

```
bReadMsg = ReadMsgQueue(hMsgq, &DeveDtls, sizeof(DeveDtls),
&size,
INFINITE, // Wait until a message appears
&flags);

if (bReadMsg == FALSE)
{
dwLastError = GetLastError();
}
else
{
// Do what you need to do if the device interface appears
}
```

Notification via WM_DEVICECHANGE

This method of handling Device Manager notifications has some drawbacks. The first is that the arrival of the message is unpredictable. The Windows message queue, which is not the same as the message queue point to point, is handled by GWES and arrives like any windows message to the windows procedure. The other limitation is that an application handling notifications this way has to be a Windows application implementing a window procedure. Your device may not have a graphic user interface at all and the device may not support implementation of windows applications. The following implementation sample in Listing 6-4 checks that the WM_DEVICECHANGE message arrived for the appearance of the device interface you require:

Listing 6-4. *Sample code for receiving device notifications via Windows message queue*

```
PDEV_BROADCAST_HDR pHdr;
PDEV_BROADCAST_DEVICEINTERFACE pDevInf;
GUID guid = DEVCLASS_STREAM_GUID;      // or any relevant device interface GUID
:
:
case WM_DEVICECHANGE:
{
    if ( DBT_DEVICEARRIVAL == wParam ||
DBT_DEVICEREMOVECOMPLETE == wParam )
    {
        pHdr = (PDEV_BROADCAST_HDR)lParam;
        if ( pHdr->dbch_devicetype == DBT_DEVTYP_DEVICEINTERFACE)
        {
            pDevInf = (PDEV_BROADCAST_DEVICEINTERFACE)pHdr;
            if (pDevInf->dbcc_classguid == guid)
            {
                // Do what you plan to do
            }
        }
    }
}
```

The `DEV_BROADCAST_DEVICEINTERFACE` structure contains all the information that is needed and is defined in C:\WINCE700\public\COMMON\sdk\inc\dbt.h.

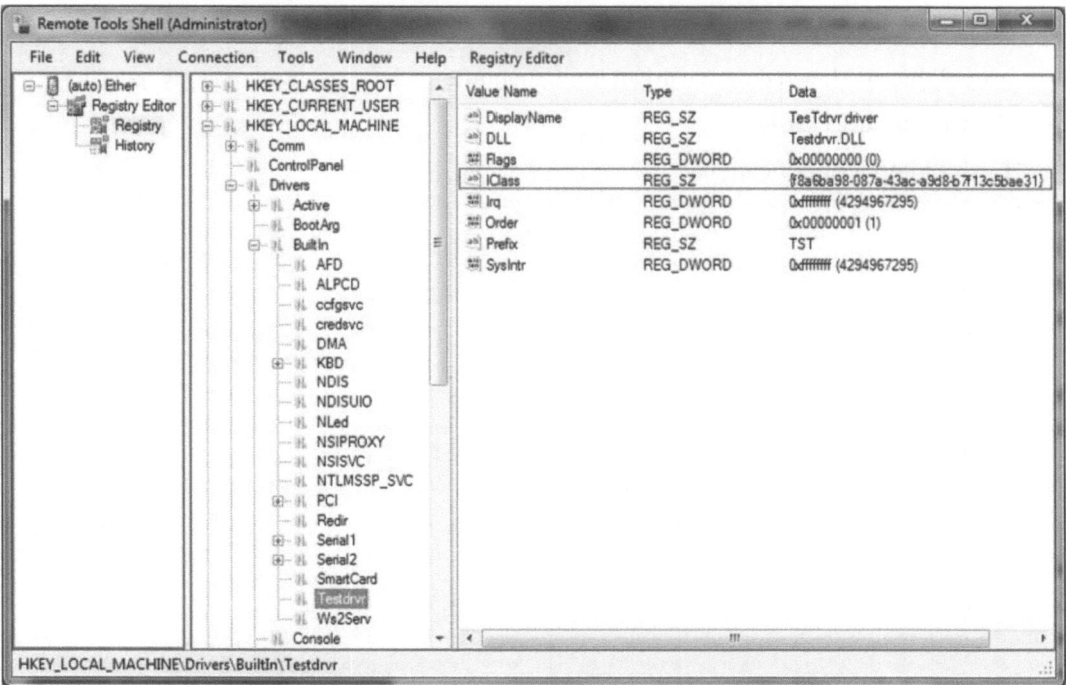

Figure 6-2. *Registry "IClass" value for Testdrvr device driver*

Chapter Summary

Device driver in Windows Embedded Compact 7, as in previous versions of Windows CE, can be categorized in various ways. They can be categorized by the system component that loads them, by their use, by the memory space they reside in, or by how they are implemented. Native device drivers are loaded by the Graphics Windowing and Event System (GWES) while all other device drivers are loaded by Device Manager. Native device drivers are accessed by GWES and not by applications directly. Moreover native device drivers for these reasons expose a set of functions that GWES calls for. All other device drivers must uniformly expose a stream device interface so that Device Manager can access them on behalf of applications that require their services. All native device drivers being loaded by GWES therefore reside in the kernel, while stream device drivers loaded by Device Manager can either reside in the kernel or in special user mode hosts launched by Device Manager.

In this chapter we discussed topics related to device driver types and device driver notifications, including:

- Native device drivers
- Stream device drivers
- Monolithic and layered device driver implementation
- Device interface classes
- Device interface notifications

CHAPTER 7

The Essence of Stream Device Drivers

Stream interface device driver are the most frequently developed device drivers for Windows Embedded Compact 7 as it is for earlier versions of Windows CE. Stream device drivers are loaded and managed by Device Manager and provide a well-known unified interface. Therefore, it allows user mode applications to access stream interface device drivers' services. User mode applications use file system APIs such as *CreateFile* to open an instance of a stream interface device driver and file I/O APIs to read or write data from and to the device. The stream interface can be found in kernel mode device drivers as well as user mode device drivers and in this latest version of the operating system in filter device drivers.

In this chapter

- Stream interface device drivers
- Kernel mode device drivers
- Filter device drivers
- User mode device drivers

Stream Interface Device Drivers

A stream interface driver is any device driver that exposes a well-known set of entry points that compose the stream interface functions. The stream interface does not imply that the hardware device controlled by such a device driver has to handle stream data, such as a serial communication port. Because block devices, such as storage disks, are implemented using the stream interface, the stream interface functions are designed to strongly match the semantics of the file system APIs such as *ReadFile*. As a result, stream interface device drivers are indirectly exposed to applications through the file system; applications interact with the driver by opening device drivers as special files in the file system.

Device Manager translates application requests via the file system API into commands that are really calls to the related device driver entry points. The device driver encapsulates all of the information that is necessary to translate those commands into appropriate actions on the devices that it controls. All stream interface drivers, whether they manage built-in devices or installable devices, or whether they are loaded at boot time or loaded dynamically, have similar interactions with other system components. Figure 7-1 shows the interactions between system components for a generic stream interface driver that manages a built-in device.

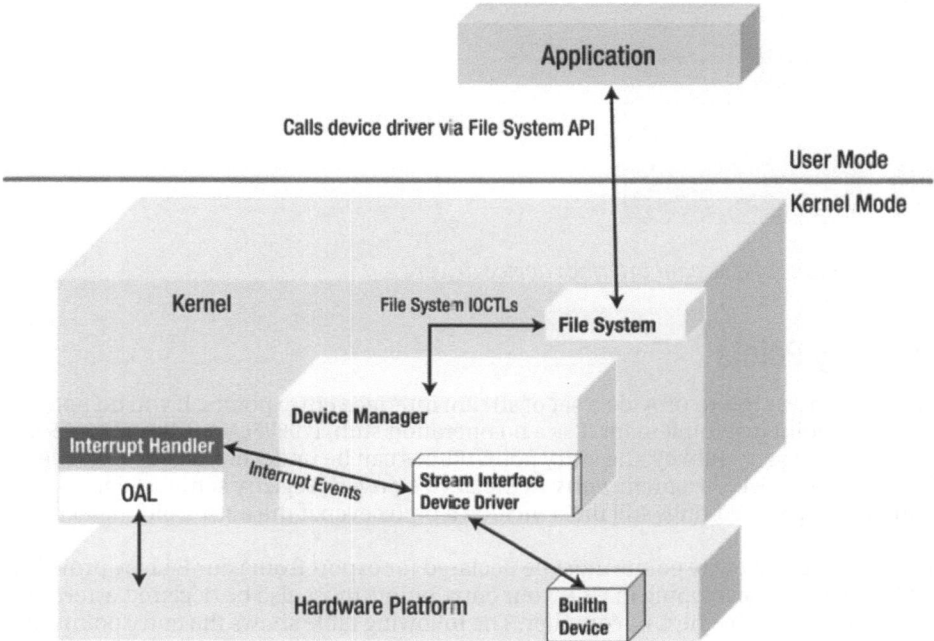

Figure 7-1. *Interaction between user mode applications and a kernel mode stream interface driver*

Structure of Stream Interface Device Drivers

Any stream interface device driver is a dynamic link library loaded and hosted by Device Manager. A stream interface device driver must expose the stream interface which is a set of well-known defined entry points that device manager is able to call in to. A visualization of the structure of stream interface device drivers is presented in Figure 7-2. In this visualization either a monolithic stream interface device driver in which the stream interface embeds the code handing the hardware device, while in a layered stream interface device driver there may be the DDSI layer and the hardware dependent code in a PDD layer.

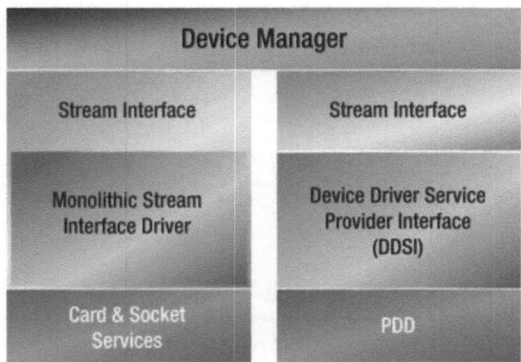

Figure 7-2. *The structure options of a stream interface device driver*

Stream Interface Entry Points

Any stream interface device driver has to provide a set of stream interface entry points. If you do not wish to implement an entry point just implement it as a no operation stub. If `DEVFLAGS_NAKEDENTRIES` is specified in the driver's Flags registry subkey, the entry point names can be undecorated; for example, Open, Close, etc. This does not preclude a prefix entry in the device driver's registry settings. For example the battery driver's registry settings still must include a prefix even if the entry point names are undecorated.

Your implementations of these entry points must be declared for export from your DLL by providing a module definition file. If you are developing in C++, your entry points must also be declared extern "C" to prevent function name mangling by the C++ compiler. The following table shows the entry points for the stream interface.

There are some notable changes in Windows Embedded Compact 7, because Device Manager provides support for asynchronous IO request. There is a new entry point that was not available before, and three entry points accept a new parameter. This new parameter is a handle for an IO request packet object.

XXX_Cancel

This function is new for Windows Embedded Compact 7; it cancels all pending asynchronous I/O requests for the specified device. In the above example the implementation is very simple. There is not much cleaning up to do because when an application calls *CancelIo* or *CancelIoEx*, Device Manger calls IO packet manager to clean everything up, because it was IO packet manager that created IO packets added them to a list it manages and all that is required of the device driver developer is to terminate the I/O request handling thread and clean up the parameters structure for this thread. Listing 7-4 shows an extremely simple implementation.

Listing 7-4. *Simple xxx_Cancel implementation*

```
BOOL TST_Cancel(DWORD dwOpenContext, HANDLE hAsyncHandle)
{
    DWORD dwRet = 0;
    PTST_DEVCONTXT pDevContxt = (PTST_DEVCONTXT)dwOpenContext;

    // TODO: Add code to implement canceling IO:
    TerminateThread(g_hAsyncThread, 0);
    return dwRet;
}
```

XXX_Close

The XXX_Close function closes the device context identified by *hOpenContext*. It is called by an application call to *CloseHandle* for the handle returned by *CreateFile*. This function is required to access the device with *CreateFile*. Listing 7-5 shows an example of closing a device driver context. If a device driver can be opened for more than one instance, you would manage a list of instances and need to delete and nullify the closing instance from the list.

Listing 7-5. *An example of XXX_Close implementation*

```
BOOL TST_Close(DWORD hOpenContext)
{
    BOOL bRet = TRUE;
    PTST_DEVCONTXT pDevContxt = (PTST_DEVCONTXT)hOpenContext;
    InterlockedDecrement(&pDevContxt->lOpenCount);
    InterlockedExchange((volatile LONG*)&pDevContxt->bOpenEx, FALSE);
    // TODO: Add code to implement closing an instance:
    return bRet;
}
```

XXX_Deinit

The XXX_Deinit function de-initializes a device. Its implementation should be a reverse process of the initialization process. XXX_Deinit is called by Device Manager. This function is required by drivers loaded by *ActivateDeviceEx, ActivateDevice*. Listing 7-6 shows a simple implementation of the XXX_Deinit function which is a reverse process of the XXX_Init in Listing 7-7.

Listing 7-6. *A simple implementation of the XXX_Deinit function*

```
BOOL TST_Deinit(DWORD hDeviceContext)
{
    BOOL bRet = TRUE;
    PTST_DEVCONTXT pDevContxt = (PTST_DEVCONTXT)hDeviceContext;

    // TODO: Add code to implement Deinitialization:

    // Destroy IST procedure and free DMA buffers
    DestroyInterruptServiceThread(pDevContxt);
```

```
        DMADeInitialize(0, pDevContxt);
        FreePhysMem(pDevContxt);
        return bRet;
}
```

XXX_Init

The XXX_Init function initializes a device. It is called by Device Manager on loading the device driver. The implementation of this function has no bearing on the performance of the device driver because it is performed just once at load time. All initialization of the controlled hardware and device driver's internal information as well as setting up of interrupt service routine and interrupt service thread and memory access methods such as DMA should be performed in this function. This function is required by drivers loaded by *ActivateDeviceEx, ActivateDevice,* or *RegisterDevice.* Listing 7-7 shows a comprehensive example of an implementation of an initialization function.

Listing 7-7. *A comprehensive example of XXX_Init function implementation*

```
DWORD TST_Init(LPCTSTR pContext, LPCVOID lpvBusContext)
{
    HKEY hConfig;
    DWORD dwRet = 0;
    BOOL bRc = FALSE;
    DWORD dwStatus;
    DDKWINDOWINFO WinInfo;
    ULONG unIoSpace = 1;
    DDKISRINFO IsrInfo;
    PTST_DEVCONTXT pDevContxt = NULL;

    // Allocate device instance context structure
    DWORD dwPhAdd;
    pDevContxt = (PTST_DEVCONTXT)AllocPhysMem(sizeof(TST_DEVCONTXT),
PAGE_READWRITE, 0, 0, &dwPhAdd);
    if (pDevContxt != NULL)
    {
        InitializeCriticalSection(&pDevContxt->CriticalSection);
        pDevContxt->hDriverMan = (HANDLE)GetCurrentProcessId();
    }
    else
    {
        DEBUGMSG(ZONE_INIT, (_T("TST!not enough memory\r\n")));
        return dwRet;
    }

    // Open active device registry key to retrieve activation
    // info
    DEBUGMSG(ZONE_INIT, (_T("TST!Starting TST_Init\r\n")));
    if (hConfig = OpenDeviceKey(pContext))
    {
```

```
        // Read window information
        WinInfo.cbSize = sizeof(WinInfo);
        dwStatus = DDKReg_GetWindowInfo(hConfig, &WinInfo);
        if (dwStatus != ERROR_SUCCESS)
        {
            DEBUGMSG(ZONE_INIT, (_T("TST!Error Getting window information\r\n")));
            FreePhysMem(pDevContxt);
            return dwRet;
        }
        pDevContxt->dwBusNumber = WinInfo.dwBusNumber;
        pDevContxt->dwInterfaceType = WinInfo.dwInterfaceType;

        // Read ISR information
        IsrInfo.cbSize = sizeof(IsrInfo);
        dwStatus = DDKReg_GetIsrInfo(hConfig, &IsrInfo);
        if (dwStatus != ERROR_SUCCESS)
        {
            DEBUGMSG(ZONE_INIT,
(_T("TST!Error Getting ISR information\r\n")));
            FreePhysMem(pDevContxt);
            return dwRet;
        }
    }
    else
    {
        DEBUGMSG(ZONE_INIT,
(_T("TST!Failed to open active device key\r\n")));
        FreePhysMem(pDevContxt);
        return dwRet;
    }
    RegCloseKey(hConfig);

    // Obtain hardware I/O address - initialized to memory mapped
    // IO space
    pDevContxt->ioPhysicalBase.LowPart = WinInfo.memWindows[0].dwBase;
    pDevContxt->ioPhysicalBase.HighPart = 0;
    pDevContxt->dwIoRange = WinInfo.memWindows[0].dwLen;
    if (HalTranslateBusAddress(
(INTERFACE_TYPE)pDevContxt->dwInterfaceType,
WinInfo.dwBusNumber,
pDevContxt->ioPhysicalBase, &unIoSpace,
&pDevContxt->ioPhysicalBase))
    {
        // It is memory mapped IO and not in IO space.
        if (!unIoSpace)
        {
            pDevContxt->bIoMemMapped = TRUE;
            if ((pDevContxt->dwIoAddr =
                (DWORD)MmMapIoSpace(pDevContxt->ioPhysicalBase,
pDevContxt->dwIoRange, FALSE)) == NULL)
            {
```

```
            DEBUGMSG(ZONE_INIT,
            (_T("TST!Error mapping IO Ports failure\r\n")));
            FreePhysMem(pDevContxt);

            // You may want to disable IO device here
            return dwRet;
        }
        else
        {
            pDevContxt->bIoMemMapped = FALSE;
            pDevContxt->pIoAddr =
                (UCHAR)pDevContxt->ioPhysicalBase.LowPart;
        }
    }
}
else
{
    DEBUGMSG(ZONE_INIT,
            (_T("TST!Error HalTranslateBusAddress call
                                        failure\r\n")));
    FreePhysMem(pDevContxt);

    // You may want to disable IO device here
    return dwRet;
}
bRc = DMAInitialize(0, pDevContxt);   // a device driver
                                      // local function
if (!bRc)
{
    FreePhysMem(pDevContxt);
    return 0;
}
pDevContxt->dwIstPriority = 75;
pDevContxt->dwIstQuantum = 50;

// Setup SYSINTR ID from registry
pDevContxt->dwSysIntr = IsrInfo.dwSysintr;

// Creat IST procedure (a call to a device driver local
// function)
dwRet =
   CreateInterruptServiceThread((PTST_DEVCONTXT)pDevContxt);
if (dwRet != 0)
{
    FreePhysMem(pDevContxt);
    return 0;
}
```

```
    // We got here if all succeded so return the device context
    // pointer
    dwRet = (DWORD)pDevContxt;
    return dwRet;
}
```

XXX_IOControl

The XXX_IOControl function sends a command to a device, or handles device driver-specific functionality that is not accessible by the file system APIs. An implementation of this function may or may not be required, depending on the device capabilities that the driver exposes. This function is called as a result of an application calling *DeviceIoControl* which is exposed by Device Manager. Note that this function is one of three entry points that can support asynchronous I/O requests. This is a new capability introduced in Windows Embedded Compact 7 and is facilitated by a new input argument which is a handle to an I/O packet. Listing 7-8 is an example of a simple implementation of XXX_IOControl function sporting a device driver private IO control code.

Listing 7-8. *An example of a simple implementation of XXX_IOControl function*

```
PINPUT pInput = g_pBufIn;
...
BOOL TST_IOControl(DWORD hOpenContext, DWORD dwCode, PBYTE pBufIn, DWORD dwLenIn, PBYTE
pBufOut, DWORD dwLenOut, PDWORD pdwActualOut, HANDLE hAsyncRef)
{
    PTST_DEVCONTXT pDevContxt = (PTST_DEVCONTXT)hOpenContext;
    BOOL bRet = TRUE;
    DWORD dwErr = 0;
    HRESULT hr = E_WASNEVERSET;

    // TODO: Add code to implement IOCTL codes:

    switch (dwCode)
    {
        case IOCTL_DEMODRVR_FOO1:
hr = CeOpenCallerBuffer((PVOID*)&g_pBufIn,
(PVOID)pBufIn,
                                            dwLenIn, ARG_I_PTR, FALSE);
            // Enter critical section if needed otherwise erase
            EnterCriticalSection(&pDevContxt->CriticalSection);
            // Add implementation code

            LeaveCriticalSection(&pDevContxt->CriticalSection);
            hr = CeCloseCallerBuffer((PVOID) pBufIn, (PVOID)pBufIn, dwLenIn, ARG_I_PTR);


            break;
        default:
            break;
    }
```

```
    // pass back appropriate response codes
    SetLastError(dwErr);
    If((dwErr != ERROR_SUCCESS) && (dwErr != ERROR_IO_PENDING))
    {
        bRet = FALSE;
    }
    else
    {
        bRet = TRUE;
    }

    return bRet;
}
```

XXX_Open

The XXX_Open function opens a device application related context for reading, writing, or both. An application indirectly invokes this function when it calls *CreateFile* to obtain a handle to a device. In this function you can decide if multiple applications can access the device driver services or if only one application can access at the time. If multiple applications can access the device driver services you need to implement housekeeping code for each open context so that each application gets the appropriate services for its context. This function is required to access the device with *CreateFile*. Listing 7-9 demonstrates the implementation of restricting a device driver to one open context.

Listing 7-9. *An example of XXX_Open restricting open contexts*

```
DWORD TST_Open(DWORD hDeviceContext, DWORD AccessCode,
DWORD ShareMode)
{
    DWORD dwRet = DRVR_INVALID_HANDLE;
    PTST_DEVCONTXT pDevContxt = (PTST_DEVCONTXT)hDeviceContext;
    if (pDevContxt == NULL)
    {
        SetLastError(ERROR_INVALID_HANDLE);
        return dwRet;
    }
    InterlockedIncrement(&pDevContxt->lOpenCount);
    EnterCriticalSection(&pDevContxt->CriticalSection);
    // The following code prevents opening more than one instance
    if (pDevContxt->bOpenEx == TRUE)
    {
        if (pDevContxt->lOpenCount > 0)
        {
            DEBUGMSG(ZONE_OPEN,
(_T("TST!There is already an open instance.\r\n")));
        }
    }
```

```
    else
    {
        pDevContxt->bOpenEx = TRUE;
        // TODO: Add code to implement opening an instance:

        dwRet = (DWORD)pDevContxt;
    }
    LeaveCriticalSection(&pDevContxt->CriticalSection);
    if (dwRet == DRVR_INVALID_HANDLE) // Not Opened
    {
        InterlockedDecrement(&pDevContxt->lOpenCount);
    }
    return dwRet;
}
```

XXX_PowerDown

Implementation of XXX_PowerDown is optional. This function ends power to the device. It is useful only with devices that can be shut off under software control. Non-power-managed drivers are suspended using the XXX_PowerDown entry point when the system has no support for API calls and running in single thread mode. Therefore this function should not call any functions and it should return as quickly as possible.

XXX_PowerUp

Implementation of XXX_PowerUp is optional. This function restores power to a device. This function is called on system resume when it is still running in single thread mode. The kernel resumes non-power-managed drivers using the XXX_PowerUp entry point.

XXX_PreClose

Implementation of XXX_PreClose is optional; however it is extremely important if lengthy asynchronous I/O is taking place in other threads. This function marks the closing handle as invalid and resumes any blocking threads. For an explanation see the note "Closing and deintializing device drivers."

XXX_PreDeinit

The XXX_PreDeinit function prepares for unloading the device driver by resumes any blocking threads allowing the release of associated resources before final call to *XXX_Deinit*. This function is required if the *XXX_PreClose* function is implemented.

CLOSING AND DEINTIALIZING DEVICE DRIVERS

Device drivers may have threads blocking, these threads may not be able to release resources associated with the handle or device instance because they block. This creates race conditions while trying to close a context instance or unloading the device driver.

A race condition may occur in between I/O operations going on in one thread and another thread calling *CloseHandle*. When Device Manager calls the *XXX_Close* entry point, drivers should resume threads blocked on a handle and free the associated resources with this handle. A device driver may crash should Device Manager call an I/O entry point, such as *XXX_IOControl,* after *XXX_Close* has been called from another thread.

Another race condition may occur if Device Manager attempts to unload a device when the device driver's *XXX_Deinit* function executes in one thread while another thread attempts to open a handle. In these cases, from the device driver's standpoint, *XXX_Deinit* is called before *XXX_Open.* This may take place during lengthy and heavy CPU loads or when drivers are unloading and reloading frequently.

XXX_Read

The XXX_Read function reads data from the device identified by the open context. This function might or might not be required, depending on the device capabilities that the driver exposes. Note that this function is one of three entry points that can support asynchronous I/O requests. This is a new capability introduced in Windows Embedded Compact 7 and is facilitated by a new input argument which is a handle to an I/O packet. See Listing 7-5 for an example.

XXX_Write

The XXX_Write function writes data to the device. This function might or might not be required, depending on the device capabilities that the driver exposes. Note that this function is one of three entry points that can support asynchronous I/O requests. This is a new capability introduced in Windows Embedded Compact 7 and is facilitated by a new input argument which is a handle to an I/O packet. See Listing 7-10 for an example.

Listing 7-10. *Example of XXX_Write handling asynchronous I/O request*

```
DWORD TST_Write(DWORD hOpenContext,
LPCVOID pSourceBytes,
DWORD NumberOfBytes, HANDLE hAsyncRef)
{
    DWORD dwRet = 0;
    PTST_DEVCONTXT pDevContxt = (PTST_DEVCONTXT)hOpenContext;
    HANDLE hAsyncIO = NULL;
    // TODO: Add code to implement write:
    if (hAsyncRef)
    {
```

```
hAsyncIO = CreateAsyncIoHandle(hAsyncRef,
(LPVOID*)pSourceBytes, 0);
    }
    CeOpenCallerBuffer((PVOID*)(&g_AsyncTestParams.pBufIn),
                            (PVOID)pSourceBytes,
NumberOfBytes, ARG_O_PTR, TRUE);
    g_AsyncTestParams.hAsyncIO = hAsyncIO;
    g_AsyncTestParams.dwInLen = NumberOfBytes;
    g_hAsyncThread = CreateThread(NULL,163840,
(LPTHREAD_START_ROUTINE)AsyncTestThread,
(LPVOID)&g_AsyncTestParams,
CREATE_SUSPENDED |
STACK_SIZE_PARAM_IS_A_RESERVATION, NULL);
        if (g_hAsyncThread == NULL)
        {
                DEBUGMSG(ZONE_IOCTL,
(_T("TST! Failed to create thread\r\n")));
                return FALSE;
        }
        ResumeThread(g_hAsyncThread);
        return dwRet;
}
```

XXX_Seek

The XXX_Seek function moves the data pointer in the device. This function might or might not be required, depending on the device capabilities that the driver exposes. An application gets access to this function by calling *SetFilePointer*.

Loading of Stream Interface Device Drivers

Loading stream interface device drivers is wholly dependent on the registry. The device driver loading process starts with Device Manager reading the registry root key which is at HKLM\Drivers\BuiltIn to obtain the root path for driver loading. See Listing 7-11 for these registry entries. The driver located at this key is BusEnum.dll which is the Bus Enumerator implemented as a bus device driver. Device Manager then calls *ActivateDeviceEx* to activate the Bus Enumerator. Once the Bus Enumerator is activated it iterates on all the nodes directly under the RootKey will be automatically loaded at boot by the Bus Enumerator. See Listing 7-12 for an example. These stream device drivers are typically referred to as "Built in" drivers. Built in drivers often include other bus drivers such as PCI, USB etc that each manage their own buses.

Listing 7-11. *Registry keys for Bus Enumerator*

```
[HKEY_LOCAL_MACHINE\Drivers]
    "RootKey"="Drivers\\BuiltIn"
    "ProcName"="udevice.exe"
    "ProcVolPrefix"="$udevice"
```

```
[HKEY_LOCAL_MACHINE\Drivers\BuiltIn]
    "Dll"="BusEnum.dll"
    "BusName"="BuiltIn"
    "Flags"=dword:8
    "BusIoctl"=dword:2a0048
    "InterfaceType"=dword:0
    "IClass"=multi_sz:
"{B3CC6EBA-5507-4196-8E41-2BF42E4A47C9}=%b",
"{6F40791D-300E-44E4-BC38-E0E63CA8375C}=%b"
```

Listing 7-12. An example of a stream device driver under the RootKey

```
; DemoDrvr driver
[HKEY_LOCAL_MACHINE\Drivers\BuiltIn\Demodrvr]
    "Prefix"="TST"
    "DLL"="Demodrvr.DLL"
    "SysIntr"=dword:1A
    "Irq"=dword:10
    "MemBase"=dword:80220000
    "MemLen"=dword:100
    "Order"=dword:0
    "DisplayName"="DemoDrvr driver"
    "Flags"=dword:0
```

The loading process is synchronous and therefore may take time since device drivers are loaded one after the other according to the device driver's load order value. The bus enumerator iterates on the device driver nodes under the RootKey and loads first all the device driver with a load order of value 0, then it will iterate and load all the drivers with load order value 1 until it has loaded all the device driver that are marked for loading.

Asynchronous I/O Request Handling

New in this latest version of Windows CE, Windows Embedded Compact 7, is the introduction of device driver support for I/O requests. In previous versions of Windows CE device drivers were able to fulfill I/O requests such as *ReadFile* in a synchronous fashion only. That is, an application called into *ReadFile* to read the device driver's retrieved data, waited until the read operation was completed before *ReadFile* returned. This also put some extra difficulty on application developers porting applications from the desktop Windows operating systems to Windows CE. Because, the pointer to the **OVERLAPPED** structure was ignored, so the developer had to set it to **NULL**. The **OVERLAPPED** structure in desktop Windows operating systems is used by the developers to get I/O operation completion notification without having to wait for this operation to complete synchronously. This allows an application to continue its flow of logic specially when there is a lengthy I/O operation. Figure 7-3 shows the difference between synchronous and asynchronous I/O request handling.

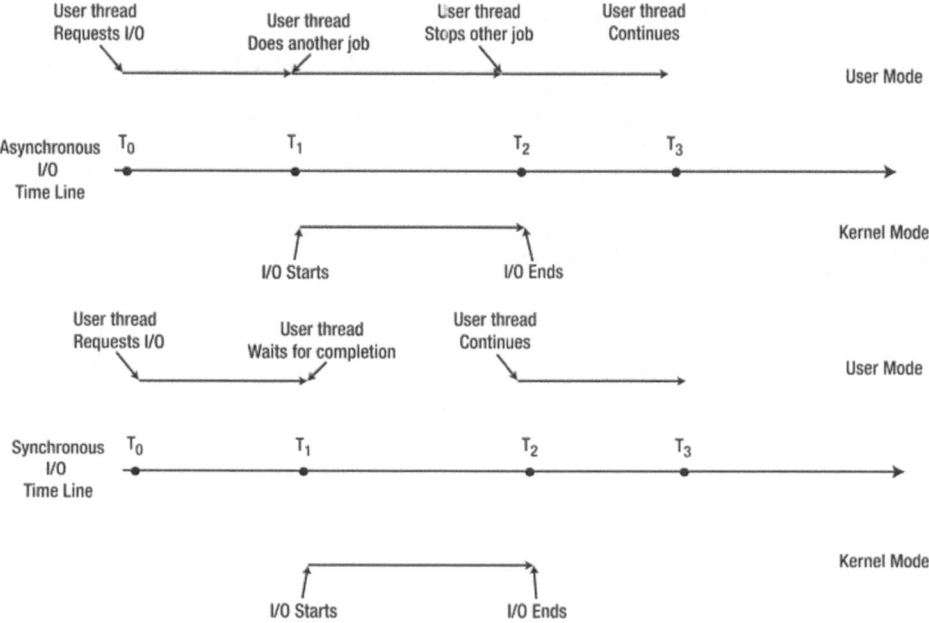

Figure 7-3. Asynchronous and synchronous I/O request handling

Motivation and Implementation Notes

Not every device driver has to provide support for asynchronous I/O request handling. The only reason to add this capability to a device driver would be if the size of data transfers between the caller process and the device driver is so large that it would cause the caller process to be halted while a lengthy I/O request is being processed. This is the motivation you would have as a device driver designer to incorporate the extra complexity needed to support asynchronous I/O request handling.

One of the said complexities is setting up threads to handle asynchronous I/O requests. Because such requests are initiated by the caller process passes an initialized OVERLAPPED structure to the device driver which to respond correctly for multiple such requests and therefore each such request needs to be handled separately. As tempting as it may be to use the IST as a handler for input requests, beware of this practice. The reason is that an IST is initialized during device driver initialization and has no information about the event object passed in the OVERLAPPED structure by the caller process. More than that, an IST is triggered by an interrupt caused by the peripheral hardware and not as a result of a caller process request.

The tasks of the IST are discussed in Chapter 8, and by no means take on the role of handling I/O requests by the caller process, because the caller process has no prior knowledge of hardware interaction with the device driver. Therefore if the IST completed handling an interrupt request as initialized by the hardware it is done. When a caller process requests to read this data the device drivers returns the data buffer to the caller. If the buffers are large enough to warrant asynchronous I/O request handling it should create a dedicated thread for this request and terminate the thread on completion.

The complexity of trying to avoid creating dedicated threads for asynchronous I/O requests outweighs the code required to implement these threads.

Implementing Asynchronous I/O Request Handling

In Windows Embedded Compact 7 Device Manger implementation has been extended to support this asynchronous mode of I/O handling and if a device driver is implemented to support it an application can call *ReadFile* which will return immediately while the device driver will launch the read I/O operation and Device Manager will set an event, created by the calling application and provided to the device driver by implementing the OVERLAPPED structure, to notify the application that the read operation has completed.

The following flow diagram in Figure 7-4 shows how Device Manager processes the OVERLAPPED structure and passes the information to the device driver.

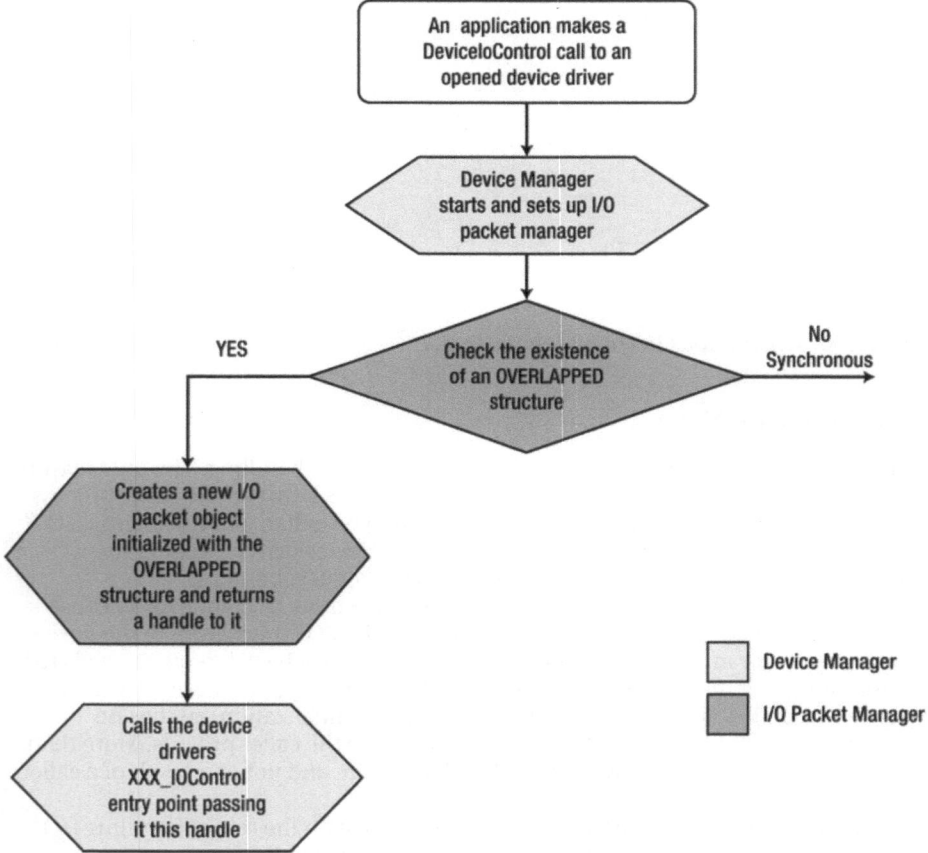

Figure 7-4. Asynchronous I/O call handling by Device Manager

Device Manager exposes three new functions that can be used by kernel mode device drivers to support asynchronous I/O requests:

- **CreateAsyncIoHandle** - This function is used by a device driver to change *XXX_Read*, *XXX_Write* and *XXX_IOControl* entry points implementations to support asynchronous I/O

- **CompleteAsyncIo** - This function signals completion of asynchronous I/O and updates the final count of bytes that were completed by asynchronous I/O

- **SetIoProgress** - This function is used by an asynchronous device driver to update the status and progress on an asynchronous I/O request

The following code example shows how to implement an asynchronous I/O operation within a device driver and a possible processing of such asynchronous I/O processing. In this example a device driver implements a long write operation (not really that long in the example, still), within the *XXX_IOControl* entry point. To perform the long write operation the device driver creates a special thread that actually copies the input buffer to the device driver's local buffer. Not to smart, but really drives the point home. The only code that distinguishes this device driver from any other kernel mode stream device driver is this particular behavior. The following in Listing 7-1 is a snippet of code which demonstrates the implementation of the *XXX_IOControl* entry point. The code marked in red signifies the special additions that Device Manager provides for device drivers developers to support asynchronous I/O handling. The first thing to notice is the new argument passed to the *XXX_IOControl* entry point, the *hAsyncRef* handle that points to an IO packet object. The next offering by Device Manager is the function *CreateAsyncIoHandle*. This function connects the IO packet to an asynchronous buffer to allocate a copy buffer, in this instance just the input buffer.

In Listing 7-2 the code sets up parameters to be passed on to thread that will process the I/O operation, and create the thread and run it. The rest is up to the thread. The code here is simple and leaves the thread at 251 priority level. When designing your driver you may want to change the priority of this thread if the I/O operation is huge. However you should remember the impact this will have on the system, and consider the priority of the user mode caller thread.

The thread itself performs the I/O operation and when it completes it, the code calls another function exposed by Device Manager *CompleteAsyncIo* to notify the caller process that the I/O operation has completed. As a result the event that was created by the caller process is signaled.

The process itself is a very simple console application that opens the device driver, creates an OVERLAPPED structure and an event and calls *DeviceIoControl* and is shown in Listing 7-3, most of the time the code listing omits debug messages to make for clarity of code. The code in bold red fonts emphasizes the code specific to asynchronous I/O request support.

▪ **Warning to Application Developers** An application must not modify the memory buffers used for asynchronous I/O requests before the device driver has notified the completion of the I/O operation, because it may lead to unpredictable results.

Listing 7-1. Adding asynchronous I/O handling support

```
BOOL TST_IOControl(DWORD hOpenContext, DWORD dwCode, PBYTE pBufIn, DWORD dwLenIn, PBYTE
pBufOut, DWORD dwLenOut, PDWORD pdwActualOut, HANDLE hAsyncRef)
{
    PTST_DEVCONTXT pDevContxt = (PTST_DEVCONTXT)hOpenContext;
    BOOL bRet = TRUE;
    DWORD dwErr = 0;

    HANDLE hAsyncIO = NULL;

    switch (dwCode)
    {
        case IOCTL_TESTDRVR_ASYNCTEST:
            if (hAsyncRef)
            {
                hAsyncIO = CreateAsyncIoHandle(hAsyncRef,
                                          (LPVOID*)pBufIn, 0);
            }
        g_AsyncIOParams.pSrcBufIn = (PBYTE)pBufIn;

    CeOpenCallerBuffer((PVOID*)(&g_AsyncTestParams.pBufIn),
                                (PVOID)pBufIn,  dwLenIn,
                            ARG_I_PTR, TRUE);

            g_AsyncTestParams.hAsyncIO = hAsyncIO;
            g_AsyncTestParams.dwInLen = dwLenIn;

            g_hAsyncThread =
                    CreateThread(NULL,163840,
(LPTHREAD_START_ROUTINE)AsyncTestThread,
                        (LPVOID)&g_AsyncTestParams,
                    CREATE_SUSPENDED |
                    STACK_SIZE_PARAM_IS_A_RESERVATION,
                        NULL);
                if (g_hAsyncThread == NULL)
                {
                    DEBUGMSG(ZONE_IOCTL,(_T("TST!failed …\r\n")));
                    return FALSE;
                }

        // Raise asyn thread priority if you want IO
            // operation to not last ethernity
            CeSetThreadPriority(g_hAsyncThread, 150);

            ResumeThread(g_hAsyncThread);
dwErr = ERROR_IO_PENDING;
```

```
break;
        default:
            break;
    }

    // pass back appropriate response codes
    SetLastError(dwErr);

    return bRet;
}
```

The following code shows the thread parameters and the thread itself. Of course this is a very simple example and you may want to consider having an array of parameter structures to allow for more than one thread at the time. You may also want the structure to hold output buffer pointer and length so that this structure is generic for both input and output I/O request handling threads. The pSrcBufIn field is there to allow closing the pointer to the marshalled caller buffer that was created in TST_IOControl function.

Listing 7-2. *Thread for I/O handling*

```
// Parameters structure for I/O thread
typedef struct _IOCTLWTPARAMS_tag
{
        volatile HANDLE hAsyncIO;
        PBYTE pSrcBufIn;
        volatile PBYTE pBufIn;
        volatile DWORD  dwInLen;
}IOCTLWTPARAMS, *PIOCTLWTPARAMS;


// Global variables
HANDLE g_hInstance;
IOCTLWTPARAMS  g_AsyncTestParams;
HANDLE g_hAsyncThread;


DWORD AsyncTestThread(LPVOID lpParameter)
{
        PIOCTLWTPARAMS pParam = (PIOCTLWTPARAMS)lpParameter;
        TCHAR buf[65536];
        BOOL bComplete = 0;

        PBYTE pBuf = pParam->pBufIn;
        for (int i = 0; i < (int)pParam->dwInLen; i++)
        {
                buf[i] = *pBuf++;
            if (i % 100 == 0)
            {
                SetIoProgress(pParam->hAsyncIO, i);
                    Sleep(50);
            }
}
```

```
        if (pParam->hAsyncIO != NULL)
        {
                bComplete = CompleteAsyncIo(pParam->hAsyncIO, pParam->dwBufLen, 0);

        }
// Remember that we didn't close the caller buffer in
// TST_IOControl
        hRes = CeCloseCallerBuffer(pParam->pBufIn,
                                        pParam->pSrcBufIn,
                                        pParam->dwInLen, ARG_I_PTR);

    return 0;
}
```

The following code is a very simple demonstration application that calls for the asynchronous I/O operation. In Figure 7-5 you can see the output resulting from running this demo application.

Listing 7-3. *User mode application to demonstrate asynchronous I/O handling*

```
#define WRITE_TEST_STRING_SIZE 65536
TCHAR szBuf[WRITE_TEST_STRING_SIZE];

int _tmain(int argc, TCHAR *argv[], TCHAR *envp[])
{
        BOOL bRet = FALSE;
        volatile OVERLAPPED ovlpd;
        HANDLE hCompltEvent = NULL;
        HANDLE hTstDrvr = INVALID_HANDLE_VALUE;
        DWORD dwBytes = 0;

        memset((void*)&ovlpd, 0, sizeof(ovlpd));

        // Try open an instance of TestDrvr
        hTstDrvr = CreateFile(_T("TST1:"),
GENERIC_READ | GENERIC_WRITE,
0,NULL,OPEN_EXISTING,0,NULL);
    if (INVALID_HANDLE_VALUE == hTstDrvr)
    {
         DWORD bdw = GetLastError();
         // Format message and printf it
      return FALSE;
    }

    // Create a completion event for IOControl IO operation
    ovlpd.hEvent = CreateEvent(NULL, TRUE, FALSE, NULL);
    if (!ovlpd.hEvent)
    {
        DWORD bdw = GetLastError();
          // Format message and printf it
```

```
    return FALSE;
      }
      for (int i = 0; i <  WRITE_TEST_STRING_SIZE; i++)
      {
          szBuf[i] = i;
      }
      bRet = DeviceIoControl(hTstDrvr,IOCTL_TESTDRVR_ASYNCTEST,
szBuf, WRITE_TEST_STRING_SIZE, NULL,
0,NULL,(LPOVERLAPPED)&ovlpd);

    while (!bRet)         // I/O is not done yet
    {
        bRet = GetOverlappedResult(hTstDrvr,
                                    (LPOVERLAPPED)&ovlpd,
&dwBytes, FALSE);
        if (!bRet )
        {
          _tprintf(_T("Asynch IO is not yet completed %d
bytes written\r\n"),
ovlpd.InternalHigh);
        }
        else
        {
_tprintf(_T("DeviceIoControl has completed
                              operation\r\n"));
        }
    }
    CloseHandle(hTstDrvr);
    CloseHandle(ovlpd.hEvent);
    return 0;
}
```

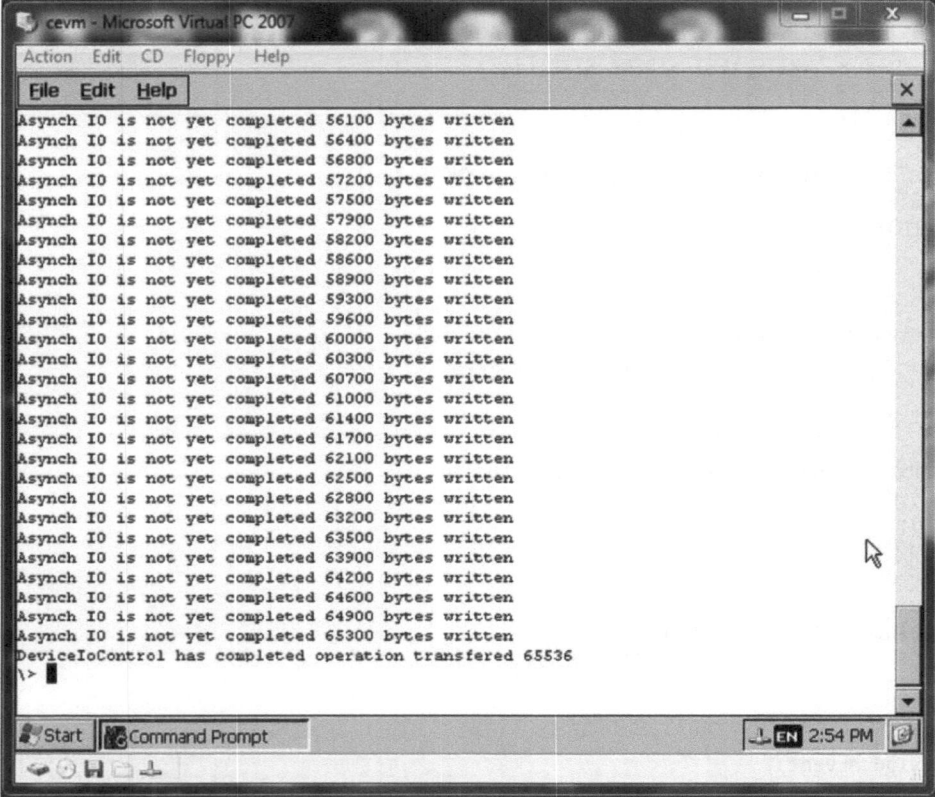

Figure 7-5. *Running the asynchronous IO request demo application*

Kernel Mode Device Drivers

The Device Manager loads all stream device drivers into kernel space as kernel mode drivers accept for device drivers that set the DEVFLAGS_LOAD_AS_USERPROC flag in the registry. Kernel mode drivers provide the best performance since they can call kernel APIs directly using the kernel version of coredll.dll named k.coredll.dll.

Kernel mode device drivers must be robust because they have unlimited access to kernel data structures and kernel space memory. A faulty kernel mode device driver can corrupt kernel memory thus causing a system crash. Kernel mode device drivers can synchronously access user buffers very quickly because user memory is directly available.

Access Checking

A stream device driver can accept input and output buffers from a calling user mode process, which presents a problem mapping these user mode virtual memory pointers to kernel mode virtual memory pointers. In Windows CE 6.0 and later, the kernel performs a full access check on pointer parameters, thus, drivers only need to access check embedded pointers. An embedded pointer, means that a user mode process has embedded a user mode virtual address pointer within the buffer it passes to the device driver. Listing 7-13 is an excerpt from commented code generated by the device driver wizard for the XXX_IOControl function to demonstrate accessing an embedded pointer. Figure 7-6 shows a visually diagrammatic access check.

Listing 7-13. *Code snippet demonstrating embedded pointer access*

```
// The following code should guide you to handle access to
// embedded pointers Structure with an embedded pointer
typedef struct _INPUT_tag
{
    UCHAR *pEmbedded;
    DWORD dwSize;
}INPUT, *PINPUT;

PUCHAR g_pMappedEmbedded

// Code implementation
HRESULT hr = E_WASNEVERSET;
PINPUT pInput = pBufIn;
hr = CeOpenCallerBuffer((PVOID*)&g_pMappedEmbedded,
pInput->pEmbedded,
pInput->dwSize,
ARG_I_PTR,
FALSE);
// Fail if FAILED(hr) == true

// When done processing using the embedded pointer
hr = CeCloseCallerBuffer((PVOID)g_pMappedEmbedded,
pInput->pEmbedded,
pInput->dwSize,
ARG_I_PTR);
```

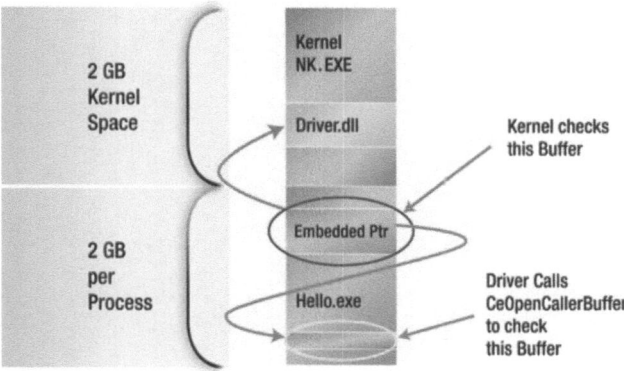

Figure 7-6. *Diagrammatic of access check process*

Marshalling

Marshalling is the transformation of data objects stored in one memory space into usable data object of another memory space. In Windows CE 6.0 and later this process of moving data objects between user mode processes and kernel mode device drivers depends on whether the pointers to these objects are used synchronously or asynchronously. This should not be confused with the subject we discussed earlier on asynchronous I/O request handling but rather of the fact that synchronous means accessing the caller's buffer on the caller's thread context. Asynchronous means that either the device driver is processing the buffer in another thread or it continues to process it after the call has returned to the user process. This really is the foundation for asynchronous I/O request handling but it was introduced with the change of architecture that occurred in Windows CE 6.0. However in Windows Embedded Compact 7 (which is really Windows CE 7.0) additional capabilities have been introduced to the Device Manager to enable user processes to be notified of completion of I/O operations, monitor progress and canceling such I/O processing before it completes. Figures 7-7 and 7-8 show a visually diagrammatic scheme of synchronous and asynchronous access.

Pointers are used synchronously

- The caller's address space is accessible for the lifetime of the call

- Eliminates any marshalling needs for both embedded and pointer parameters

- Employs Direct Access Marshalling

Pointers are used asynchronously

- It's critical that the caller buffer is accessible when the caller's address space is unavailable

- Use the new OS marshalling helper APIs CeAllocAsynchronousBuffer/CeFreeAsynchronousBuffer

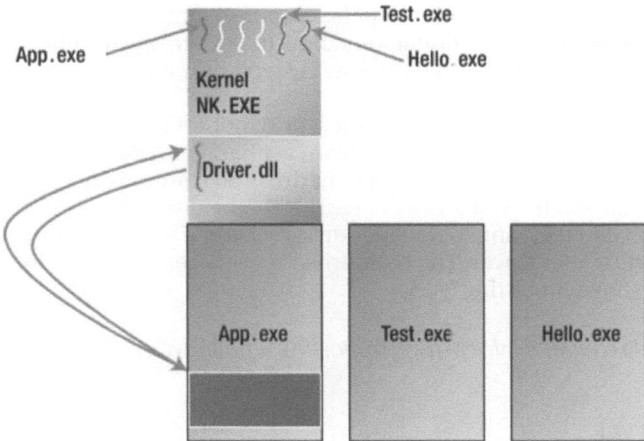

Figure 7-7. *Diagrammatic of synchronous access*

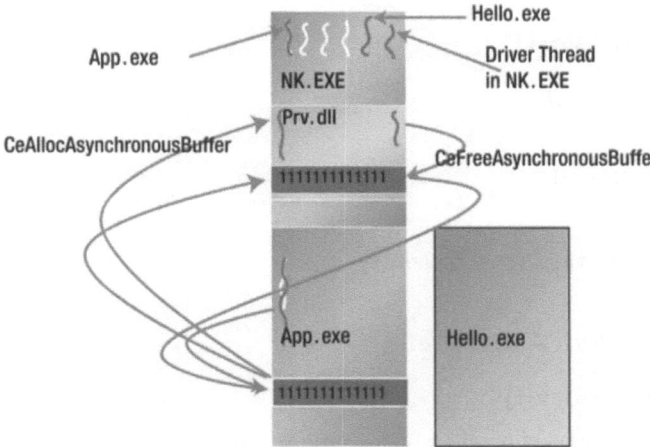

Figure 7-8. *Diagrammatic of asynchronous access*

Filter Device Drivers

Filter device drivers are a new feature in Windows Embedded Compact 7. Filter device drivers are optional and basically insert themselves "in front" of a device driver to filter I/O requests to this device driver. The documentation in Windows Embedded Compact resembles the Windows Driver Model (WDM) documentation; however there is little comparison to the desktop model. Filter device drivers can relate to bus device drivers, kernel mode device drivers, user mode device drivers, or device drivers loaded by GWES.

A useful example of such a filter device driver would be a finite impulse response filter driver for some sampling low level stream device driver. The best way to understand how to develop such a filter device driver would be to understand how Device Manager handles its loading, and how it relates to the device driver which I/O it filters.

Unlike the desktop where filter drivers are inserted into the driver stack, in Windows Embedded Compact, Device Manager has a new component: Filter manager. Filter manager handles a list of filter drivers chained together by registry settings. When you want to relate a filter driver to some stream device driver, or any device driver for that matter, you have to add a "Filter" key to the device driver's registry setting and the value assigned to it is a GUID relating to the filter driver. Listing 7-14 shows the registry settings for a device driver that supports a filter driver. The filter driver registry settings entry for the filter device driver for that device driver is shown in Listing 7-15.

Listing 7-14. *Registry settings entry for a sample stream device driver supporting a filter driver*

```
; TesTdrvr driver
[HKEY_LOCAL_MACHINE\Drivers\BuiltIn\Testdrvr]
    "Prefix"="TST"
    "DLL"="Testdrvr.DLL"
    "Order"=dword:0
    "DisplayName"="TesTdrvr driver"
    "Flags"=dword:0
    "Filter"="{fbf9a438-f6c8-46dc-a278-df2900638f3f}"
```

Listing 7-15. *Registry settings entry for a sample filter driver*

```
[HKEY_LOCAL_MACHINE\Drivers\Filters\
{fbf9a438-f6c8-46dc-a278-df2900638f3f}\FIRFilter]
    "DLL"="Firfilterdrvr.dll"
    "InitEntry"="FIRFilterInit"
; You may want to change the loading order as this is a temporary
; value
    "Order"=dword:0
; Add this line to the registry settings of device driver being
; filtered
    ;"Filter"="{fbf9a438-f6c8-46dc-a278-df2900638f3f}"
```

The stream device driver is my faithful example used previously, with the addition of a new IOCTL code to help demonstrate the filtering process. The filter driver was created using the Windows CE Device Driver Wizard hence the last two lines of the listing. Figure 7-10 shows how to create a filter driver using the Windows CE Device Driver Wizard.

Device Manager starts its device driver loading process and BusEnum loads Testdrvr.dll by calling *ActivateDeviceEx*. In essence Device Manager starts the process of loading the stream device driver within an internal function *LoadLib*. It loads first Testdrvr.dll and assigns all of its entry points and goes on to load the related filter driver. Once the filter driver dll is loaded it calls the function pointed to by the "InitEntry" key in the registry settings of the filter driver. And really both drivers are initially loaded. Figure 7-9 shows the call stack of the loading process. Now Device Manager calls the *Init* entry point and this is where it becomes interesting because both device drivers are chained and the filter driver Init entry point is called first and if it does what it does to initialize the filter driver and would not trigger the call to *TST_Init Device Manager will not call it by itself. See Listing 7-17 for an example of a FilterInit function.*

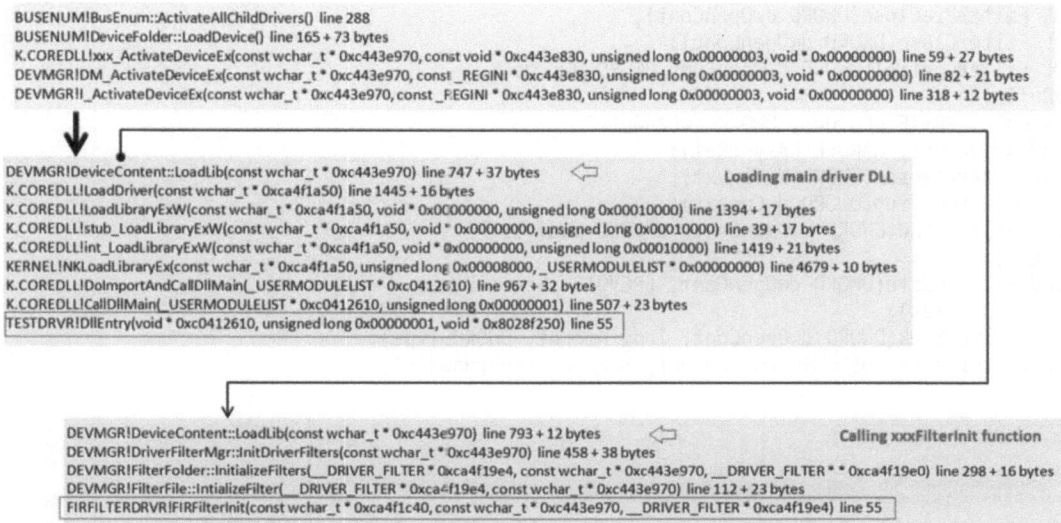

Figure 7-9. *Stream device driver loading and the related filter driver loading and initializing*

The filter driver provides a FIR filter (really very rudimentary for the example) that will handle sampling data from the stream device driver. The filter driver is implemented as a C++ class derived from *DriverFilterBase* class which Microsoft provides in C:\WINCE700\public\common\ddk\inc\drfilter.h. Listing 7-16 shows a jumpstart filter driver generated by the device driver wizard.

Listing 7-16. *An example filter driver class*

```
class FIRFilter : public DriverFilterBase
{
protected:
    // Value returned from xxx_Init()
    DWORD m_initReturn;
        // The pointer to the device driver that this filters
        PDRIVER_FILTER m_pNext;

public:
        FIRFilter(LPCTSTR lpcFilterRegistryPath,
LPCTSTR lpcDriverRegistryPath,
PDRIVER_FILTER pNextFilterParam);
        ~FIRFilter();

    DWORD FilterInit(DWORD dwContext,LPVOID lpParam);
    BOOL FilterPreDeinit(DWORD dwContext);
    BOOL FilterDeinit(DWORD dwContext);
    DWORD FilterOpen(DWORD dwContext, DWORD AccessCode,
DWORD ShareMode);
```

```
    BOOL FilterPreClose(DWORD dwOpenCont);
    BOOL FilterClose(DWORD dwOpenCont);
    BOOL FilterControl(DWORD dwOpenCont,DWORD dwCode,
PBYTE pBufIn,
DWORD dwLenIn, PBYTE pBufOut, DWORD dwLenOut,
PDWORD pdwActualOut, HANDLE hAsyncRef);
    void FilterPowerdn(DWORD dwConext);
    void FilterPowerup(DWORD dwConext);
    DWORD FilterRead(DWORD dwOpenCont, LPVOID pBuffer,
DWORD Count);
    DWORD FilterWrite(DWORD dwOpenCont, LPCVOID pSourceBytes,
DWORD NumberOfBytes);
    DWORD FilterSeek(DWORD dwOpenCont, long Amount, DWORD Type);
    BOOL FilterCancelIo(DWORD dwOpenCont, HANDLE hAsyncHandle);
};
```

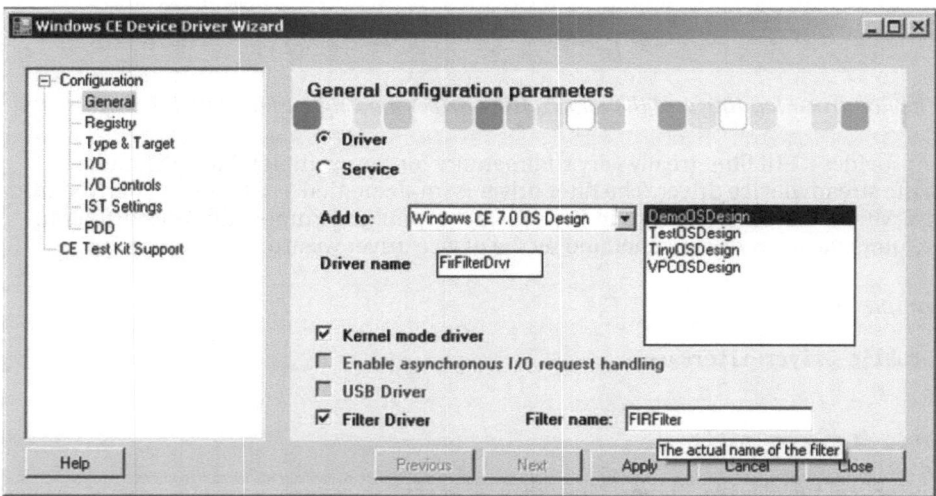

Figure 7-10. *Using Windows CE Device Driver Wizard to create a filter driver*

A simplified basic implementation of the Init entry point, which is the only function exposed by the filter driver, is seen in Listing 7-17. All it does is create a new instance of the *FirFilter* class saves the pointer to the next filter which is really a pointer to our stream device driver, and returns the pointer to the filter driver object.

Listing 7-17. A sample Init entry to the filter driver.

```
extern "C" PDRIVER_FILTER FIRFilterInit(LPCTSTR lpcFilterRegistryPath, LPCTSTR
lpcDriverRegistryPath, PDRIVER_FILTER pNextFilter)
{

FIRFilter* pFIRFilter = NULL;

        InitializeCriticalSection(&g_CriticalSection);
DEBUGMSG(ZONE_INIT,
(L"FIRFilter: Creating new filter driver
            for <%s>\r\n",
lpcDriverRegistryPath));
        EnterCriticalSection(&g_CriticalSection);

pFIRFilter = new FIRFilter(lpcFilterRegistryPath,
                                        lpcDriverRegistryPath,pNextFilter);
        if (!pFIRFilter)
        {
        DEBUGMSG(ZONE_ERROR,
(L"FIRFilter: Error, Unable to allocate memory.  %s cannot be initialized\r\n",
lpcDriverRegistryPath));
        goto done;
    }

done:
pFIRFilter->pNextFilter = pNextFilter;
        LeaveCriticalSection(&g_CriticalSection);
        return (PDRIVER_FILTER)pFIRFilter;
}
```

Following in Listing 7-18 is an example of *FIRFilter::FilterInit* entry point implementation that uses the pointer to the stream device driver that we saved to call into its Init entry point, in this case *TST_Init*. Be careful not to implement a filter driver for a device driver that can have multiple instances opened.

Listing 7-18. A sample FilterInit entry point

```
DWORD FIRFilter::FilterInit(DWORD dwContext,LPVOID lpParam)
{
        DWORD dwRet = 0;

        m_initReturn = pNextFilter->fnInit(dwContext, lpParam,
this);

        return m_initReturn;
}
```

User Mode Device Drivers

User mode device drivers run in the context of a user mode process and are therefore restricted from calling kernel only APIs. User mode device drivers are loaded into user mode device driver host process called udevice.exe. This isolates the driver from the system kernel increasing overall stability at the expense of performance. Basically user mode device drivers are ordinary stream device drivers that have `DEVFLAGS_LOAD_AS_USERMODE` flag value added to the flags registry settings. User mode device drivers do not have access to kernel mode memory and therefore have restrictions on the kinds of pointers and asynchronous memory accesses they can perform. Figure 7-11 shows a block diagram of how user mode device drivers interact with Device Manager.

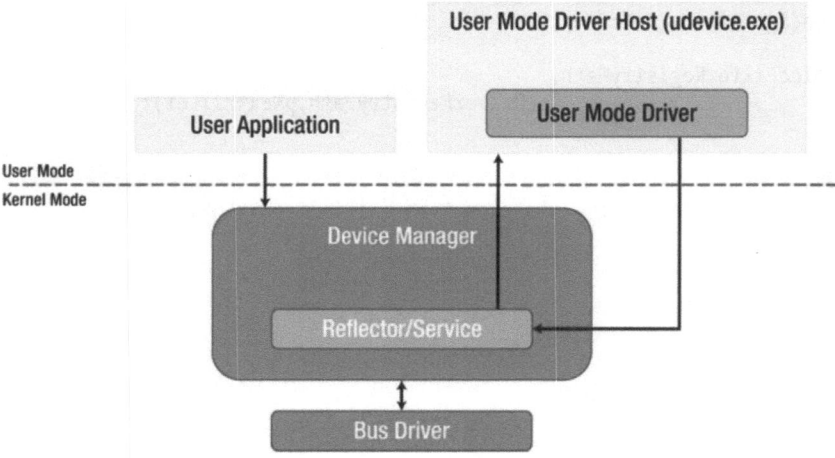

Figure 7-11. *User mode device driver architecture*

Restrictions on User Mode Device Drivers

User mode device drivers should not use embedded pointers. The user mode device driver reflector will perform the marshalling necessary for pointer parameters in function calls to be dereferenced. However the reflector is not able to marshal embedded pointers in a data structure so the user mode driver has to perform the necessary marshalling which is tough. For example, if the driver is called by a kernel mode component the embedded pointer would point to a kernel address which the user mode driver can't access. The portable solution to this problem is to ensure that all data is passed into the driver in a single flat structure that does not contain pointers.

User mode drivers should not be designed to implement asynchronous memory accesses to client buffers. The reflector in the kernel will marshal the pointer parameter during the synchronous call but the buffer can't be marshalled for asynchronous access. User mode drivers can marshal embedded pointers for asynchronous use themselves, but only if they point to user address space.

Implementing a User Mode Device Driver

Implementing a user mode device driver is no different from implementing a kernel mode stream device driver. The main concern is to remember the restrictions just discussed and deciding on the user mode host. A user mode device driver is hosted by a user mode process Udevice.exe, however you can decide if you want your device driver to be hosted by its own host, or be hosted by a host that contains a group of user mode device drivers. Once this decision was taken, the only way for Device Manager to treat your device driver as a user mode device driver, is setting the "Flags" key value to include the DEVFLAGS_LOAD_AS_USERPROC. The registry settings example in Listing 7-19 is for a user mode device driver that will be hosted in its own Udevice process. While the registry settings example in Listing 7-20 is for a user mode device driver that will be hosted in a shared Udevice process. The "ProcGroup" key in the latter signifies that it will be hosted by Udevice process registered as process group 3 which defined in the registry by Microsoft see Listing 7-21.

Listing 7-19. *Registry settings for a user mode device driver hosted by its own private Udevice process*

```
; Umdemodrvr driver
[HKEY_LOCAL_MACHINE\Drivers\BuiltIn\Umdemodrvr]
    "Prefix"="UMD"
    "DLL"="Umdemodrvr.DLL"
    "Order"=dword:5
    "DisplayName"="Umdemodrvr driver"
    "Flags"=dword:10
```

Listing 7-20. *Registry settings for a user mode device driver hosted by a shared Udevice process*

```
; Umdemodrvr2 driver
[HKEY_LOCAL_MACHINE\Drivers\BuiltIn\Umdemodrvr2]
    "Prefix"="UMD"
    "DLL"="Umdemodrvr2.DLL"
    "Order"=dword:8
    "DisplayName"="Umdemodrvr2 driver"
    "Flags"=dword:10
    "ProcGroup"=dword:3
```

Listing 7-21. *Registry settings for a shared Udevice process defined as process group 3*

```
; udevice.exe running in default chamber, commonly elevated, for MS Drivers
#define PROCGROUP_DRIVER_MSFT_DEFAULT    3
[HKEY_LOCAL_MACHINE\Drivers\ProcGroup_0003]
    "ProcName"="udevice.exe"
    "ProcVolPrefix"="$udevice"
```

However you can create your own process group just as well, for example say process group 4 the same way: [HKEY_LOCAL_MACHINE\Drivers\ProcGroup_0004].

Loading and Initializing a User Mode Device Driver

Loading user mode device drivers starts the same way as any stream device driver loading process. Figure 7-12 helps explain the process of loading a user mode device driver. It shows the loading process progression in the upper call stack including the creation of the reflector, in the lower call stack is the progression of the driver initialization process until the *xxx_Init* entry point of the user mode device driver is called.

Note that the red squares in the figure actually start the process once BusEnum calls *ActivateDeviceEx* to load the device driver. The first step is calling *LoadLib* which triggers first either finding a running Udevice process if our device drivers is to run in a shared host or create a new Udevice host process. This process now creates a new reflector service for our device driver (This process occurred in the call to CreateReflector in line 5 of the top block in the figure). The reflector eventually loads the device driver DLL. If it loaded successfully the Init function for the reflector trigger a call to the device driver xxx_Init entry point. If the Init function of the device driver does not fail the device driver is active and running in the host Udevice process.

Figure 7-12. *Loading process of a user mode device driver*

One of the options of Windows CE Device Driver Wizard is to create a jumpstart user mode device driver. Listing 7-22 shows an example of such code. To make things silly I added a private IOCTL to this driver to demonstrate the ability of user mode device drivers to display GUI, note that allocating memory in *UMD_Init* is done by using *VirtuAlloc* as opposed to *AllocPhysMem*. Also note that PAGE_NOCACHE is used. Listing 7-23 shows a simple application opening the device driver and calling this specific IOCTL to display a silly message box.

The result of the call is displayed in Figure 7-13.

Listing 7-22. *Sample code for two entry points in a user mode driver*

```
DWORD UMD_Init(LPCTSTR pContext, LPCVOID lpvBusContext)
{
    HKEY hConfig;
    DWORD dwRet = 0;
    BOOL bRc = FALSE;
    DWORD dwStatus;
    DDKWINDOWINFO WinInfo;
    PUMD_DEVCONTXT pDevContxt;

    // Allocate device instance context structure
    pDevContxt = (PUMD_DEVCONTXT)VirtualAlloc(NULL,
sizeof(PUMD_DEVCONTXT), MEM_COMMIT,
                                PAGE_NOCACHE |
PAGE_EXECUTE_READWRITE);
    if (pDevContxt != NULL)
    {
        InitializeCriticalSection(&pDevContxt->CriticalSection);
        pDevContxt->hDriverMan = (HANDLE)GetCurrentProcessId();
    }
    else
    {
        DEBUGMSG(ZONE_INIT, (_T("UMD!not enough memory\r\n")));
        return dwRet;
    }

    // Open active device registry key to retrieve activation
    // info
    DEBUGMSG(ZONE_INIT, (_T("UMD!Starting UMD_Init\r\n")));
    if (hConfig = OpenDeviceKey(pContext))
    {
```

```
        // Read window information
        WinInfo.cbSize = sizeof(WinInfo);
        dwStatus = DDKReg_GetWindowInfo(hConfig, &WinInfo);
        if (dwStatus != ERROR_SUCCESS)
        {
            DEBUGMSG(ZONE_INIT,
(_T("UMD!Error Getting window information\r\n")));
            VirtualFree(pDevContxt, sizeof(UMD_DEVCONTXT),
MEM_DECOMMIT);
            return dwRet;
        }
        pDevContxt->dwBusNumber = WinInfo.dwBusNumber;
        pDevContxt->dwInterfaceType = WinInfo.dwInterfaceType;
    }
    else
    {
        DEBUGMSG(ZONE_INIT,
(_T("UMD!Failed to open active device key\r\n")));
        VirtualFree(pDevContxt, sizeof(UMD_DEVCONTXT),
MEM_DECOMMIT);
        return dwRet;
    }
    RegCloseKey(hConfig);
    // We got here if all succeded so return the device context
    // pointer
    dwRet = (DWORD)pDevContxt;
    return dwRet;
}
....
....
BOOL UMD_IOControl(DWORD hOpenContext, DWORD dwCode,
 PBYTE pBufIn,
                    DWORD dwLenIn, PBYTE pBufOut, DWORD dwLenOut,
                    PDWORD pdwActualOut, HANDLE hAsyncRef)
{
    PUMD_DEVCONTXT pDevContxt = (PUMD_DEVCONTXT)hOpenContext;
    BOOL bRet = TRUE;
    DWORD dwErr = 0;

    // TODO: Add code to implement IOCTL codes:
    switch (dwCode)
    {
```

```
            case IOCTL_UMDEMODRVR_FOO1:
                // Enter critical section if needed otherwise erase
                // EnterCriticalSection(
                //              &pDevContxt->CriticalSection);
                // Add implementation code
                // LeaveCriticalSection(
                //              &pDevContxt->CriticalSection);
                    MessageBox(NULL,
_T("User Driver Message Box"),
_T("User Mode Device Driver"), MB_OK);
                break;
            default:
                break;
        }
}
```

Listing 7-23. *Sample code of an application calling a user mode device driver to display a message box*

```
int _tmain(int argc, TCHAR *argv[], TCHAR *envp[])
{
        BOOL bRet = FALSE;
        HANDLE hTstDrvr = INVALID_HANDLE_VALUE;

        // Try open an instance of TestDrvr
        hTstDrvr = CreateFile(L"UMD1:",
GENERIC_READ | GENERIC_WRITE,0,
NULL,OPEN_EXISTING,0,NULL);
    if (INVALID_HANDLE_VALUE == hTstDrvr) {
                DWORD bdw = GetLastError();
        return FALSE;
    }

        bRet = DeviceIoControl(hTstDrvr,IOCTL_UMDEMODRVR_FOO1,
NULL, 0, NULL, 0, NULL, NULL);

        return 0;
}
```

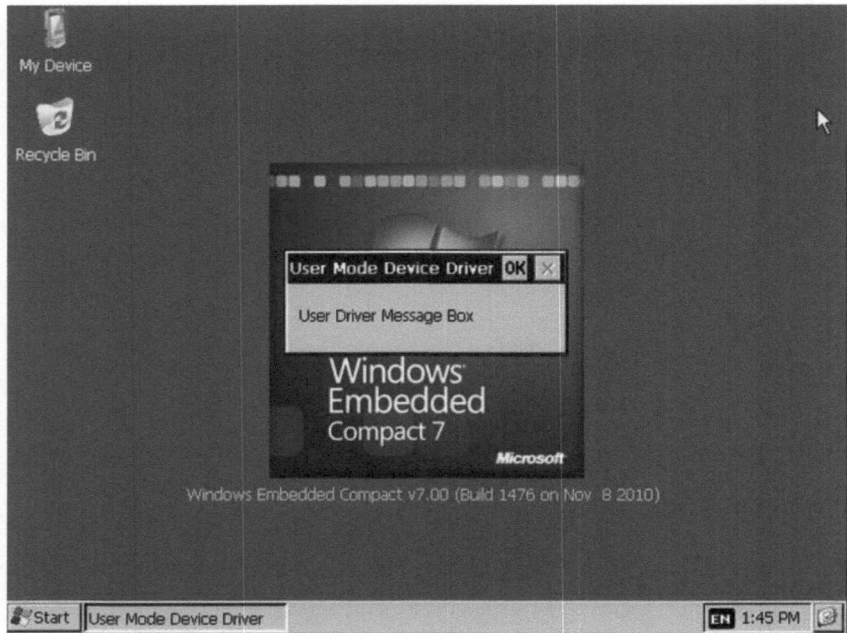

Figure 7-13. *User mode device driver displaying a message box*

Chapter Summary

The stream device driver has been the mainstay of Windows CE throughout its existence. The main difference between earlier versions of Windows CE leading to Windows CE 6.0 and Windows CE 6.0 and its successor Windows Embedded Compact 7, is that in the older versions stream device drivers where user mode drivers because of the architecture. However in the last two versions stream device drivers reside either in kernel space or in user space, thus having kernel mode stream device drivers and user mode stream device drivers. The former providing better performance, and the latter providing robustness, especially for installable device drivers. This latest version of Windows CE Device Manager enables us to develop device drivers that support asynchronous I/O request handling. Device Manager allows creating filter drivers for various capabilities.

CHAPTER 8

Device Driver I/O and Interrupts

The essence of any computer system is to accept input data, process it, and produce output. How the system accepts input data is critical for real-time embedded systems. Because it needs to process the input data and output a response within a determined time interval. The most accurate way to achieve this would be to poll an input source constantly for data. This however puts a heavy burden on the CPU, limiting the system to just one task. Waiting for input data to arrive and react on it alleviates this burden and frees CPU resources. To be able to wait and react, we need hardware support for getting CPU attention away from its flow of processing.

Hardware triggered interrupts cause the CPU to stop the flow of execution and jump to a specific entry in the code that handles the interrupt. The arrival of an interrupt is not predictable; therefore it can occur at any time even when another interrupt is being handled. Once the interrupt was processed the CPU resumes from the point it stopped.

In this chapter

- Interrupt model
- Interrupt processing
- I/O memory mapping

Interrupt Model

I/O hardware triggers an interrupt whenever it needs the CPU's attention, because its I/O registers changed state. Interrupts may be categorized into maskable, non-maskable, inter-processor, and software interrupts.

- Maskable interrupt – hardware interrupt that may be ignored if masked by setting a specific bit in the Interrupt Mask Register (IMR)
- Non-Maskable interrupt (NMI) – hardware interrupt that cannot be ignored

- Inter-Processor interrupt (IPI) – an interrupt triggered by one processor to another in a multiprocessor environment. Mainly used to implement cache coherence. In Windows Embedded Compact 7 it has become relevant as it supports multicore processors.

- Software interrupt – an exception triggered by some CPU instruction. Used as a trap to execute system calls since the CPU switches to kernel mode.

Hardware interrupts may be edge triggered or level triggered. As with everything in life there are pros and cons to each of these. Edge triggered interrupts occur when there is a level transition of a pulse on the interrupt request line, a rising edge trigger occurs when the transition is from low (0) to high (1), and falling edge trigger occurs when the transition is from high (1), to low (0). The major failing of edge triggered interrupts is that noise may be misinterpreted or interrupts may be missed altogether. Modern hardware really solves this problem using interrupt status registers. These should be scanned by well-implemented device drivers to check that there are no missed interrupts. Level triggered interrupts transition the interrupt request line to an active state (maybe high or low) and keep it until it receives a command to go inactive. The main failing for level triggered interrupts is handling of shared interrupt request line. If a lower level request is kept level active, it is a problem to detect a request from another I/O device even if it has a higher request level.

Windows Embedded Compact 7 and its predecessors need to provide OS services to handle these interrupts to allow the operating system itself and processes to perform their purpose. A physical interrupt is a signal arriving over a hardware line connected to the CPU, and the OEM Adaptation Layer (OAL) implementation maps hardware assigned interrupts to logical interrupts understood by the operating system to allow interrupt handling code to service correctly each interrupt.

Interrupt Architecture

The interrupt model for Windows Embedded Compact 7 is that all interrupts get vectored into the kernel. Windows Embedded Compact 7 interrupt architecture tries to balance simplicity with performance by splitting the interrupt processing into an extremely fast (and "lightweight") Interrupt Service Routine (ISR) and a device driver provided thread that processes the bulk of the interrupt processing. Because extended processing in an ISR delays the servicing of other interrupts and may result in jitter the ISR does very little but acknowledges the interrupt and differs most of the interrupt processing to the IST. Because the IST is scheduled like any other thread in the system it is assigned a scheduling priority fitting the priority of the interrupt that it serves. This greatly improves real-time performance by reducing jitter and simplifies locking and scheduling by the kernel.

The kernel component that handles all interrupts is the exception handler. When an interrupt occurs, the CPU transfers control to the kernel exception handler. The exception handler in turn calls the ISR which is registered to handle the current interrupt. The ISR should return the interrupts logical interrupt identifier, which it passes to the kernel as its return value. The kernel sets an event associated with the logical interrupt, which causes an interrupt service thread (IST) to be scheduled. Code in the IST is responsible for servicing the device interrupt. The IST runs in the context of a thread in Device Manager and is essentially a typical thread running at a high priority.

Interrupt Processing

The diagram in Figure 8-1 shows the sequence of state transitions on a timeline going from right to left. Starting with the arrival of the hardware triggered interrupt all the way to completion of the interrupt processing and releasing the blocked interrupt hardware to handle another incomming interrupt. The following 5 steps are echoed in the diagram.

1. Device raises registered hardware interrupt

2. Kernel gets exception, calls associated Interrupt Service Routine (ISR)

3. Interrupt Service Routine (ISR) quickly deals with pending interrupt

4. Interrupt Service Thread (IST) in driver is signaled to process interrupt

5. Interrupt Service Thread (IST) completes processing and

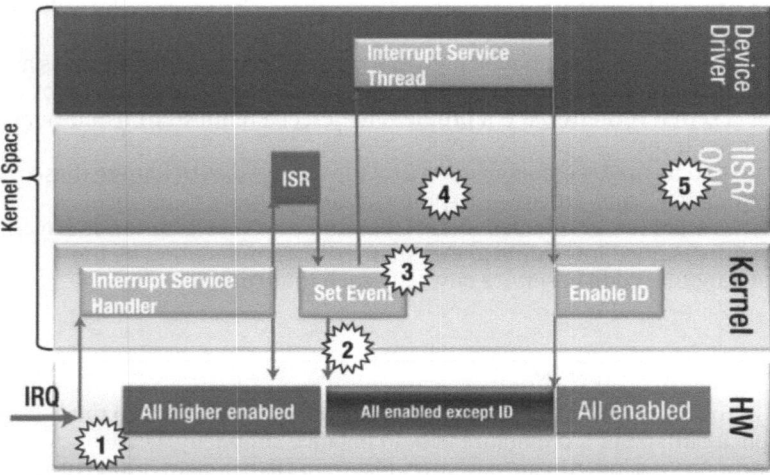

Figure 8-1. Interrupt processing in Windows Embedded Compact 7

The Interrupt Service Routine - ISR

ISRs in WEC 7 must be small and fast because ISRs execute with all interrupts turned off, they cannot call any kernel functions, they cannot use any stack, and depending on the CPU architecture they may not even use all of the registers. More than that, ISRs cannot cause any nested exception. ISRs can return back to the kernel with a return value which either tells the kernel that the interrupt has been handled so to speak by returning SYSINTR_NOP, or asks it to schedule a specific IST by returning a SYSINTR corresponding to it.

There two categories of Interrupt Service Routines acceptable for WEC 7 based devices:

- Interrupt handlers within the OAL created by the hardware OEM that provide interrupt handlers for BSP device drivers.

- Installable ISRs developed if needed by ISVs for example; however the OEM has to provide support within the OAL for chaining installable ISRs.

The OAL and Interrupt Handling

The OEM Adaptation Layer (OAL) implementation provides the operating system's kernel with access to the OEMs hardware. The OAL implementation contains a set of more than a dozen functions to initialize, map, enable, and disable interrupts and translate between interrupt request values and logical IDs. Hardware architectures may support a single interrupt line handled by a single ISR for example the ARM architecture where the OEM is responsible for implementing this single ISR named *OEMInterruptHandler*. This function must be implemented specifically for each ARM base SoC (System on Chip) as each such SoC has its own set of control registers. Listing 8-1 shows such an implementation where repetitive code has been shorthanded by "....." strings and profiling support has been removed. Other hardware, exemplified by the x86 architecture where interrupts are handled by a Programmable Interrupt Controller (PIC), have multiple ISRs for multiple interrupts. In such cases the OAL does not implement the **OALIntrMapInit** function. However, it is interesting to look at the actual ISR provided for the x86 platform *PeRPISR* which is common for all x86 based devices. Listing 8-2 shows the x86 ISR where profiling and ILTiming support has been removed.

Listing 8-1. *OEMInterruptHandler implementation for the OMAP 35xx platform*

```
UINT32 OEMInterruptHandler(UINT32 ra)
{
    UINT32 irq = OAL_INTR_IRQ_UNDEFINED;
    UINT32 sysIntr = SYSINTR_NOP;
    UINT32 mask,status;

    if (g_oalILT.active) g_oalILT.interrupts++;

    // Get pending interrupt
    irq = INREG32(&s_intr.pICLRegs->INTC_SIR_IRQ);

    if (irq == IRQ_GPIO1_MPU)
        {
        // mask status with irq enabled GPIO's to make sure only
        // interrupts which generated by a new interrupt is handled
        status = INREG32(&s_intr.pGPIORegs[0]->IRQSTATUS1);
        status &= INREG32(&s_intr.pGPIORegs[0]->IRQENABLE1);
        for (irq = IRQ_GPIO_0, mask = 1; mask != 0; mask <<= 1, irq++)
            {
            if ((mask & status) != 0) break;
            }
        OUTPORT32(&s_intr.pGPIORegs[0]->IRQSTATUS1, mask);
        OUTPORT32(&s_intr.pGPIORegs[0]->IRQSTATUS2, mask);
        OUTPORT32(&s_intr.pGPIORegs[0]->CLEARIRQENABLE1, mask);
        OUTPORT32(&s_intr.pGPIORegs[0]->CLEARWAKEUPENA, mask);
        OEMEnableIOPadWakeup((irq - IRQ_GPIO_0), FALSE);
        }
    else if (irq == IRQ_GPIO2_MPU)
        {
        status = INREG32(&s_intr.pGPIORegs[1]->IRQSTATUS1);
        status &= INREG32(&s_intr.pGPIORegs[1]->IRQENABLE1);
        for (irq = IRQ_GPIO_32, mask = 1; mask != 0; mask <<= 1, irq++)
            {
```

```
            if ((mask & status) != 0) break;
                }
        OUTPORT32(&s_intr.pGPIORegs[1]->IRQSTATUS1, mask);
        OUTPORT32(&s_intr.pGPIORegs[1]->IRQSTATUS2, mask);
        OUTPORT32(&s_intr.pGPIORegs[1]->CLEARIRQENABLE1, mask);
        OUTPORT32(&s_intr.pGPIORegs[1]->CLEARWAKEUPENA, mask);
        OEMEnableIOPadWakeup((irq - IRQ_GPIO_0), FALSE);
        }
    else if (irq == IRQ_GPIO3_MPU)
        {
                .....
        }
    else if (irq == IRQ_GPIO4_MPU)
        {
                .....
        }
    else if (irq == IRQ_GPIO5_MPU)
        {
                .....
        }
    else if (irq == IRQ_GPIO6_MPU)
        {
                .....
        }
    else if (irq < 32)
        {
        SETPORT32(&s_intr.pICLRegs->INTC_MIR0, 1 << irq);
        }
    else if (irq < 64)
        {
        SETPORT32(&s_intr.pICLRegs->INTC_MIR1, 1 << (irq - 32));
        }
    else if (irq < 96)
        {
        SETPORT32(&s_intr.pICLRegs->INTC_MIR2, 1 << (irq - 64));
        }

    // Acknowledge interrupt
    OUTREG32(&s_intr.pICLRegs->INTC_CONTROL, IC_CNTL_NEW_IRQ);

    // Check if this is timer IRQ
    if (irq == g_oalTimerIrq)
        {
        if (g_oalILT.active)
                        g_oalILT.interrupts--;

        // Call timer interrupt handler
        sysIntr = OALTimerIntrHandler();

        // re-enable interrupts
        OALIntrDoneIrqs(1, &irq);
        }
```

```
        else if (irq == g_oalPrcmIrq)
            {
            // call prcm interrupt handler
            sysIntr = OALPrcmIntrHandler();

            // re-enable interrupts
            if (sysIntr == SYSINTR_NOP)
                            OALIntrDoneIrqs(1, &irq);
            }
        else if (irq == g_oalSmartReflex1)
            {
            // call prcm interrupt handler
            sysIntr = OALSmartReflex1Intr();

            // re-enable interrupts
            if (sysIntr == SYSINTR_NOP)
                            OALIntrDoneIrqs(1, &irq);
            }
        else if (irq == g_oalSmartReflex2)
            {
                    .....
            }
        else if (irq != OAL_INTR_IRQ_UNDEFINED)
            {
            // We don't assume IRQ sharing, use static mapping
            sysIntr = OALIntrTranslateIrq(irq);
            }
        return sysIntr;
    }
```

Listing 8-2. *PeRPISR implementation of the x86 ISR function*

```
static ULONG PeRPISR()
{
    ULONG ulRet = SYSINTR_NOP;
    UCHAR ucCurrentInterrupt;

    ucCurrentInterrupt = PICGetCurrentInterrupt();

    if (ucCurrentInterrupt == INTR_TIMER0)
    {

        if (PProfileInterrupt)
        {
            ulRet= PProfileInterrupt();
        }

        if (!PProfileInterrupt || ulRet == SYSINTR_RESCHED)
        {
            if (sgTimeAdvance)
            {
```

```
                CurMSec += g_dwBSPMsPerIntr;

                CurTicks.QuadPart += g_dwOALTimerCount;
            }

            if ((int) (CurMSec - dwReschedTime) >= 0)
                ulRet = SYSINTR_RESCHED;
        }

        // Check if a reboot was requested.
        if (dwRebootAddress)
        {
            RebootHandler();
        }

    }
    else if (ucCurrentInterrupt == INTR_RTC)
    {
        // Check to see if this was an alarm interrupt
        UCHAR cStatusC = CMOS_Read( RTC_STATUS_C);

        if((cStatusC & (RTC_SRC_IRQ|RTC_SRC_AS)) ==
(RTC_SRC_IRQ|RTC_SRC_AS))
            ulRet = SYSINTR_RTC_ALARM;
    }
    else if (ucCurrentInterrupt <= INTR_MAXIMUM)
    {
        // Mask off interrupt source
        PICEnableInterrupt(ucCurrentInterrupt, FALSE);

        // We have a physical interrupt ID, but want to return a
        // SYSINTR_ID Call interrupt chain to see if any
          // installed ISRs handle this interrupt
        ulRet = NKCallIntChain(ucCurrentInterrupt);

        // IRQ not claimed by installed ISR; translate into
  // SYSINTR
        if (ulRet == SYSINTR_CHAIN)
        {
            ulRet = OALIntrTranslateIrq (ucCurrentInterrupt);
            if (!OALIsInterruptEnabled(ulRet))
            {
                // This default IST is not intialized.
                ulRet = (ULONG)SYSINTR_UNDEFINED;
            }
        }
```

```
        if (ulRet == SYSINTR_NOP)
        {
            // If SYSINTR_NOP, IRQ claimed by installed ISR, but
            //   no further action required
            PICEnableInterrupt(ucCurrentInterrupt, TRUE);
        }
        else if (ulRet == SYSINTR_UNDEFINED ||
!NKIsSysIntrValid(ulRet))
        {
            // If SYSINTR_UNDEFINED, ignore
            // If SysIntr was never initialized, ignore
            OALMSGS(OAL_WARN&&OAL_INTR,
(L"Spurious interrupt on IRQ %d\r\n",
 ucCurrentInterrupt));
            ulRet = OALMarkUnknownIRQ(ucCurrentInterrupt);
        }
    }

    OEMIndicateIntSource(ulRet);

    // Disable interrupts before issuing the EOI, that way if the
    // interrupt source hasn't been properly serviced we will
    // spin trying to service the interrupt rather than
    // infinitely nesting here until the stack overflows. Prior
    // to adding this cli when running under Virtual Server 2005
    // we saw the timer interrupt immediately interrupting after
    // the EOI causing fatal interrupt nesting here.
    //
    __asm {
        cli
    }

    if (ucCurrentInterrupt > 7 || ucCurrentInterrupt == -2)
    {
        __asm {
            mov al, 020h      ; Nonspecific EOI
            out 0A0h, al
        }
    }

    __asm {
        mov al, 020h          ; Nonspecific EOI
        out 020h, al
    }
    return ulRet;
}
```

Installable ISRs

Installable ISRs as the name suggests can be installed on a running device, without the need to
implement the code within the OAL. This allows ISVs to add ISRs to the system without the need to

engage the OEM. Furthermore, installable ISRs allow multiple devices to share interrupts on a single interrupt request line. This means that the OEM has to implement support within the OAL code exposing an IRQ that installable ISRs can hook to.

Listing 8-3 shows how a device driver installs an ISR that is set in the registry settings from within its xxx_Init entry point.

Listing 8-3. *Installing an ISR sample code*

```
// We make sure we got a good result from DDKReg_GetIsrInfo
if (IsrInfo.szIsrDll[0] != 0)
{
    if (IsrInfo.szIsrHandler[0]!= 0 &&
                            IsrInfo.dwIrq == IRQ_UNSPECIFIED &&
                                    IsrInfo.dwSysintr == SYSINTR_UNDEFINED)
    {
        DEBUGMSG(ZONE_INIT,
                (_T("TMP!Corrupted or missing installable ISR
settings\r\n")));
        FreePhysMem(pDevContxt);
        return dwRet;
    }
    else
    {
        pDevContxt->hInstISR =
LoadIntChainHandler(IsrInfo.szIsrDll,
                            IsrInfo.szIsrHandler,
                    (BYTE)IsrInfo.dwIrq);
        if (!pDevContxt->hInstISR)
        {
            DEBUGMSG(ZONE_INIT,
(_T("TMP!Failed to install ISR handler\r\n")));
            FreePhysMem(pDevContxt);
            return dwRet;
        }
        else
        {
            GIISR_INFO Info;
            PHYSICAL_ADDRESS PortAddress =
pDevContxt->ioPhysicalBase;
            pDevContxt->dwSysIntr = IsrInfo.dwSysintr;

            // Set up ISR handler
            Info.SysIntr = IsrInfo.dwSysintr;
            Info.CheckPort = TRUE;
            Info.PortIsIO = pDevContxt->bIoMemMapped;
            Info.UseMaskReg =  FALSE;
            Info.PortAddr = pDevContxt->pIoAddr;
            Info.PortSize = sizeof(DWORD);
            Info.MaskAddr = 0x0000;
```

```
            if (!KernelLibIoControl(pDevContxt->hInstISR,
IOCTL_GIISR_INFO,                                        &Info, sizeof(Info), NULL, 0, NULL))
            {
                DEBUGMSG(ZONE_ERROR,
(_T("TMP!KernelLibIoControl call
failed.\r\n")));
            }
        }
    }
}
```

LoadIntChainHandler basically loads the DLL for the ISR, calls the mandatory *CreateInstance,* and adds the ISR to the end of the list of ISRs. In most cases the generic installable ISR implemented in %WINCEROOT%\public\COMMON\oak\drivers\giisr is sufficient to recognize the triggering device and returning the correct SYSINTR. If you need to extend the capabilities of your installable ISR beyond returning the correct SYSINTR you can implement your own ISR handler. It must be implemented within a DLL, exposing four functions:

- ISRHandler—Actual ISR

- CreateInstance - Returns a value that references a particular instance of the ISR.

- DestroyInstance - Remove from list by the index returned by CreateInstance

- IOControl—Handler for any IST calls with KernelLibIOControl

Following in listing 8-4 is an extremely simple example of an installable ISR.

Listing 8-4. *Oversimplified installable ISR handler*

```
DWORD ISRHandler(DWORD InstanceIndex)
{
        BYTE Value;
        Value = READ_PORT_UCHAR((PUCHAR)PortAddress);
        // If interrupt bit set, return corresponding SYSINTR
        if ( Value & 0x01 )
        {
                return SYSINTR_DEMO;
        }
        else
        {
                return SYSINTR_CHAIN;
        }
}
```

The ISR handler code uses a port I/O call to check the status of the device. You may have a scenario that requires a much more complex implementation. An example of such an ISR can be found in %WINCEROOT%\public\COMMON\oak\drivers\serial\isr16550. If the device is not the source of the interrupt, the return value will be SYSINTR_CHAIN. This return value tells the *NKChainIntr* function that our device was not the source of the interrupt and that other ISRs in the chain should be evaluated. If a valid SYSINTR is returned by the ISR, then *NKChainIntr* will immediately return and not call any other ISRs on the list. This provides a priority ordering. The first loaded installable ISR is loaded first on the list, or highest interrupt request level, subsequent installable ISRs are then added to the bottom of the list.

The highest interrupt request level installable ISR in the chain should be installed first for both priority and speed of execution.

Nested ISRs

Because Windows Embedded Compact 7 is an RTOS it needs to service highest interrupt request level interrupts as soon as these are triggered to prevent loss or delay, therefore the kernel employs nesting for interrupts. Nested interrupts allow interrupt requests of a higher interrupt request level to preempt IRQs of a lower interrupt request level. The following steps are taken by the kernel to handle nested interrupts:

- The kernel disables all other IRQs with the same or lower IRQ level as the IRQ that invoked the current ISR call.

- If a higher IRQ level arrives before the current ISR completes processing, the kernel saves the current ISR state (The state includes only those registers that are supported for use in an ISR to save time).

- The kernel calls the IRQ level ISR to handle the new request.

- The kernel restores the original ISR's state and continues processing.

The Interrupt Service Thread - IST

The IST is a thread that is scheduled when the related SYSINTR is returned by the ISR. Once it completes its processing of the interrupt it signals the kernel to re-enable the physical interrupt on the I/O device related to this IST, and blocks until another interrupt needs to be processed.

The following steps are typical in creating and launching an IST:

- Create an event

- Associate the event with the corresponding SYSINTR

- Create the IST itself

- Set the ISTs priority

- Optionally set the ISTs quantum

Listing 8-5 shows a sample code generated by the device driver wizard to create and launch an interrupt service thread.

Listing 8-5. *Sample implementation for creating an IST*

```
DWORD CreateInterruptServiceThread(PDMO_DEVCONTXT pDevCntxt)
{
    pDevCntxt->hIstEvent = CreateEvent(NULL, FALSE, FALSE, NULL);
    if (pDevCntxt->hIstEvent == NULL)
    {
        DEBUGMSG(ZONE_INIT,
(_T("DMO!IST Create: Event creation failed\r\n")));
        return -1;
    }
```

```
    // Associate the event with the interrupt ID
    //
    if (!InterruptInitialize(pDevCntxt->dwSysIntr,
pDevCntxt->hIstEvent, NULL,0))
    {
        DEBUGMSG(ZONE_INIT,
(_T("DMO!IST Create: Failed to associate event ..\r\n")));
        return -1;
    }

    // Create the Interrupt Service Thread
    //
    pDevCntxt->hIst = CreateThread(NULL,0,
(LPTHREAD_START_ROUTINE)DMOInterruptServiceThread,
(LPVOID)pDevCntxt, CREATE_SUSPENDED,
NULL);
    if (pDevCntxt->hIst == NULL)
    {
        DEBUGMSG(ZONE_INIT,(_T("DMO!IST Create: Failed to create
IST\r\n")));
        return -1;
    }
    // Set the thread priority
    //
    if( !CeSetThreadPriority(pDevCntxt->hIst,
pDevCntxt->dwIstPriority))
    {
        DEBUGMSG(ZONE_INIT,
(_T("DMO!IST Create: Failed to set IST thread priority\r\n")));
        return -1;
    }
    // Set the thread quantum
    //
    if(!CeSetThreadQuantum(pDevCntxt->hIst,
pDevCntxt->dwIstQuantum))
    {
        DEBUGMSG(ZONE_INIT,
(_T("DMO!IST Create: Failed to set IST thread
quantum\r\n")));
        return -1;
    }
    // Start IST
    //
    ResumeThread(pDevCntxt->hIst);
    return 0;
}
```

The IST itself blocks on this event and when the kernel sets the event as a result of the corresponding interrupt being triggered, it processes the interrupt by retrieving the data that it needs to retrieve and calls *InterruptDone* to re-enable the corresponding hardware interrupt. Listing 8-6 shows the device driver wizard generated implementation of the IST that was created in listing 8-5.

Listing 8-6. Sample implementation of a skeleton IST

```
DWORD DMOInterruptServiceThread(LPVOID lpParameter)
{
    PDMO_DEVCONTXT pParam = (PDMO_DEVCONTXT)lpParameter;
    while(WaitForSingleObject(pParam->hIstEvent, INFINITE))
    {
        if (pParam->bShutDown)
        {
            ExitThread(0);
        }
        // TODO: Write code to process interrupt

        // Complete interrupt and reanable interrupt
        InterruptDone(pParam->dwSysIntr);
    }
    return 0;
}
```

I/O Memory Mapping

An important part of interrupt processing is retrieving the data that its arrival caused the interrupt to trigger. A peripheral I/O device provides a set of ports or registers via which data can be retrieved. Accessing these ports means that we need some way to address these ports or registers and read them, or write to them. Addressing these locations on peripheral I/O devices is the subject of this section. The two methods of performing I/O between the CPU and peripheral I/O devices depending on the architecture are memory-mapped I/O and port-mapped I/O.

I/O base address and length information is cardinal to develop device drivers. I/O base address would be the address where the first register of the peripheral device is located, be it memory mapped or I/O space mapped. The length is better known as the range of registers the peripheral device occupies. So for example the classic example of COM1 port on a PC (remember it is I/O space) has a base address of 0x3F8 and length of 8 since its range is 0x3F8 to 0x3FF. Length is always denoted in bytes. So if a peripheral device can be described by the following structure in listing 8-7 it would have a length of 32 bytes.

Listing 8-7. A demo peripheral device 'C' structure description

```
typedef  struct
{
    volatile UINT32 REG0;          // offset 0x0000, REG0
    volatile UINT32 Reserved[3];
    volatile UINT32 REG1;          // offset 0x0010, REG1
    volatile UINT32 REG2;          // offset 0x0014, REG2
    volatile UINT32 REG3;          // offset 0x0018, REG3
    volatile UINT32 REG4;          // offset 0x001C, REG4
} DEMO_REGS *PDEMO_REGS;
```

The best practice while developing device drivers is to set these values in the registry like the following registry entries example in listing 8-8. Note that this example describes a device driver for an x86 platform where IoBase denote I/O space addresses. If these were settings for a device driver where I/O is memory mapped it would have "MemBase" and "MemLen" setting values instead.

Listing 8-8. *Registry entries for a demo device driver*

```
; DemoDrvr driver
[HKEY_LOCAL_MACHINE\Drivers\BuiltIn\Demodrvr]
    "Prefix"="DMO"
    "DLL"="Demodrvr.DLL"
    "SysIntr"=dword:20
    "Irq"=dword:13
    "IoBase"=dword:F0
    "IoLen"=dword:16
    "Order"=dword:0
    "DisplayName"="DemoDrvr driver"
    "IsrDll"="giisr.dll"
    "IsrHandler"="ISRHandler"
    "Flags"=dword:0
    "IClass"="{A32942B7-920C-486b-B0E6-92A702A99B35}"
```

Port-mapped I/O

Port-mapped I/O uses a special set of CPU instructions specifically for performing I/O. Typically found on x86 architecture, specifically the IN and OUT instructions which can read and write one to four bytes to a peripheral I/O device. Peripheral I/O devices have a separate address space from the systems memory space, which is accomplished by an extra pin on the CPU's physical interface. Because the address space for I/O is isolated from the main memory, this is also referred to as isolated I/O.

Kernel mode device driver developers should use a set of functions for reading from and writing to port mapped I/O ports declared in ceddk.h to read and write from and to these ports. An example of such a function is **READ_PORT_UCHAR** which reads a byte from a byte wide port on a peripheral device. Listing 8-9 is the declaration in ceddk.h. The implementation in ddk_io library is simple and demonstrates using the special instructions for port mapped I/O, see listing 8-10.

Listing 8-9. *Declaration of READ_PORT_UCHAR*

```
NTKERNELAPI
UCHAR
READ_PORT_UCHAR(
    __in volatile const UCHAR * const  Port
);
```

Listing 8-10. *Implementation of READ_PORT_UCHAR in ddk_io library*

```
UCHAR
READ_PORT_UCHAR(
    volatile const UCHAR * const  Port
    )
{
```

```
#if defined(x86)
   __asm {
     mov          dx, word ptr Port
     in           al, dx
   }
#else
     return *(volatile UCHAR * const)Port;
#endif
}
```

For an example of using these macros see listing 8-11 which is part of an implementation of a device driver that reads data from GPIO port 1on an eBox3300 based device.

Listing 8-11. *using WRITE_PORT_UCHAR and READ_PORT_UCHAR macros*

```
UCHAR chVal = 0;

// set GPIO port1 as input direction
WRITE_PORT_UCHAR(0x2E, 0xF3);
WRITE_PORT_UCHAR(0x2F, 0xFF);

// read data from GPIO port1
WRITE_PORT_UCHAR(0x2E, 0xF4);
chVal = READ_PORT_UCHAR(0x2F);
```

The following is a table of port mapped I/O port access support by the CEDDK:

- **READ_PORT_BUFFER_UCHAR** - This function reads a number of bytes from the specified port I/O address into a buffer.

- **READ_PORT_BUFFER_ULONG** - This function reads a number of ULONG values from the specified port address into a buffer.

- **READ_PORT_BUFFER_USHORT** - This function reads a number of USHORT values from the specified port address into a buffer.

- **READ_PORT_UCHAR** - This function reads a byte from the specified port address.

- **READ_PORT_ULONG** - This function reads a ULONG value from the specified port address.

- **READ_PORT_USHORT** - This function reads a USHORT value from the specified port address.

- **WRITE_PORT_BUFFER**_UCHAR - This function writes a number of bytes from a buffer to the specified port.

- **WRITE_PORT_BUFFER_ULONG** - This function writes a number of ULONG values from a buffer to the specified port address.

- **WRITE_PORT_BUFFER_USHORT** - This function writes a number of USHORT values from a buffer to the specified port address.

- **WRITE_PORT_UCHAR** - This function writes a byte to the specified port address.

- **WRITE_PORT_ULONG** - This function writes a ULONG value to the specified port address.

- **WRITE_PORT_USHORT** - This function writes a USHORT value to the specified port address.

Memory-mapped I/O

In memory-mapped I/O the peripheral devices registers are part of the system address space, accessed the same way that any memory location is accessed and become part of the virtual address space of the kernel. The base address for a set of registers for a peripheral device is denoted by the hardware mapping address. When developing we have to translate it to kernel space virtual memory base address. This is done by calling *MmMapIoSpace*. This function is called to map the physical base address of a register set to a non-paged, kernel virtual address space directly mapped, to the device.

Device driver developers should call this function in the device driver initialization code to get a virtual address for the device driver's memory range if a call to *HalTranslateBusAddress* indicates that the device memory range for the bus can map to a system memory address. Listing 8-12 demonstrates a code snippet from a device driver's initialization code.

Note the implementation in Listing 8-10, the implementation for non x86 platforms is simply reading a memory address. Reading and writing to memory mapped I/O registers is naturally served by using the READ_REGISTER_UCHAR instead as its implementation is straight forward and simple as can be seen in Listing 8-13.

Listing 8-12. *Sample code mapping physical address space to virtual address space*

```
ULONG unIoSpace = 1;

// Obtain hardware I/O address - initialized to memory mapped IO space
pDevContxt->ioPhysicalBase.LowPart = WinInfo.memWindows[0].dwBase;
pDevContxt->ioPhysicalBase.HighPart = 0;
pDevContxt->dwIoRange = WinInfo.memWindows[0].dwLen;
if (HalTranslateBusAddress(
(INTERFACE_TYPE)pDevContxt->dwInterfaceType,
                        WinInfo.dwBusNumber,
pDevContxt->ioPhysicalBase,
                        &unIoSpace,
&pDevContxt->ioPhysicalBase))
{
    // Is it memory mapped IO or in IO space.
    if (!unIoSpace)
    {
        pDevContxt->bIoMemMapped = TRUE;
        if ((pDevContxt->dwIoAddr = (DWORD)MmMapIoSpace(
pDevContxt->ioPhysicalBase,
                                        pDevContxt->dwIoRange,
                                        FALSE)) == NULL)
        {
            DEBUGMSG(ZONE_INIT,
(_T("DMO!Error mapping IO Ports failure\r\n")));
            FreePhysMem(pDevContxt);
```

```
            // You may want to disable IO device here
            return dwRet;
        }
    }
    else
    {
        pDevContxt->bIoMemMapped = FALSE;
        pDevContxt->IoAddr = pDevContxt->ioPhysicalBase.LowPart;
    }
}
else
{
    DEBUGMSG(ZONE_INIT,
                        (_T("DMO!Error HalTranslateBusAddress call
failure\r\n")));
    FreePhysMem(pDevContxt);
    // You may want to disable IO device here
    return dwRet;
}
```

Listing 8-13. *Implementation of READ_REGISTER_UCHAR in ddk_io library*

```
UCHAR
READ_REGISTER_UCHAR(
    volatile const UCHAR * const  Register
    )
{
    return (*(volatile UCHAR * const)Register);
}
```

A similar set of such functions is implemented by CEDDK and provides quick and efficient access to memory-mapped I/O registers.

- **READ_REGISTER_BUFFER_UCHAR** - This function reads a number of bytes from the specified register memory address into a buffer.

- **READ_REGISTER_BUFFER_ULONG**- This function reads a number of ULONG values from the specified register address into a buffer.

- **READ_REGISTER_BUFFER_USHORT**- This function reads a number of USHORT values from the specified register address into a buffer.

- **READ_REGISTER_UCHAR** - This function reads a byte from the specified register address.

- **READ_REGISTER_ULONG** - This function reads a ULONG value from the specified register address.

- **READ_REGISTER_USHORT** - This function reads a USHORT value from the specified register address.

- **WRITE_REGISTER_BUFFER_UCHAR** - This function writes a number of bytes from a buffer to the specified register.

- **WRITE_REGISTER_BUFFER_**ULONG - This function writes a number of ULONG values from a buffer to the specified register.

- **WRITE_REGISTER_BUFFER_USHORT**- This function writes a number of USHORT values from a buffer to the specified register.

- **WRITE_REGISTER_UCHAR** - This function writes a byte to the specified address.

- **WRITE_REGISTER_ULONG** - This function writes a ULONG value to the specified address.

- **WRITE_REGISTER_USHORT** - This function writes a USHORT value to the specified address.

Chapter Summary

Modern real-time systems have switched from polling for input to waiting on input to arrive. This is possible because hardware has advanced so much and latencies for processing input from the point in time it arrives to the point in time it has been processed have been reduced by huge margins. Real-time systems these days are capable of minimal interrupt latencies, and more importantly, these systems keep jitter to an acceptable level.

This chapter discussed the interrupt model for Windows Embedded Compact 7, which is very much the same as for Windows CE 6.0 and quite similar to previous versions such as Windows CE 5.0. A very minimally coded and fast ISR triggered by the kernel exception handler, deferred interrupt processing by a run of the mill thread that should release the interrupt once it has completed processing it. The fact that such a thread can be assigned a scheduling priority that correlates to the interrupt request level it is associated to, allows for consistent and good real-time performance.

Additionally, to enhance real-time performance ISR execution can be preempted by the kernel to allow an ISR for a higher interrupt request level to execute before returning to complete its execution. This is called nested interrupt. This assures that interrupts for critical I/O devices are serviced ahead of less critical devices.

I/O devices resources are accessed either by mapping these resources to the system memory or are accessed specifically by special CPU instructions if mapped to specific I/O memory range like the x86 architecture supports.

C H A P T E R 9

Device I/O Control Handling

Stream device drivers are accessed by applications using the file system API. This really limits the interface capabilities of device drivers. All that the file system interface allows the developer to perform are read, write, or seek operations. This is fine for real file I/O, but stream device drivers, though regarded as files are completely different. To allow the device driver to communicate custom operations it can perform on the peripheral device it controls, a special mode of operation was created. This method is not unique to Windows Embedded Compact 7 or Windows CE, it is part of the Win32 API and it has been part of UNIX and UNIX like systems since 1979, and allows stream device drivers to communicate custom operations to an application by calling the *DeviceIoControl* function. This function is implemented by Device Manager and exposed by it so it can be called from within user mode applications.

In this chapter

- What are IOCTLs

- Adding Device IOCTLs

- Processing Device IOCTLs

What Is an IOCTL

IOCTL literally means Input Output ConTroL. Stream device drivers can be regarded as device files which represent physical devices. Physical devices are used for input, output or both, so there has to be some mechanism for device drivers in the kernel to communicate with user mode processes. Since opening a stream device driver as a file using file system APIs means that we can use file system API *WriteFile* to send data from a user mode application to a peripheral device for output. However what happens if a user mode application needs to communicate with the same peripheral device not for sending data out but to get the device status for example? This is where the "control" part of the IOCTL comes in. It really gives user mode applications a way to directly control the peripheral device programmatically.

So what is an IOCTL exactly from a technical aspect? IOCTL is a 32-bit value divided into four fields that becomes a unique system IOCTL:

Device Type	Required Access	Function Code	Method

31   16   14   2   0

- **Device Type** - This is the type of device the IOCTL belongs to. This can be user defined by setting the Common bit. This must match the device type of the device object. Windows Embedded Compact specific device types:

  - FILE_DEVICE_HAL

  - FILE_DEVICE_CONSOLE

  - FILE_DEVICE_PSL

  - FILE_DEVICE_SERVICE

- **Required Access** - This is the required access for the device such as FILE_READ_DATA, FILE_WRITE_DATA, etc.

- **Function Code** - This is the function code that the system or the user defined depending on the custom bit.

- **Method** - This is the data transfer method to be used in Windows Embedded Compact only METHOD_BUFFERED should be used.

Kernel IOCTLs

The kernel, like kernel mode device drivers offers a method to communicate control requests from kernel mode components via the *KernelIoControl* kernel API. Because I/O control means control over the hardware, this call basically calls into an OEM supplied function *OEMIoControl* which is really the actual function that implements these IOCTLs. Remember that this is founded on the premise that a Windows Embedded Compact device is not generic and is based on, mostly unique hardware combinations. Therefore only the OEM can provide coherent I/O control over its hardware.

OEMIoControl implements a number of standard IOCTLs defined by Microsoft. These IOCTLs provide mechanisms for callbacks into the OAL at strategic points in the boot process, retrieving system information from the OAL, managing interrupt identifiers etc. The IOCTL interface may be extended by the OEM to implement any other custom functionality the OEM sees fit for advanced operation of the system. For example, the OAL is sometimes used to manage access to shared systemwide resources such as GPIO.

Windows Embedded Compact 7 Platform Builder provides in it platform common sources the implementation of OEMIoControl. Listing 9-1 shows the implementation of *OEMIoControl* function provided in the platform common sources. The function is called by a kernel device driver that calls KernelIoControl. This function's sole purpose is to allow an OEM device driver to communicate with kernel mode code.

Listing 9-1. Common implementation of OEMIoControl

```
BOOL OEMIoControl(DWORD code, VOID *pInBuffer, DWORD inSize,
                  VOID *pOutBuffer, DWORD outSize, DWORD *pOutSize)
{
    BOOL rc = FALSE;
    UINT32 i;

    OALMSG(OAL_IOCTL&&OAL_FUNC,
                  (L"+OEMIoControl(0x%x, 0x%x, %d, 0x%x, %d, 0x%x)\r\n", code, pInBuffer, ⏎
 inSize, pOutBuffer, outSize, pOutSize));

    //Initialize g_ioctlState.cs when IOCTL_HAL_POSTINIT is
    // called. By this time, the kernel is up and ready to handle
    // the critical section initialization.
    if (!g_ioctlState.postInit && code == IOCTL_HAL_POSTINIT)
    {
        // Initialize critical section
        InitializeCriticalSection(&g_ioctlState.cs);
        g_ioctlState.postInit = TRUE;
    }

    // Search the IOCTL table for the requested code.
    for (i = 0; g_oalIoCtlTable[i].pfnHandler != NULL; i++)
    {
        if (g_oalIoCtlTable[i].code == code) break;
    }

    // Indicate unsupported code
    if (g_oalIoCtlTable[i].pfnHandler == NULL)
    {
        NKSetLastError(ERROR_NOT_SUPPORTED);
        OALMSG(OAL_IOCTL,
                      (L"OEMIoControl: Unsupported Code 0x%x -
                       device 0x%04x func %d\r\n", code, code >> 16,
                       (code >> 2)&0x0FFF));
        goto cleanUp;
    }

    // Take critical section if required (after postinit & no
    // flag)
    if (g_ioctlState.postInit &&
        (g_oalIoCtlTable[i].flags & OAL_IOCTL_FLAG_NOCS) == 0)
    {
        rc = DoOEMIoControlWithCS(i,code, pInBuffer, inSize,
                                  pOutBuffer, outSize, pOutSize);
    }
```

```
    else
    {
        rc = g_oalIoCtlTable[i].pfnHandler(code, pInBuffer,
                                    inSize,
                                    pOutBuffer, outSize,
                                    (UINT32 *)pOutSize);
    }

cleanUp:
    OALMSG(OAL_IOCTL&&OAL_FUNC,
                (L"-OEMIoControl(rc = %d)\r\n", rc ));
    return rc;
}
```

A new feature for Windows Embedded Compact 7 is the template BSP located under the PLATFORM root. The first tutorial provides a sample jumpstart code for implementing the coding of OEM IOCTLs for a specific BSP. Listing 9-2 shows the sample code for this implementation.

Listing 9-2. the contents of %PLATFORMROOT% \BSPTemplate\tutorial\1\oal\oallib\ioctl.c

```
#include <windows.h>
// This contains IOCTL codes needed by oal_ioctl_tab.h
#include <pkfuncs.h>
// This is the platform\common ioctl header.
#include <oal_ioctl.h>
#include <oemglobal.h>


// ---------------------------------------------------------------
// OEMIoControl: REQUIRED
//
// This function provides a generic I/O control code (IOCTL) for
// OEM-supplied information.
//
// OEMIoControl is supplied by a platform\common library in this
// tutorial, so we should not implement it here in the BSP.


// ---------------------------------------------------------------
// g_oalIoCtlTable: REQUIRED
//
// The platform\common implementation requires that we define
// this variable describing which IOCTLs we support.
//
const OAL_IOCTL_HANDLER g_oalIoCtlTable[] = {
// Required Termination
{ 0,                                    0,  NULL                    }
};
```

```
// ----------------------------------------------------------
// OEMKDIoctl: OPTIONAL
//
// This function supports requests from the kernel debugger.
//
BOOL OEMKDIoctl(DWORD dwCode, LPVOID pBuf, DWORD cbSize)
{
  // Fill in IOCTL code here.

  return TRUE;
}

// ----------------------------------------------------------
// OEMIsProcessorFeaturePresent: OPTIONAL
//
// This function provides information about processor features
// and support.
//
BOOL OEMIsProcessorFeaturePresent(DWORD dwProcessorFeature)
{
  // Fill in processor feature code here.

  return TRUE;
}
```

An example of implementing this code can be found in the ebox3300 BSP and it demonstrates how the OEM relates BSP specific functions to various predefined IOCTLs, and a custom handler for IOCTL_HAL_POSTINIT. Listing 9-3 is an abbreviated version in which I omitted some code that is irrelevant for understanding the sample code but left most of the comments. Notice the marked in bold and underline line of code that connects the IOCTL to the function that is implemented later in the code.

Listing 9-3. *The partial contents of %PLATFORM%\ebox3300\src\oal\oallib\ioctl.c*

```
#include <windows.h>
#include <pkfuncs.h>
#include <oal.h>
// This is the platform\common ioctl headers.
#include <oal_intr.h>
#include <oal_io.h>
#include <oal_ioctl.h>
#include <x86ioctl.h>

// Cache Information for Vortex86DX (A9121) rev. D and
// Vortex86MX/DX-II chips
//
const CacheInfo Vortex86MXCacheInfo =
{
......
......
};
```

```
// Declaration of x86 common libraries in platform\common
void  RTCPostInit();

// forward declarations of custom IOCTL handler functions
BOOL BSPIoCtlPostInit(
    UINT32 code, VOID *lpInBuf, UINT32 nInBufSize,
    VOID *lpOutBuf, UINT32 nOutBufSize, UINT32 *lpBytesReturned
);

BOOL BSPIoCtlHalGetCacheInfo (
    UINT32 code, VOID *lpInBuf, UINT32 nInBufSize,
    VOID *lpOutBuf, UINT32 nOutBufSize, UINT32 *lpBytesReturned
);

// g_pPlatformManufacturer: REQUIRED
// The platform\common implementation requires that we define
// this variable for device info ioctl handler.
LPCWSTR g_pPlatformManufacturer = L"DMP";          // OEM Name

// g_pPlatformName: REQUIRED
// The platform\common implementation requires that we define
// this variable for device info ioctl handler.
LPCWSTR g_pPlatformName        = L"VDX";    // Platform Name

// g_oalIoCtlPlatformType: REQUIRED
// The platform\common implementation requires that we define
// this variable for device info ioctl handler.
LPCWSTR g_oalIoCtlPlatformType = L"VDX";      // changeable by
                                              // IOCTL

// g_oalIoCtlPlatformOEM: REQUIRED
// The platform\common implementation requires that we define
// this variable for device info ioctl handler.
LPCWSTR g_oalIoCtlPlatformOEM  = L"VDX"; // constant, should've
                                         // never changed

// g_pszDfltProcessorName: REQUIRED
// The platform\common implementation requires that we define
// this variable for processor info ioctl handler.
LPCWSTR g_pszDfltProcessorName = L"Vortex86DX";

static BOOL g_fPostInit;

// ----------------------------------------------------------------
// OEMIoControl: REQUIRED
//
// This function provides a generic I/O control code (IOCTL) for
// OEM-supplied information.
//
// OEMIoControl is supplied by a platform\common library,
// so we should not implement it here in the BSP.
```

```
// ------------------------------------------------------------
// g_oalIoCtlTable: REQUIRED
//
// The platform\common implementation requires that we define
// this variable describing which IOCTLs we support.
//
const OAL_IOCTL_HANDLER g_oalIoCtlTable[] = {
    { IOCTL_HAL_REQUEST_SYSINTR, 0, OALIoCtlHalRequestSysIntr},
    { IOCTL_HAL_RELEASE_SYSINTR, 0, OALIoCtlHalReleaseSysIntr },
    { IOCTL_HAL_REQUEST_IRQ, 0, OALIoCtlHalRequestIrq},
    { IOCTL_HAL_DDK_CALL, 0, OALIoCtlHalDdkCall},
    { IOCTL_HAL_DISABLE_WAKE, 0, x86PowerIoctl},
    { IOCTL_HAL_ENABLE_WAKE, 0, x86PowerIoctl},
    { IOCTL_HAL_GET_WAKE_SOURCE, 0, x86PowerIoctl},
    { IOCTL_HAL_PRESUSPEND, 0, x86PowerIoctl},
    { IOCTL_HAL_GET_POWER_DISPOSITION, 0, x86IoCtlGetPowerDisposition},
    { IOCTL_HAL_GET_CACHE_INFO, 0, BSPIoCtlHalGetCacheInfo},
    { IOCTL_HAL_GET_DEVICEID, 0, OALIoCtlHalGetDeviceId},
    { IOCTL_HAL_GET_DEVICE_INFO, 0,  OALIoCtlHalGetDeviceInfo},
    { IOCTL_HAL_GET_UUID, 0, OALIoCtlHalGetUUID},
    { IOCTL_HAL_GET_RANDOM_SEED, 0, OALIoCtlHalGetRandomSeed},
    { IOCTL_PROCESSOR_INFORMATION, 0, x86IoCtlProcessorInfo},
    { IOCTL_HAL_INIT_RTC, 0, x86IoCtlHalInitRTC},
    { IOCTL_HAL_REBOOT, 0, x86IoCtlHalReboot},
    { IOCTL_HAL_ILTIMING, 0, x86IoCtllTiming},
    { IOCTL_HAL_POSTINIT, 0, BSPIoCtlPostInit},
    { IOCTL_HAL_INITREGISTRY, 0, x86IoCtlHalInitRegistry},

    // Required Termination
    { 0, 0, NULL}
};

// ------------------------------------------------------------
// BSPIoCtlPostInit: CUSTOM
//
// IOCTL_HAL_POSTINIT is called by the kernel and implemented in
// the OAL to provide the OEM with a last chance to perform an
// action before other processes are started.
//
// The handler initialize the critical section for RTC common
// library here.
BOOL BSPIoCtlPostInit (
    UINT32 code, VOID *lpInBuf, UINT32 nInBufSize,
    VOID *lpOutBuf, UINT32 nOutBufSize, UINT32 *lpBytesReturned
)
{
    if (lpBytesReturned) {
        *lpBytesReturned = 0;
    }
```

```
        RTCPostInit();

        g_fPostInit = TRUE;

        return TRUE;
}
......
......
```

Adding Device Specific IOCTLs

The DDK provides the developer with a macro `CTL_CODE` that defines a systemwide unique IOCTL. This macro should be used to define IOCTLs by all developers so that values do not overlap by different developers. This macro simply sets the four fields into a 32 bit value:

```
#define CTL_CODE( DeviceType, Function, Method, Access) (
  ((DeviceType) << 16) | ((Access) << 14) | ((Function) << 2) | (Method))
```

Listing 9-4 is an example of defining IOCTLs for a demo device driver using the `CTL_CODE`.

Listing 9-4. *Defining IOCTLs*

```
#ifndef __DEMODRVRSDK_H__
#define __DEMODRVRSDK_H__

#ifdef __cplusplus
extern "C"
{
#endif

#include <winioctl.h>

//
// Device IOControl codes definitions we define 2048 as base since 0-2047 is reserved for
Microsoft
//
#define IOCTLDEVTYPE_DEVICE_DEMODRVR      2048

/////////////////////////////////////////////////////////////////
//
// Specific driver IOCTL codes
//
//
// IOCTL_DEMODRVR_FOO1
//
#define IOCTL_DEMODRVR_FOO1\
        CTL_CODE(IOCTLDEVTYPE_DEVICE_DEMODRVR, 0x100,
                        METHOD_BUFFERED, FILE_ANY_ACCESS)
```

```
//
// IOCTL_DEMODRVR_FOO2
//
#define IOCTL_DEMODRVR_FOO2\
        CTL_CODE(IOCTLDEVTYPE_DEVICE_DEMODRVR, 0x101,
                        METHOD_BUFFERED, FILE_ANY_ACCESS)


}
#endif  /* __DEMODRVRSDK_H__ */
```

The file example in Listing 9-4 was generated by the device driver wizard entering needed IOCTL function code text and selecting the required access as can be seen in Figure 9-1. This header file is separated from the other files of the device driver implementation so it can be distributed to application developers to use in code controlling the specific device driver.

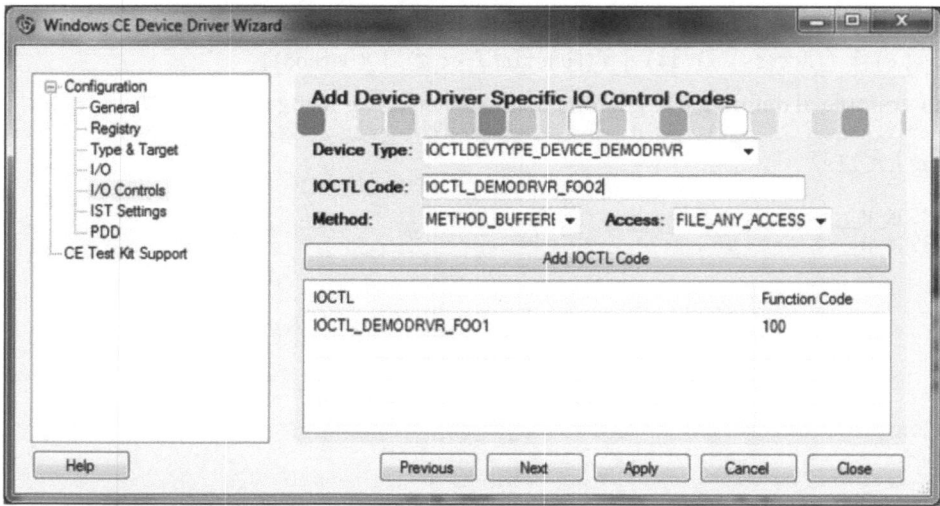

Figure 9-1. *Defining and adding IOCTLs to device driver definitions*

Processing Device Specific IOCTLs

Suppose IOCTL_DEMODRVR_FOO1 defined in Listing 9-4 handles some asynchronous I/O operation. Implementing this functionality has to be coded within the xxx_*IOControl* entry point of your stream device driver. Listing 9-5 is a skeleton generated by the device driver wizard; it allows the developer to add device driver specific functionality to the code to handle asynchronous I/O.

Listing 9-5. *Skeleton implementation of xxx_IOControl entry point*

```
BOOL DMO_IOControl(DWORD hOpenContext, DWORD dwCode, PBYTE pBufIn,
                        DWORD dwLenIn, PBYTE pBufOut, DWORD dwLenOut,
                        PDWORD pdwActualOut, HANDLE hAsyncRef)
{
    PDMO_DEVCONTXT pDevContxt = (PDMO_DEVCONTXT)hOpenContext;
    BOOL bRet = TRUE;
    DWORD dwErr = 0;

    switch (dwCode)
    {
        case IOCTL_DEMODRVR_FOO1:
            // Enter critical section if needed otherwise erase
            // EnterCriticalSection(
            //              &pDevContxt->CriticalSection);
            // Add implementation code
                bRet = Foo1(hAsyncRef, pDevContxt);
                if (!bRet)
                {
                        // Handle error
                }
            // LeaveCriticalSection(
            //              &pDevContxt->CriticalSection);
            break;
                    ...
                    ...
                    ...

        default:
            break;
    }
        return bRet;
}
```

The bold, underlined lines of code in Listing 9-5 actually provide the required functionality. The function Foo1 is an internal function shown in Listing 9-6. However you can just insert the code contained in this function directly into the case handling of the IOCTL. However, this IOControl entry point, may become cumbersome to track and difficult to maintain.

Listing 9-6. *Sample implementation of Foo1*

```
BOOL Foo1(HANDLE _hAsyncRef, PDMO_DEVCONTXT _pDevContxt)
{
        HANDLE hAsyncIO = NULL;
        if (_hAsyncRef)
        {
                hAsyncIO = CreateAsyncIoHandle(
                    hAsyncRef, (LPVOID*)pBufIn, 0);
        }
```

```
CeOpenCallerBuffer(
                    (PVOID*)(&g_AsyncParams.pBufIn),
                    (PVOID)pBufIn,
                        dwLenIn, ARG_O_PTR, TRUE);
EnterCriticalSection(&_pDevContxt->CriticalSection);
g_AsyncParams.hAsyncIO = hAsyncIO;
g_AsyncParams.dwInLen = dwLenIn;
LeaveCriticalSection(&_pDevContxt->CriticalSection);

g_hAsyncThread = CreateThread(NULL,163840,
                        (LPTHREAD_START_ROUTINE)AsyncThread,
                        (LPVOID)&g_AsyncParams,
                        CREATE_SUSPENDED |  STACK_SIZE_PARAM_IS_A_RESERVATION, NULL);
if (g_hAsyncThread == NULL)
{
        DEBUGMSG(ZONE_IOCTL,
            (_T("DMO! AsyncThread: Failed to create
                thread\r\n")));
        return FALSE;
}
ResumeThread(g_hAsyncThread);
return TRUE;
}
```

Power Management Support

A good example of using IOCTLs to provide custom device control is power management I/O control handling by device drivers that support power management. Power management support is provided by specific IOCTLs that Power Manger calls into to retrieve information about device specific capabilities - `IOCTL_POWER_CAPABILITIES`. Power Manger calls into to retrieve device power state - `IOCTL_POWER_GET`. Power Manger calls into to request to change the device power state from on state to another - `IOCTL_POWER_SET`. Previous versions of Windows CE had one more IOCTL that is deprecated for Windows Embedded Compact 7 - `IOCTL_POWER_QUERY`. Listing 9-7 is a typical implementation of the first three power management IOCTLs.

Listing 9-7. *Power management IOCTLs implementation*

```
case IOCTL_POWER_CAPABILITIES:
    // Tell power manager about this.
    if (pBufOut != NULL &&
                    dwLenOut >= sizeof(POWER_CAPABILITIES) &&
                        pdwActualOut != NULL)
    {
        __try {
            PPOWER_CAPABILITIES ppc =
                    (PPOWER_CAPABILITIES) pBufOut;
            memset(ppc, 0, sizeof(POWER_CAPABILITIES));
            ppc->DeviceDx = 0x11;        // support D0, D4
            ppc->WakeFromDx = 0x00;      // No wake capability
            ppc->InrushDx = 0x00;        // No in rush requirement
```

```
                ppc->Power[D0] = 600;        // 0.6W
                ppc->Power[D1] = (DWORD) PwrDeviceUnspecified;
                ppc->Power[D2] = (DWORD) PwrDeviceUnspecified;
                ppc->Power[D3] = (DWORD) PwrDeviceUnspecified;
                ppc->Power[D4] = 0;
                ppc->Latency[D0] = 0;
                ppc->Latency[D1] = (DWORD) PwrDeviceUnspecified;
                ppc->Latency[D2] = (DWORD) PwrDeviceUnspecified;
                ppc->Latency[D3] = (DWORD) PwrDeviceUnspecified;
                ppc->Latency[D4] = 0;
                ppc->Flags = 0;
                *pdwActualOut = sizeof(POWER_CAPABILITIES);
                dwErr = ERROR_SUCCESS;
            }
            __except(EXCEPTION_EXECUTE_HANDLER)
            {
                DEBUGMSG(ZONE_IOCTL,
                    (_T("DMO!Exception in ioctl.\r\n")));
            }
        }
        break;
    case IOCTL_POWER_SET:
        if (pBufOut != NULL &&
                        dwLenOut >= sizeof(POWER_CAPABILITIES) &&
                             pdwActualOut != NULL)
        {
            EnterCriticalSection(&pDevContxt->CriticalSection);
            __try {
                CEDEVICE_POWER_STATE NewDx =
                            *(PCEDEVICE_POWER_STATE)pBufOut;
                if(VALID_DX(NewDx))
                {
                    *(PCEDEVICE_POWER_STATE) pBufOut = NewDx;
                    *pdwActualOut = sizeof(CEDEVICE_POWER_STATE);
                    pDevContxt->psPowerState = NewDx;
                    dwErr = ERROR_SUCCESS;
                }
                DEBUGMSG(ZONE_IOCTL,
                (_T("DMO!IOCTL_POWER_SET %u %s passing back %u\r\n"),
                NewDx, dwErr == ERROR_SUCCESS ? _T("succeeded") :
                _T("failed"), pDevContxt->psPowerState));
            }
            __except(EXCEPTION_EXECUTE_HANDLER)
            {
                DEBUGMSG(ZONE_IOCTL,
                        (_T("DMO!Exception in ioctl.\r\n")));
            }
            LeaveCriticalSection(&pDevContxt->CriticalSection);
        }
        break;
```

```
case IOCTL_POWER_GET:
    if (pBufOut != NULL &&
                    dwLenOut >= sizeof(POWER_CAPABILITIES) &&
                        pdwActualOut != NULL)
    {
        EnterCriticalSection(&pDevContxt->CriticalSection);
        __try {
            CEDEVICE_POWER_STATE NewDx =
                        *(PCEDEVICE_POWER_STATE) pBufOut;
            *(PCEDEVICE_POWER_STATE) pBufOut =
                        pDevContxt->psPowerState;
            *pdwActualOut = sizeof(CEDEVICE_POWER_STATE);
            dwErr = ERROR_SUCCESS;
            DEBUGMSG(ZONE_IOCTL,
                (_T("DMO!IOCTL_POWER_GET %s passing back %u\r\n"),
                dwErr == ERROR_SUCCESS ? _T("succeeded") :
                _T("failed"), pDevContxt->psPowerState));
        }
        __except(EXCEPTION_EXECUTE_HANDLER)
        {
            DEBUGMSG(ZONE_IOCTL,
                    (_T("DMO!Exception in ioctl.\r\n")));
        }
        LeaveCriticalSection(&pDevContxt->CriticalSection);
    }
    break;
```

Chapter Summary

I/O control is a mechanism that allows user mode applications to communicate custom requests to a kernel mode device driver. This is also true for user mode device drivers. It is the device driver implementation that dictates which IOCTLs can be handled by the device driver. There are Microsoft predefined IOCTLs for various device driver classes, so it is good practice to check those if you are writing a device driver such as a storage disk device driver for example, because you will have to implement those predefined IOCTLs. You can create custom I/O control codes for the device driver you are implementing but remember to provide a header file that defines these custom IOCTLs so application developers can compile the code that uses these.

Device Manager exposes a special function `DeviceIoControl` for applications to call and pass IOCTL codes and buffers for either input or output or both if required by a custom IOCTL. This function accepts an OVERLAPPED structure in Windows Embedded Compact 7 so your device driver implementation can provide asynchronous I/O support for such I/O requests.

CHAPTER 10

Network Driver Interface Specification and Network Device Drivers

The Network Driver Interface Specification (NDIS) is the specification for network driver architecture that allows transport protocols such as TCP/IP, Native ATM, IPX, and NetBEUI to communicate with an underlying network adapter. The implementation of this specification is an applicative framework for developing network device drivers. Network device drivers provide access for Windows Embedded Compact 7 based devices to local and wide area networks. The Windows Embedded Compact-based communications architecture supports network device drivers' implemented using Network Driver Interface Specification (NDIS) framework as well as technologies such as Remote NDIS (RNDIS), NDISWAN, Token Ring, Wi-Fi, IrDA, and Bluetooth.

In this chapter

- The OSI model

- NDIS as a programming framework

- NDIS miniport drivers

Overview

Networks allow a multitude of computers to communicate data between them over some physical lines of communication, and yes I have heard of wireless communications too. Obviously this presents some obstacles, as huge chunks of data will create traffic jams. How does one computer weed out the data so it takes in only the data that is directed to it? Most of these problems were solved by packet switching networking, where data was broken up into small chunks, called packets, and sent individually. Historically, the biggest advance was made in the early 1980s. Funded by the DoD's Advanced Research Projects Agency (ARPA) the ARPANET has evolved and the ARPA internetworking protocol better known as TCP/IP has become the standard. Figure 10-1 shows the TCP/IP protocol flow, where the network interface layer is responsible for transacting frames with the physical network, the Internet layer encapsulate packets into Internet datagrams and deals with routing. The transport layer provides communication sessions between computers, and the application layer provides APIs for the application to connect to the transport layer.

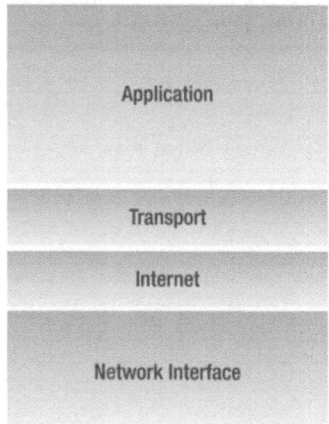

Figure 10-1. TCP/IP

This still presented a heavy load of implementation for both top and bottom layers, which motivated the formation of the ISO Open Systems Interconnection (OSI) model (shown in comparison to TCP/IP in Figure 10-2).

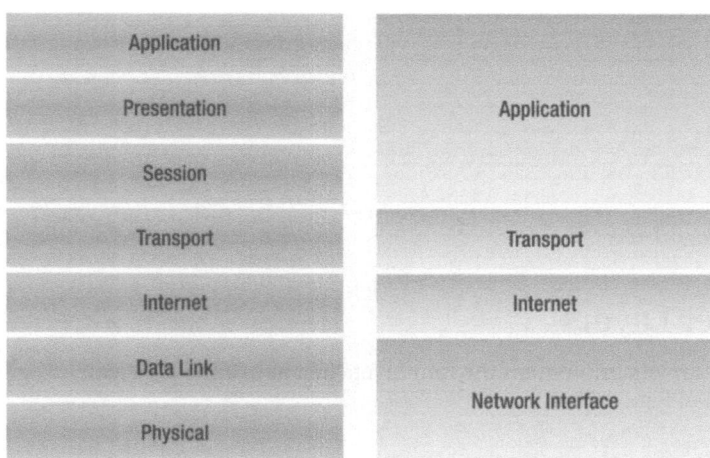

Figure 10-2. OSI model in relation to TCP/IP

The OSI model is the basis to the networking architecture of Windows Embedded Compact 7.

NDIS

The Network Driver Interface Specification (NDIS) framework abstracts the network hardware from network drivers. NDIS also specifies a standard interface between layered network drivers, thereby abstracting lower-level drivers that manage hardware from upper-level drivers, such as network transports. NDIS maintains state information and parameters for network drivers, including pointers to functions, handles, and parameter blocks for linkage, and various system values. Figure 10-3 demonstrates how the NDIS framework relates to network drivers using it.

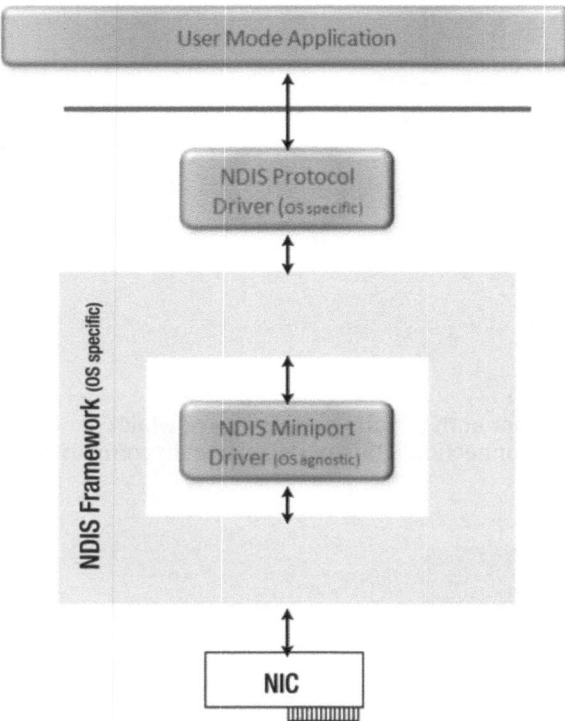

Figure 10-3. NDIS framework and network drivers

The Network Device Driver Layers

In all Windows OS versions the network drivers implement the four layers just above the physical communication medium as can be seen in Figure 10-4.

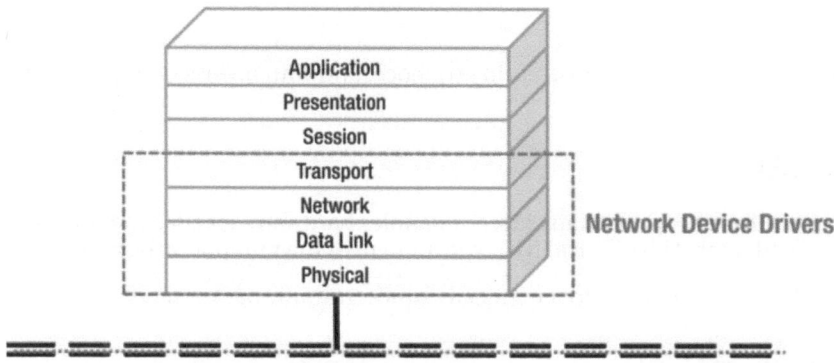

Figure 10-4. *Network device drivers as related to the OSI model*

Physical Layer

This layer manages the reception and transmission of the unstructured raw bit stream over a physical medium. The physical layer is implemented by the network interface card (NIC), its transceiver, and the medium to which the NIC is attached

Data Link Layer

The data link layer is composed of two sub layers:

- LLC - Logical Link Control

    - The LLC sub-layer provides error-free transfer of data frames from one node to another

- MAC - Media Access Control

    - The MAC sub-layer manages access to the physical layer, checks frame errors, and manages address recognition of received frames

Network Layer

This layer determines the physical path that the data should take, based on the following:

- Network conditions

- Priority of service

Other factors include routing, traffic control, frame fragmentation and reassembly, logical-to-physical address mapping, and usage accounting.

Transport Layer

This layer ensures that messages are delivered error-free, in sequence, and with no loss or duplication

NDIS Miniport Driver

A miniport driver implements the lower edge data link layer. It handles hardware-specific operations necessary to manage a network adapter. The physical NIC type influences the miniport driver adapter.

- Bus master DMA NIC - The miniport driver typically supports multi-packet sends and receives.

- Subordinate DMA NIC - The miniport driver uses the system DMA controller to manage the transfer of packet data to and from the network.

- Programmed I/O NIC - The miniport driver uses NDIS functions to move outgoing frames byte by byte, or other types to device registers and then causes the device to send the data. It is very rare these days to find such network cards and highly unlikely that you will implement such drivers.

- Onboard shared memory NIC - The miniport driver must map the NIC's shared memory to host memory and then copy outgoing packets to the NIC memory. It copies incoming frames from NIC memory to buffers that upper layer protocol drivers supply.

NDIS miniport NIC driver communicates with its NIC and with higher-level drivers through the NDIS framework see Figure 10-3. NDIS framework functions export a full set of functions, typically prefixed by "Ndis", these functions encapsulate all the operating system functions that a miniport needs to call. The NDIS miniport driver, in turn, must export a set of entry points, that the NDIS framework calls for its own purposes or on behalf of higher-level drivers to access the miniport.

A miniport driver sustains information about its capabilities and status, and information about the NIC that it controls. An object identifier (OID) is system-defined constant and identifies each information type.

NDIS Miniport Driver Functions

This is a set of entry points that are mostly required by a miniport driver so that the NDIS framework can call into to perform various tasks required by either the framework or on behalf of NDIS protocol drivers. The miniport driver is required to implement these entry points for robust operation.

DriverEntry

This is the first function called by NDIS after the NDIS device driver (NDIS.DLL) is loaded and initialized by Device Manager. At the minimum this function must register the driver with NDIS by calling *NdisMRegisterMiniportDriver* after setting the miniport driver's characteristic structure; NDIS_MINIPORT_DRIVER_CHARACTERISTICS. An example for implementing *DriverEntry* is in Listing 10-1.

Listing 10-1. *DriverEntry implementation example*

```
NDIS_HANDLE     g_NdisMiniportDriverHandle = NULL;
NDIS_HANDLE     g_MiniportDriverContext = NULL;

NDIS_STATUS DriverEntry(IN PDRIVER_OBJECT DriverObject, IN PUNICODE_STRING RegistryPath)
{
    NDIS_STATUS Status;
    NDIS_MINIPORT_DRIVER_CHARACTERISTICS MPChar;

    // Fill in the Miniport characteristics structure
    NdisZeroMemory(&MPChar, sizeof(MPChar));

    MPChar.Header.Type = NDIS_OBJECT_TYPE_MINIPORT_DRIVER_CHARACTERISTICS,
    MPChar.Header.Size = sizeof(NDIS_MINIPORT_DRIVER_CHARACTERISTICS);
    MPChar.Header.Revision = NDIS_MINIPORT_DRIVER_CHARACTERISTICS_REVISION_1;

    MPChar.MajorNdisVersion = MP_NDIS_MAJOR_VERSION;
    MPChar.MinorNdisVersion = MP_NDIS_MINOR_VERSION;
    MPChar.MajorDriverVersion = NIC_MAJOR_DRIVER_VERSION;
    MPChar.MinorDriverVersion = NIC_MINOR_DRIVER_VERISON;

    MPChar.SetOptionsHandler            = MPSetOptions;
    MPChar.InitializeHandlerEx          = MPInitialize;
    MPChar.HaltHandlerEx                = MPHalt;
    MPChar.UnloadHandler                = MPUnload,
    MPChar.PauseHandler                 = MPPause;
    MPChar.RestartHandler               = MPRestart;
    MPChar.OidRequestHandler            = MPOidRequest;
    MPChar.DevicePnPEventNotifyHandler  = MPPnPEventNotify;
    MPChar.ShutdownHandlerEx            = MPShutdown;
    MPChar.CheckForHangHandlerEx        = MPCheckForHang;
    MPChar.ResetHandlerEx               = MPReset;

    Status = NdisMRegisterMiniportDriver(DriverObject, RegistryPath,
                            (PNDIS_HANDLE)g_MiniportDriverContext,
                        &MPChar, &g_NdisMiniportDriverHandle);
    return Status;
}
```

MiniportSetOptions

At present there is no NDIS support for miniport optional characteristic or chimney offload capabilities in Windows Embedded Compact 7 version of NDIS. So the implementation of this function should do nothing and just return a NDIS_STATUS_SUCCESS value.

MiniportInitializeEx

This function is called by the NDIS framework after the call to *DriverEntry* returned successfully. In the example in Listing 10-1 this entry point is named *MPInitialize* therefore NDIS will call this function. This function intializes both hardware and registers the miniport adapter's attributes and interrupt characteristics with the NDIS framework. Listing 10-2 is an example of an implementation specific for Windows Embedded Compact 7 and is stripped of debug messages and other debug handling. Some of the code calls into local functions that initialize the hardware and allocate memory. Note that most of the code sets up NDIS framework structures and calls into NDIS functions to set attributes and interrupts and such.

■ **Implementation Note** The do-while block is implemented for ease of maintenace because it is easier to break out of the block than returning from each fail condition.

Listing 10-2. Example of MiniportInitializeEx function implementation

```
NDIS_STATUS MPInitialize(IN NDIS_HANDLE MiniportAdapterHandle,
                         IN NDIS_HANDLE MiniportDriverContext,
                  IN PNDIS_MINIPORT_INIT_PARAMETERS  MiniportInitParameters)
{
    NDIS_STATUS Status = NDIS_STATUS_SUCCESS;
    NDIS_MINIPORT_INTERRUPT_CHARACTERISTICS Interrupt;
    NDIS_MINIPORT_ADAPTER_REGISTRATION_ATTRIBUTES RegistrationAttributes;
    NDIS_MINIPORT_ADAPTER_GENERAL_ATTRIBUTES GeneralAttributes;
    NDIS_PNP_CAPABILITIES PowerManagementCapabilities;
    NDIS_TIMER_CHARACTERISTICS Timer;

    PMP_ADAPTER Adapter = NULL;   // local structure abstarcting the adapter
    ULONG ulInfoLen;

    do
    {
        // Allocate MP_ADAPTER structure (local function)
        Status = MpAllocAdapterBlock(&Adapter, MiniportAdapterHandle);
        if (Status != NDIS_STATUS_SUCCESS)
        {
            break;
        }

        Adapter->AdapterHandle = MiniportAdapterHandle;

        NdisZeroMemory(&RegistrationAttributes,
                    sizeof(NDIS_MINIPORT_ADAPTER_REGISTRATION_ATTRIBUTES));
        NdisZeroMemory(&GeneralAttributes,
                    sizeof(NDIS_MINIPORT_ADAPTER_GENERAL_ATTRIBUTES));
```

```
// setting registration attributes
RegistrationAttributes.Header.Type =
            NDIS_OBJECT_TYPE_MINIPORT_ADAPTER_REGISTRATION_ATTRIBUTES;
RegistrationAttributes.Header.Revision =
            NDIS_MINIPORT_ADAPTER_REGISTRATION_ATTRIBUTES_REVISION_1;
RegistrationAttributes.Header.Size =
            sizeof(NDIS_MINIPORT_ADAPTER_REGISTRATION_ATTRIBUTES);
RegistrationAttributes.MiniportAdapterContext = (NDIS_HANDLE)Adapter;
RegistrationAttributes.AttributeFlags =
            NDIS_MINIPORT_ATTRIBUTES_HARDWARE_DEVICE |
            NDIS_MINIPORT_ATTRIBUTES_BUS_MASTER;
RegistrationAttributes.CheckForHangTimeInSeconds = 2;
RegistrationAttributes.InterfaceType =
        NIC_INTERFACE_TYPE;

Status =
    NdisMSetMiniportAttributes(MiniportAdapterHandle,
            (PNDIS_MINIPORT_ADAPTER_ATTRIBUTES)&RegistrationAttributes);
if (Status != NDIS_STATUS_SUCCESS)
{
    break;
}

// Read the registry parameters (local function)
Status = NICReadRegParameters(Adapter);
if (Status != NDIS_STATUS_SUCCESS)
{
    break;
}

        // Find the physical adapter (local function)
Status = MpFindAdapter(Adapter,
        MiniportInitParameters->AllocatedResources);
if (Status != NDIS_STATUS_SUCCESS)
{
    break;
}

// Map bus-relative IO range to system IO space
Status = NdisMRegisterIoPortRange(
                    (PVOID *)&Adapter->PortOffset,
                            Adapter->AdapterHandle,
                            Adapter->IoBaseAddress,
                            Adapter->IoRange);
if (Status != NDIS_STATUS_SUCCESS)
{
    NdisWriteErrorLogEntry(Adapter->AdapterHandle,
            NDIS_ERROR_CODE_BAD_IO_BASE_ADDRESS, 0);
    break;
}
```

```c
// Read additional info from NIC such as MAC address
// (local function)
Status = NICReadAdapterInfo(Adapter);
if (Status != NDIS_STATUS_SUCCESS)
{
    break;
}

// set up generic attributes
GeneralAttributes.Header.Type =
                    NDIS_OBJECT_TYPE_MINIPORT_ADAPTER_GENERAL_ATTRIBUTES;
GeneralAttributes.Header.Revision =
                    NDIS_MINIPORT_ADAPTER_GENERAL_ATTRIBUTES_REVISION_1;
GeneralAttributes.Header.Size =
                    sizeof(NDIS_MINIPORT_ADAPTER_GENERAL_ATTRIBUTES);
GeneralAttributes.MediaType = NIC_MEDIA_TYPE;
GeneralAttributes.MtuSize = NIC_MAX_PACKET_SIZE - NIC_HEADER_SIZE;
GeneralAttributes.MaxXmitLinkSpeed = NIC_MEDIA_MAX_SPEED;
GeneralAttributes.MaxRcvLinkSpeed = NIC_MEDIA_MAX_SPEED;
GeneralAttributes.XmitLinkSpeed = NDIS_LINK_SPEED_UNKNOWN;
GeneralAttributes.RcvLinkSpeed = NDIS_LINK_SPEED_UNKNOWN;
GeneralAttributes.MediaConnectState = MediaConnectStateUnknown;
GeneralAttributes.MediaDuplexState = MediaDuplexStateUnknown;
GeneralAttributes.LookaheadSize = NIC_MAX_PACKET_SIZE -
                                            NIC_HEADER_SIZE;

MPFillPoMgmtCaps(Adapter, &PowerManagementCapabilities,
                &Status, &ulInfoLen);
if (Status == NDIS_STATUS_SUCCESS)
{
    GeneralAttributes.PowerManagementCapabilities =
                                            &PowerManagementCapabilities;
}
else
{
    GeneralAttributes.PowerManagementCapabilities = NULL;
}
// do not fail the call because of failure to get PM caps
Status = NDIS_STATUS_SUCCESS;

GeneralAttributes.MacOptions = NDIS_MAC_OPTION_COPY_LOOKAHEAD_DATA |
                            NDIS_MAC_OPTION_TRANSFERS_NOT_PEND |
                            NDIS_MAC_OPTION_NO_LOOPBACK;

GeneralAttributes.SupportedPacketFilters = NDIS_PACKET_TYPE_DIRECTED
                                        | NDIS_PACKET_TYPE_MULTICAST
                                        | NDIS_PACKET_TYPE_ALL_MULTICAST
                                        | NDIS_PACKET_TYPE_BROADCAST;
GeneralAttributes.MaxMulticastListSize =
                NIC_MAX_MCAST_LIST;
GeneralAttributes.MacAddressLength =
                ETH_LENGTH_OF_ADDRESS;
```

```
    NdisMoveMemory(GeneralAttributes.PermanentMacAddress,
                Adapter->PermanentAddress,
                ETH_LENGTH_OF_ADDRESS);
    NdisMoveMemory(GeneralAttributes.CurrentMacAddress,
                Adapter->CurrentAddress,
                ETH_LENGTH_OF_ADDRESS);

    GeneralAttributes.PhysicalMediumType =
                NdisPhysicalMediumUnspecified;
    GeneralAttributes.RecvScaleCapabilities = NULL;
      // NET_IF_ACCESS_BROADCAST for a typical ethernet adapter
    GeneralAttributes.AccessType = NET_IF_ACCESS_BROADCAST;
      // NET_IF_DIRECTION_SENDRECEIVE for a typical ethernet
      // adapter
    GeneralAttributes.DirectionType =
                NET_IF_DIRECTION_SENDRECEIVE;
      // NET_IF_CONNECTION_DEDICATED for a typical ethernet
      // adapter
    GeneralAttributes.ConnectionType =
                NET_IF_CONNECTION_DEDICATED;
      // IF_TYPE_ETHERNET_CSMACD for a typical ethernet adapter
      // (regardless of speed)
    GeneralAttributes.IfType = IF_TYPE_ETHERNET_CSMACD;
      // RFC 2665 TRUE if physical adapter
    GeneralAttributes.IfConnectorPresent = TRUE;
    GeneralAttributes.SupportedStatistics =
                        NDIS_STATISTICS_XMIT_OK_SUPPORTED
                      | NDIS_STATISTICS_RCV_OK_SUPPORTED
                      | NDIS_STATISTICS_XMIT_ERROR_SUPPORTED
                      | NDIS_STATISTICS_RCV_ERROR_SUPPORTED
                      | NDIS_STATISTICS_RCV_CRC_ERROR_SUPPORTED
                      | NDIS_STATISTICS_RCV_NO_BUFFER_SUPPORTED
                      | NDIS_STATISTICS_TRANSMIT_QUEUE_LENGTH_SUPPORTED
                      | NDIS_STATISTICS_GEN_STATISTICS_SUPPORTED;
    GeneralAttributes.SupportedOidList = NICSupportedOids;
    GeneralAttributes.SupportedOidListLength =
            sizeof(NICSupportedOids);

    Status =
        NdisMSetMiniportAttributes(MiniportAdapterHandle,
                    (PNDIS_MINIPORT_ADAPTER_ATTRIBUTES)&GeneralAttributes);
    // Allocate all other memory blocks including shared
    // memory (local function)
    Status = NICAllocAdapterMemory(Adapter);
    if (Status != NDIS_STATUS_SUCCESS)
    {
        break;
    }
    // Init send data structures (local function)
    NICInitSend(Adapter);
    // Init receive data structures (local function)
    Status = NICInitRecv(Adapter);
```

```
if (Status != NDIS_STATUS_SUCCESS)
{
    break;
}
// Map bus-relative registers to virtual system-space
Status = NdisMMapIoSpace((PVOID *)&(Adapter->CSRAddress),
                          Adapter->AdapterHandle,
                                 Adapter->MemPhysAddress,
                                 NIC_MAP_IOSPACE_LENGTH);
if (Status != NDIS_STATUS_SUCCESS)
{
    NdisWriteErrorLogEntry(Adapter->AdapterHandle,
                           NDIS_ERROR_CODE_RESOURCE_CONFLICT,
                           1, ERRLOG_MAP_IO_SPACE);
    break;
}

// Disable interrupts here which is as soon as possible
// (local function)
NICDisableInterrupt(Adapter);

// Register the interrupt
// the embedded NDIS interrupt structure is already
// zero'ed out within adapter structure
NdisZeroMemory(&Interrupt,
                         sizeof(NDIS_MINIPORT_INTERRUPT_CHARACTERISTICS));

Interrupt.Header.Type =
          NDIS_OBJECT_TYPE_MINIPORT_INTERRUPT;
Interrupt.Header.Revision =
          NDIS_MINIPORT_INTERRUPT_REVISION_1;
Interrupt.Header.Size =
                         sizeof(NDIS_MINIPORT_INTERRUPT_CHARACTERISTICS);
Interrupt.InterruptHandler = MPIsr;
Interrupt.InterruptDpcHandler = MPHandleInterrupt;
Interrupt.MsiSupported = FALSE;
Interrupt.MsiSyncWithAllMessages = FALSE;

Status = NdisMRegisterInterruptEx(Adapter->AdapterHandle,
                          Adapter,
                          &Interrupt,
                          &Adapter->NdisInterruptHandle);
if (Status != NDIS_STATUS_SUCCESS)
{
    NdisWriteErrorLogEntry(Adapter->AdapterHandle,
                NDIS_ERROR_CODE_INTERRUPT_CONNECT, 0);
    break;
}
Adapter->Flags |=  F_MP_ADAPTER_INTERRUPT_IN_USE;

// Test our adapter hardware (local function)
Status = NICSelfTest(Adapter);
```

```
if (Status != NDIS_STATUS_SUCCESS)
{
    break;
}

// Init the hardware and set up everything (local
// function)
Status = NICInitializeAdapter(Adapter);
if (Status != NDIS_STATUS_SUCCESS)
{
    break;
}

// initial state is paused
Adapter->AdapterState = NicPaused;
// Set the link detection flag
Adapter->Flags |= F_MP_ADAPTER_LINK_DETECTION;
// Increment the reference count so halt handler will
// wait
NdisInterlockedIncrement(&(Adapter)->RefCount);

// Enable the interrupt (local function)
NICEnableInterrupt(Adapter);

// Minimize initialization time
NdisZeroMemory(&Timer,
        sizeof(NDIS_TIMER_CHARACTERISTICS));

Timer.Header.Type =
    NDIS_OBJECT_TYPE_TIMER_CHARACTERISTICS;
Timer.Header.Revision =
    NDIS_TIMER_CHARACTERISTICS_REVISION_1;
Timer.Header.Size = sizeof(NDIS_TIMER_CHARACTERISTICS);
Timer.AllocationTag = NIC_TAG;
  // Local timer function for postponed link negotiation
Timer.TimerFunction = MpLinkDetectionDpc;
Timer.FunctionContext = Adapter;

Status = NdisAllocateTimerObject(Adapter->AdapterHandle,
                    &Timer,
                    &Adapter->LinkDetectionTimerHandle);

if (Status != NDIS_STATUS_SUCCESS)
{
    break;
}

liDueTime.QuadPart = NIC_LINK_DETECTION_DELAY;
isTimerAlreadyInQueue = NdisSetTimerObject(
                        Adapter->LinkDetectionTimerHandle,
                        liDueTime, 0, NULL);
ASSERT(!isTimerAlreadyInQueue);
```

```
    } while (FALSE); // end of do while block

    if (Adapter && (Status != NDIS_STATUS_SUCCESS))
    {
        // Undo everything if it failed
        NdisInterlockedDecrement(&(Adapter)->RefCount);
        MpFreeAdapter(Adapter);
    }
    return Status;
}
```

MiniportHaltEx

The NDIS framework calls a miniport driver's *MiniportHaltEx* function to stop the hardware and deallocate resources when a miniport adapter is removed. Since this may happen any time so you should consider checking if it is a surprise hardware remove and handle it accordingly. Listing 10-3 is an example of a possible implementation of a miniport driver's halt function.

Listing 10-3. *Example of MiniportHaltEx function implementation*

```
VOID MPHalt(IN NDIS_HANDLE MiniportAdapterContext,
            IN NDIS_HALT_ACTION HaltAction)
{
    LONG Count;

    PMP_ADAPTER Adapter = (PMP_ADAPTER)MiniportAdapterContext;

    if (HaltAction == NdisHaltDeviceSurpriseRemoved)
    {
        // You may want to  ascertain that halt will not rely
        // on hardware to generatean interrupt in order to
        // complete a pending operation, for example.
    }

    ASSERT(Adapter->AdapterState == NicPaused);
    Adapter->Flags |= F_MP_ADAPTER_HALT_IN_PROGRESS;

    // Call Shutdown handler to disable interrupts and turn the
    // hardware off
    MPShutdown(MiniportAdapterContext, NdisShutdownPowerOff);

    // Deregister interrupt so interrupts will not be processed
    if ((Adapter->Flags & F_MP_ADAPTER_INTERRUPT_IN_USE) != 0)
    {
        NdisMDeregisterInterruptEx(Adapter->NdisInterruptHandle);
            Adapter->Flags &= ~ F_MP_ADAPTER_INTERRUPT_IN_USE;
    }
```

```
        NdisCancelTimerObject(Adapter->LinkDetectionTimerHandle);

        // Decrement the ref count which was incremented in
        // MPInitialize
        Count = NdisInterlockedDecrement(&(Adapter)->RefCount);

        // Possible non-zero ref counts mean that there may be
        // pending async shared memory allocation or maybe
        // MPHandleInterrupt is not done
        if (Count)
        {
            while (TRUE)
            {
                if (NdisWaitEvent(&Adapter->ExitEvent, 2000))
                {
                    break;
                }
            }
        }

        // Reset the PHY transceiver chip.
        ResetPHYceiver(Adapter);

        // Free the entire adapter object, including the shared memory
        // structures.
        MpFreeAdapter(Adapter);
}
```

MiniportDriverUnload

The implementation of this function needs to release resources before the system completes a driver unload operation and is extremely simple as you can see for yourself in Listing 10-4.

Listing 10-4. *Example of MiniportDriverUnload function implementation*

```
VOID MPUnload(IN PDRIVER_OBJECT DriverObject)
{
    // Deregister Miniport driver
    NdisMDeregisterMiniportDriver(g_NcisMiniportDriverHandle);
}
```

MiniportPause

This function is called to stop the network data flow through the miniport adapter. It basically sets the adapter's state and frees and completes the pending send packets in SendWaitQueue. It then decrements the receive count and if receive count is null it set adapter's state to paused and returns success otherwise it returns status pending to inform the framework that receive data is still there. Listing 10-5 is an example of how to pause a miniport adapter.

Listing 10-5. *Example of MiniportPause function implementation*

```
NDIS_STATUS MPPause(IN NDIS_HANDLE MiniportAdapterContext,
                    IN PNDIS_MINIPORT_PAUSE_PARAMETERS MiniportPauseParameters)
{
    PMP_ADAPTER Adapter = (PMP_ADAPTER)MiniportAdapterContext;
    NDIS_STATUS Status;
    LONG Count;

    ASSERT(Adapter->AdapterState == NicRunning);

    NdisAcquireSpinLock(&Adapter->RcvLock);
    Adapter->AdapterState = NicPausing;
    NdisReleaseSpinLock(&Adapter->RcvLock);

    // Complete all the pending sends
    NdisAcquireSpinLock(&Adapter->SendLock);

    MpFreeQueuedSendNetBufferLists(Adapter);
    NdisReleaseSpinLock(&Adapter->SendLock);

    NdisAcquireSpinLock(&Adapter->RcvLock);
    Count = --(Adapter->RcvRefCount);
    if (Count ==0)
    {
        Adapter->AdapterState = NicPaused;
        Status = NDIS_STATUS_SUCCESS;
    }
    else
    {
        Status = NDIS_STATUS_PENDING;
    }
    NdisReleaseSpinLock(&Adapter->RcvLock);

    return Status;
}
```

MiniportRestart

This function is called to restart a paused miniport adapter. This function is very simple as it mainly has to handle some restart attributes and increment receive count and set state to running. Listing 10-6 is an example of how to restart a paused miniport adapter.

Listing 10-6. *Example of MiniportRestart function implementation*

```
NDIS_STATUS MPRestart(IN NDIS_HANDLE MiniportAdapterContext,
              IN PNDIS_MINIPORT_RESTART_PARAMETERS MiniportRestartParameters)
{
    PMP_ADAPTER Adapter = (PMP_ADAPTER)MiniportAdapterContext;
    PNDIS_RESTART_ATTRIBUTES NdisRestartAttributes;
```

```
        PNDIS_RESTART_GENERAL_ATTRIBUTES NdisGeneralAttributes;

        NdisRestartAttributes =
                MiniportRestartParameters->RestartAttributes;

        // If NdisRestartAttributes is not NULL, then miniport can
        // modify generic attributes and add new media specific info.
        // attributes at the end Otherwise, NDIS framework restarts
        // the miniport because of other reasons. The miniport driver
        // should not try to modify/add attributes
        if (NdisRestartAttributes != NULL)
        {
            ASSERT(NdisRestartAttributes->Oid ==
            OID_GEN_MINIPORT_RESTART_ATTRIBUTES);
            NdisGeneralAttributes =
            (PNDIS_RESTART_GENERAL_ATTRIBUTES)
                            NdisRestartAttributes->Data;
            // Check if  any attributes need to be changed, maybe
            // change the current MAC address, or add media specific
            // info attributes.
        }
        NdisAcquireSpinLock(&Adapter->RcvLock);
        Adapter->RcvRefCount++;
        Adapter->AdapterState = NicRunning;
        NdisReleaseSpinLock(&Adapter->RcvLock);

        return NDIS_STATUS_SUCCESS;
}
```

MiniportOidRequest

This function is called to handle an OID (NDIS object identifiers) request to query or set information within a connectionless miniport driver. The only notable point is that handling an OID request should take place if there is no pending request and the adapter is not being removed or reset. Otherwise the request can be handled. Listing 10-7 is an example of how to handle an OID request. Note the help for the NDIS_REQUEST_TYPE enumeration for request types as quite a few have been marked as obsolete.

Listing 10-7. *Example of MiniportOidRequest function implementation*

```
NDIS_STATUS MPOidRequest(IN NDIS_HANDLE MiniportAdapterContext,
                              IN PNDIS_OID_REQUEST NdisRequest)
{
    PMP_ADAPTER Adapter = (PMP_ADAPTER)MiniportAdapterContext;
    NDIS_STATUS Status = NDIS_STATUS_SUCCESS;
    NDIS_REQUEST_TYPE RequestType;

    // Should abort the request if reset is in process
    NdisAcquireSpinLock(&Adapter->Lock);
```

```
    // If there is a request pending then assert.
    ASSERT(Adapter->PendingRequest == NULL);

    if (Adapter->Flags &
        (F_MP_ADAPTER_RESET_IN_PROGRESS |
         F_MP_ADAPTER_REMOVE_IN_PROGRESS))
    {
        NdisReleaseSpinLock(&Adapter->Lock);
        return NDIS_STATUS_REQUEST_ABORTED;
    }

    NdisReleaseSpinLock(&Adapter->Lock);

    RequestType = NdisRequest->RequestType;

    switch (RequestType)
    {
        case NdisRequestMethod:
            Status = MpMethodRequest(Adapter, NdisRequest);
            break;

        case NdisRequestSetInformation:
            Status = MpSetInformation(Adapter, NdisRequest);
            break;

        case NdisRequestQueryInformation:
        case NdisRequestQueryStatistics:
            Status = MpQueryInformation(Adapter, NdisRequest);
            break;

        default:
            // Later the entry point may by used by all the
            // requests
            Status = NDIS_STATUS_NOT_SUPPORTED;
            break;
    }
    return Status;
}
```

MiniportDevicePnPEventNotify

This function is called to notify the adapter miniport driver of Plug and Play (PnP) events. The example implementation in Listing 10-8 is a simple example that just outputs messages indicating what event occurred.

Listing 10-8. *Example of MiniportDevicePnPEventNotify function implementation*

```
VOID MPPnPEventNotify(IN NDIS_HANDLE MiniportAdapterContext,
                                     IN PNET_DEVICE_PNP_EVENT NetDevicePnPEvent)
{
    PMP_ADAPTER Adapter = (PMP_ADAPTER)MiniportAdapterContext;
    NDIS_DEVICE_PNP_EVENT PnPEvent =
            NetDevicePnPEvent->DevicePnPEvent;
    PVOID InformationBuffer =
            NetDevicePnPEvent->InformationBuffer;
    ULONG InformationBufferLength =
            NetDevicePnPEvent->InformationBufferLength;

    switch (PnPEvent)
    {
        case NdisDevicePnPEventQueryRemoved:
            DEBUGMSG(ZONE_WARN,
                ("MPPnPEventNotify: NdisDevicePnPEventQueryRemoved\n"));
            break;

        case NdisDevicePnPEventRemoved:
            DEBUGMSG(ZONE_WARN,
                ("MPPnPEventNotify: NdisDevicePnPEventRemoved\n"));
            break;

        case NdisDevicePnPEventSurpriseRemoved:
            DEBUGMSG(ZONE_WARN,
                ("MPPnPEventNotify: NdisDevicePnPEventSurpriseRemoved\n"));
            break;

        case NdisDevicePnPEventQueryStopped:
            DEBUGMSG(ZONE_WARN,
                ("MPPnPEventNotify: NdisDevicePnPEventQueryStopped\n"));
            break;

        case NdisDevicePnPEventStopped:
            DEBUGMSG(ZONE_WARN,
                ("MPPnPEventNotify: NdisDevicePnPEventStopped\n"));
            break;

        case NdisDevicePnPEventPowerProfileChanged:
            DEBUGMSG(ZONE_WARN,
            ("MPPnPEventNotify: NdisDevicePnPEventPowerProfileChanged\n"));
            break;

        default:
            DEBUGMSG(ZONE_ERROR,
                ("MPPnPEventNotify: unknown PnP event %x \n", PnPEvent));
            break;
    }
}
```

MiniportShutdownEx

This function is called when the system is shut down. It disables interrupts and put the transmission units into an idle state and try and force a reset. Listing 10-9 is an example that calls two driver local functions to perform both tasks on the NIC hardware.

Listing 10-9. *Example of MiniportShutdownEx function implementation*

```
VOID MPShutdown(IN NDIS_HANDLE MiniportAdapterContext,
                            IN NDIS_SHUTDOWN_ACTION ShutdownAction)
{
    PMP_ADAPTER Adapter = (PMP_ADAPTER)MiniportAdapterContext;

    // Disable interrupt and issue a full reset
    NICDisableInterrupt(Adapter);
    NICIssueFullReset(Adapter);
}
```

MiniportCheckForHangEx

This function does nothing more than check the internal state of the network adapter and return TRUE if it detects that the NIC adapter is not operating correctly. Listing 10-10 is an example checking for hardware errors or failure, send hang, and media state.

Listing 10-10. *Example of MiniportCheckForHangEx function implementation*

```
BOOLEAN MPCheckForHang(IN NDIS_HANDLE MiniportAdapterContext)
{
    PMP_ADAPTER Adapter = (PMP_ADAPTER) MiniportAdapterContext;
    NDIS_MEDIA_CONNECT_STATE CurrMediaState;
    PMP_TCB pMpTcb;
    BOOLEAN NeedReset = TRUE;

    do
    {
        // Skip this block if
        // the adapter is doing link detection
        if ((Adapter->Flags & F_MP_ADAPTER_LINK_DETECTION) != 0)
        {
            NeedReset = FALSE;
            break;
        }
        // any non-recoverable hardware error occured
        if ((Adapter->Flags & F_MP_ADAPTER_NON_RECOVER_ERROR)
                != 0)
        {
            break;
        }
```

```
        // any hardware failure occured
            if ((Adapter->Flags & F_MP_ADAPTER_HARDWARE_ERROR)
                    != 0)
    {
        break;
    }

    // Send hanged?
      NdisAcquireSpinLock(&Adapter->SendLock);
    if (Adapter->nBusySend > 0)
    {
        pMpTcb = Adapter->CurrSendHead;
        pMpTcb->Count++;
        if (pMpTcb->Count > NIC_SEND_HANG_THRESHOLD)
        {
                NdisReleaseSpinLock(&Adapter->SendLock);
            break;
        }
    }
    NeedReset = FALSE;

      NdisReleaseSpinLock(&Adapter->SendLock);
      NdisAcquireSpinLock(&Adapter->RcvLock);

    // Update the RFD shrink count
    if (Adapter->CurrNumRfd > Adapter->NumRfd)
    {
        Adapter->RfdShrinkCount++;
    }
      NdisReleaseSpinLock(&Adapter->RcvLock);

      NdisAcquireSpinLock(&Adapter->Lock);
    CurrMediaState = NICGetMediaState(Adapter);

    if (CurrMediaState != Adapter->MediaState)
    {
        Adapter->MediaState = CurrMediaState;
        MPIndicateLinkState(Adapter);
    }
      NdisReleaseSpinLock(&Adapter->Lock);
  }
  while (FALSE); // end of do while block

  return NeedReset;
}
```

MiniportResetEx

This function is called to reset the NIC adapter hardware device. It first checks if another reset is already in progress or being halted. It then aborts any pending requests, makes certain it will not wakeup during the reset process. Ask NDIS to remove the miniport if there is a hardware error or failure. Disable interrupts and reset hardware. Free send buffers and restart the receive unit. Listing 10-11 is an example reset function that uses driver local helper functions.

Listing 10-11. *Example of MiniportResetEx function implementation*

```
NDIS_STATUS MPReset(IN NDIS_HANDLE MiniportAdapterContext,
                                   OUT PBOOLEAN AddressingReset)
{
    NDIS_STATUS Status;
    PNDIS_OID_REQUEST PendingRequest;
    PMP_ADAPTER Adapter = (PMP_ADAPTER) MiniportAdapterContext;

    *AddressingReset = TRUE;

    NdisAcquireSpinLock(&Adapter->Lock);
    NdisDprAcquireSpinLock(&Adapter->SendLock);
    NdisDprAcquireSpinLock(&Adapter->RcvLock);


    ASSERT(!(Adapter->Flags & F_MP_ADAPTER_HALT_IN_PROGRESS)
                     != 0));

    // Is this adapter already doing a reset?
    if (Adapter->Flags & F_MP_ADAPTER_RESET_IN_PROGRESS) != 0)
    {
        Status = NDIS_STATUS_RESET_IN_PROGRESS;
        goto exit;
    }

    Adapter->Flags |= F_MP_ADAPTER_RESET_IN_PROGRESS;
    // Abort any pending request
    if (Adapter->PendingRequest != NULL)
    {
        PendingRequest = Adapter->PendingRequest;
        Adapter->PendingRequest = NULL;
        NdisDprReleaseSpinLock(&Adapter->RcvLock);
        NdisDprReleaseSpinLock(&Adapter->SendLock);
        NdisReleaseSpinLock(&Adapter->Lock);
        NdisMOidRequestComplete(Adapter->AdapterHandle,
                           PendingRequest,
                              NDIS_STATUS_REQUEST_ABORTED);
        NdisAcquireSpinLock(&Adapter->Lock);
        NdisDprAcquireSpinLock(&Adapter->SendLock);
        NdisDprAcquireSpinLock(&Adapter->RcvLock);
    }
    MPRemoveAllWakeUpPatterns(Adapter);
```

```
    // Is this adapter doing link detection?
    if (Adapter->Flags & F_MP_ADAPTER_LINK_DETECTION) != 0)
    {
        DEBUGMSG(ZONE_WARN, ("Reset is pended...\n"));
        Status = NDIS_STATUS_PENDING;
        Adapter->bResetPending = TRUE;
        goto exit;
    }
    // Is this adapter going to be removed
    if (Adapter->Flags & F_MP_ADAPTER_NON_RECOVER_ERROR) != 0)
    {
        Status = NDIS_STATUS_HARD_ERRORS;
        if (Adapter->Flags & F_MP_ADAPTER_REMOVE_IN_PROGRESS)
                        != 0)
        {
            goto exit;
        }
        // This is an unrecoverable hardware failure.
        // Need inform NDIS to remove this miniport
          Adapter->Flags |= F_MP_ADAPTER_REMOVE_IN_PROGRESS;
          Adapter->Flags &= ~ F_MP_ADAPTER_RESET_IN_PROGRESS;

        NdisDprReleaseSpinLock(&Adapter->RcvLock);
        NdisDprReleaseSpinLock(&Adapter->SendLock);
        NdisReleaseSpinLock(&Adapter->Lock);

        NdisWriteErrorLogEntry(Adapter->AdapterHandle,
                            NDIS_ERROR_CODE_HARDWARE_FAILURE, 1, ERRLOG_REMOVE_MINIPORT);

        NdisMRemoveMiniport(Adapter->AdapterHandle);
        return Status;
    }

    // Disable the interrupt and issue a reset to the NIC
    NICDisableInterrupt(Adapter);
    NICIssueSelectiveReset(Adapter);

    // release all the locks and then reacquire the send-lock,
    // clean up the send queues which involves calling Ndis
    // framework, release all the locks before grabbing the send
    // lock to avoid deadlocks
    NdisDprReleaseSpinLock(&Adapter->RcvLock);
    NdisDprReleaseSpinLock(&Adapter->SendLock);
    NdisReleaseSpinLock(&Adapter->Lock);
    NdisAcquireSpinLock(&Adapter->SerdLock);

    // Free the packets on SendWaitList
    MpFreeQueuedSendNetBufferLists(Adapter);
```

```
    // Free the packets being actively sent & stopped
    MpFreeBusySendNetBufferLists(Adapter);

    NdisZeroMemory(Adapter->MpTcbMem,
                    Adapter->NumTcb * sizeof(MP_TCB));

    // Re-initialize the send structures
    NICInitSend(Adapter);
    NdisReleaseSpinLock(&Adapter->SendLock);

    // get all the locks again in the right order
    NdisAcquireSpinLock(&Adapter->Lock);
    NdisDprAcquireSpinLock(&Adapter->SendLock);
    NdisDprAcquireSpinLock(&Adapter->RcvLock);

    // Reset the RFD list and re-start RU
    NICResetRecv(Adapter);
    Status = NICStartRecv(Adapter);
    if (Status != NDIS_STATUS_SUCCESS)
    {
        // Are we having failures in a few consecutive resets?
        if (Adapter->HwErrCount < NIC_HARDWARE_ERROR_THRESHOLD)
        {
            // It's not over the threshold yet, let it to
            // continue
            Adapter->HwErrCount++;
        }
        else
        {
            // This is an unrecoverable hardware failure.
            // We need to tell NDIS to remove this miniport
            Adapter->Flags |= F_MP_ADAPTER_REMOVE_IN_PROGRESS;
            Adapter->Flags &= ~ F_MP_ADAPTER_RESET_IN_PROGRESS;
            NdisDprReleaseSpinLock(&Adapter->RcvLock);
            NdisDprReleaseSpinLock(&Adapter->SendLock);
            NdisReleaseSpinLock(&Adapter->Lock);

            NdisWriteErrorLogEntry(Adapter->AdapterHandle,
                            NDIS_ERROR_CODE_HARDWARE_FAILURE, 1,↵
ERRLOG_REMOVE_MINIPORT);

            NdisMRemoveMiniport(Adapter->AdapterHandle);
            return Status;
        }

        return Status;
    }
    Adapter->HwErrCount = 0;
    Adapter->Flags &= ~ F_MP_ADAPTER_HARDWARE_ERROR
    NICEnableInterrupt(Adapter);
    Adapter->Flags &= ~ F_MP_ADAPTER_RESET_IN_PROGRESS;
```

```
exit:
    NdisDprReleaseSpinLock(&Adapter->RcvLock);
    NdisDprReleaseSpinLock(&Adapter->SendLock);
    NdisReleaseSpinLock(&Adapter->Lock);

    return(Status);
}
```

Physical Data Transactions

Throughout the preceding examples I used local functions for various hardware I/O interfaces abstractly. The miniport functions described provide an upper edge interface for upper layer NDIS drivers to acquire services from the miniport driver. However the miniport driver is still left with its main task of "driving" the actual Network Interface Card (NIC). That is reading and writing data and configuration attributes to the hardware ports/registers. It still needs to handle memory buffers for the transacted data.

The NDIS framework provides a lower edge for miniport driver to interface with the hardware. It provides a set of functions that a miniport network adapter (NIC) driver calls to access I/O ports. These calls provide a standard portable interface that supports the various operating systems for NDIS drivers. Functions are provided for mapping ports, for claiming I/O resources, and for reading from and writing to the mapped and unmapped I/O ports. If you decide to implement your own port mapping and resource management the NDIS framework provides a set of raw I/O port interface functions such as *NdisRawReadPortXxx* where Xxx indicates the byte size of the port. However these are specific for port I/O based architectures.

For memory mapped I/O architectures the NDIS framework provides a set of functions to map the NIC's registers to the system's memory *NdisMMapIoSpace* to map a given physical range of device RAM or registers onto a system-space virtual range, and a set of functions such as *NdisReadRegisterXxx* where Xxx indicates the byte size of the register.

NDIS Memory Management Helpers

Considering the performance of the NIC (network interface card) and its miniport driver, we have to take into account the bottleneck occurs when moving data between the NIC and the memory of the computer. The two most efficient methods for moving information from the network interface card into the computer once it has been received would be bus master DMA and shared memory. NICs providing bus master DMA a controller take charge of the system bus and transfer data from the NIC to a memory location, thus reducing the CPU load. In the shared memory option, either NICs have their own memory that the system processor can access directly, or both the CPU and NIC share a block of system memory that both can directly access.

Shared Memory

NDIS framework provides the miniport driver developer with a set of functions to implement the shared memory scheme. The focal function is *NdisMAllocateSharedMemory*. This function provides both the mapped virtual address range that the driver uses to access the shared memory block and the NDIS_PHYSICAL_ADDRESS type range that the network adapter uses. This function must be called from the *MiniportInitializeEx* entry point only. The biggest issue with shared memory is its size. On the one hand in high network traffic, a miniport driver cannot maintain high I/O throughput if it runs low on shared memory space for device-accessible data buffers. So you may try to anticipate some maximum transfer demands and set the shared memory size to accommodate these. This would create a driver with a large image and a resource usage that is very inefficient most of the time. Another problem would be failure to initialize the driver, if *NdisMAllocateSharedMemory* fails to allocate the requested size due to insufficient system memory availability. Note that even though kernel mode drivers usually use uncached memory in this case you should consider cached memory because uncached memory is sparse and therefore larger allocations should be acquired from cached memory.

Scatter Gather DMA

This is the preferred memory scheme for performance. NDIS does not map the data buffer before sending it down to the miniport driver. Instead, NDIS provides an interface for the driver to map the network data. Because of this, miniport drivers can optimize the transmission of small or highly fragmented packets by copying them to a pre-allocated buffer with a known physical address. It also avoids mapping that is not required and therefore improves system performance. NDIS can send multiple buffers to the miniport driver safely. This results in fewer calls to miniport drivers and therefore improves system performance. Lastly, miniport drivers can pre-allocate the memory for an SG list as part of the transmit descriptor blocks. Therefore, NDIS or miniport drivers are not required to allocate memory for SG lists at run time.

The NDIS framework provides the following functions to handle scatter gather DMA transactions:

NdisMAllocateNetBufferSGList

Bus-master miniport drivers call this function to obtain a scatter/gather list for the network data that is associated with a NET_BUFFER structure.

NdisMAllocateSharedMemoryAsyncEx

Miniport drivers call this function to allocate additional memory shared between the driver and its bus-master DMA NIC, usually when the miniport driver is running low on available NIC receive buffers.

NdisMRegisterScatterGatherDma

Bus master miniport drivers call this function from *MiniportInitializeEx* to initialize a scatter/gather DMA channel.

NdisMDeregisterScatterGatherDma

Bus-master miniport drivers call this function to release DMA resources that were allocated with the *NdisMRegisterScatterGatherDma* function.

NdisMFreeNetBufferSGList

Bus-master miniport drivers call this function to free scatter/gather list resources that were allocated by calling the *NdisMAllocateNetBufferSGList* function.

NDIS Protocol Driver

A protocol driver implements the network and transport layers of the OSI model (Figure 10-4). As such it ensures that messages are delivered error-free, in sequence, and with no loss or duplication. In addition it determines the physical path that the data should take, based on the following:

- Network conditions

- Priority of service

- Other factors, such as routing, traffic control, frame fragmentation and reassembly, logical-to-physical address mapping, and usage accounting

A protocol driver communicates with NDIS to send and receive network data. It implements and exports a set of *ProtocolXxx* functions at its lower edge and binds to an underlying miniport driver that exports a *MiniportXxx* interface at its upper edge. It must allocate driver resources and register the required *ProtocolXxx* functions in *DriverEntry*. To register the *ProtocolXxx* functions and the protocol driver with the NDIS framework and you have to setup the NDIS_PROTOCOL_DRIVER_CHARACTERISTICS structure and call *NdisRegisterProtocolDriver*.

NDIS protocol drivers provide the following ProtocolXxx functions; the two last functions are for send and receive operations:

ProtocolSetOptions

This is an optional function. It registers optional services and can allocate other driver resources. It calls *NdisSetOptionalHandlers* to overwrite its default entry points. It is very much like the MiniportSetOptions function described previously so you may as well not implement it at all at present.

ProtocolBindAdapterEx

This function is a required function. The NDIS framework calls this function to bind to an underlying miniport adapter. In the implementation it should create send and receive buffer list pools using *NdisAllocateNetBufferListPool* and then call *NdisOpenAdapterEx* function to set up a binding between the protocol driver and an underlying driver. If the call to *NdisOpenAdapterEx* returns NDIS_STATUS_PENDING you should wait on a signal from *ProtocolOpenAdapterCompleteEx* that indicates completion. If the call to *NdisOpenAdapterEx* returns NDIS_STATUS_SUCCESS you may proceed by calling *NdisQueryAdapterInstanceName* to retrieve the friendly name of a physical network adapter (or a virtual adapter) to which the calling protocol is bound. Using the *CurrentMacAddress* field of NDIS_BIND_PARAMETERS structure you can retrieve media connect status and MAC options.

ProtocolUnbindAdapterEx

This is a required function. It is a mirror of the *ProtocolBindAdapterEx* function; The NDIS framework calls *ProtocolUnbindAdapterEx* to release the resources that the driver allocated for network I/O operations that are specific to a binding. The implementation of this function must call the *NdisCloseAdapterEx* function to close the binding to the underlying miniport adapter. A protocol driver cannot fail an unbind operation.

ProtocolOpenAdapterCompleteEx

This is a required function. This is a completion routine for *NdisOpenAdapterEx* function. The implementation of this function simply signals the thread that made the call to open the adapter *NdisOpenAdapterEx* to indicate completion.

ProtocolCloseAdapterCompleteEx

This is a required function. Like the *ProtocolOpenAdapterCompleteEx* function this is a completion routine, but for *NdisCloseAdapterEx* function. The implementation of this function simply signals the thread that made the call to close the adapter *NdisCloseAdapterEx* to indicate completion.

ProtocolNetPnPEvent

This function is required in protocol drivers to support Plug and Play and Power Management. Implementation switches on the event type that is passed via the `NET_PNP_EVENT_NOTIFICATION` structure and processes what it needs by the design of the protocol driver. For example it can handle power management notifications or a restart notification.

ProtocolUninstall

This function is optional. If implemented this function performs cleanup before the protocol driver is 27.151 uninstalled.

ProtocolReceiveNetBufferLists

This is a required function for protocol drivers if scatter/gather DMA is implemented for the underlying miniport driver. The NDIS framework calls it after a bound miniport driver calls the *NdisMIndicateReceiveNetBufferLists* function. Net buffer list is only available for version 6.x of NDIS. If the `NDIS_RECEIVE_FLAGS_RESOURCES` flag in the *ReceiveFlags* parameter is not set, the protocol driver retains ownership of the `NET_BUFFER_LIST` structures until it calls the *NdisReturnNetBufferLists* function. The prototype for this function is in Listing 10-12.

Listing 10-12. *Prototype for ProtocolReceiveNetBufferLists function*

```
VOID ProtocolReceiveNetBufferLists(
                IN NDIS_HANDLE ProtocolBindingContext,
                IN PNET_BUFFER_LIST pNetBufferLists,
                IN NDIS_PORT_NUMBER PortNumber,
                IN ULONG NumberOfNetBufferLists,
                IN ULONG ReceiveFlags)
```

where the arguments passed to the function:

- **ProtocolBindingContext** - pointer to open context
- **pNetBufferLists** - a list of the Net Buffer lists being indicated up.
- **PortNumber** - Port on which NBLs were received
- **NumberOfNetBufferLists** - The number of NetBufferLists that are in this call
- **ReceiveFlags** - Flags associated with the receives

ProtocolSendNetBufferListsComplete

This is a required function for protocol drivers if scatter/gather DMA is implemented for the underlying miniport driver. This function executes whatever post processing is needed to complete the send operation. For example, the protocol driver can notify clients that requested to send the data that the operation is completed.

The NDIS framework calls this function after the underlying miniport driver calls the *NdisMSendNetBufferListsComplete* function. Completion of a send operation implies that the underlying miniport driver has transmitted the specified network data. The prototype for this function is in Listing 10-13.

Listing 10-13. *Prototype for ProtocolSendNetBufferListsComplete function*

```
VOID ProtocolSendNetBufferListsComplete(
                    IN NDIS_HANDLE ProtocolBindingContext,
                    IN PNET_BUFFER_LIST pNetBufferLists,
                    IN ULONG SendCompleteFlags)
```

where the arguments passed to the function:

- **ProtocolBindingContext** - pointer to open context
- **pNetBufferLists** - a list of the Net Buffer lists being indicated up
- **SendCompleteFlags** - NDIS flags that can be combined with an OR operation

NDIS Intermediate Driver

NDIS intermediate drivers are layered between upper-level protocol drivers and hardware level miniport drivers. A NDIS intermediate driver should be regarded as a layered miniport driver. A layered miniport driver exposes a miniport interface to the overlying protocol driver and a protocol driver interface to the underlying NIC miniport driver. In a layered miniport driver structure, the protocol driver communicates with a miniport driver at the bottom of the layered miniport driver. A layered miniport driver exports *MiniportXxx* functions at its upper edge and *ProtocolXxx* functions at its lower edge. The intermediate driver miniport interface may be referred to as a virtual miniport. It is "virtual" because it does not control the NIC directly. Instead, it relies on an underlying miniport driver to communicate with the physical device. Figure 10-5 is an illustration of the layered NDIS miniport driver architecture.

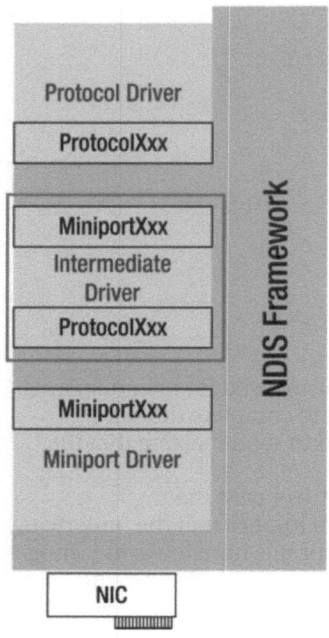

Figure 10-5. *The relationship between layered NDIS miniport driver and other drivers in NDIS architecture*

The following examples illustrate various usages for intermediate drivers:

- Media translation between an old transport driver and a miniport driver that manages a media type unknown to the transport driver

- Data filtering for security or other purposes

- Load Balancing Failover (LBFO) solutions

- Monitoring and collecting of network data statistics

An NDIS intermediate driver registers both its *MiniportXxx* functions and its *ProtocolXxx* functions in the context of its *DriverEntry* routine. To register its miniport functions, the driver must set NDIS_MINIPORT_DRIVER_CHARACTERISTICS structure Flags to NDIS_INTERMEDIATE_DRIVER flag and call the *NdisMRegisterMiniportDriver* function. Otherwise setting up the NDIS_MINIPORT_DRIVER_CHARACTERISTICS is the same as for any other miniport driver. To register its *ProtocolXxx* functions, an intermediate driver must call the *NdisRegisterProtocolDriver* function.

Registry Settings

Registry settings for NDIS network driver revolve around the NDIS device driver being loaded by Device Manager. NDIS in turn is responsible for loading and running network drivers. The registry allows NDIS to load and then call the drivers' *DriverEntry* routine and continue with initialization and operation of the drivers. Registry information for the miniport driver and adapter instance must be configured in HKEY_LOCAL_MACHINE\Comm\. Listing 10-14 is a generic template for such registry information.

Listing 10-14. *Generic registry information for a NDIS miniport driver*

```
[HKEY_LOCAL_MACHINE\Comm\<MiniportDriverName>]
    "Group"="NDIS"
    "ImagePatch"="<driver>.dll"
[HKEY_LOCAL_MACHINE\Comm\<AdapterInstanceName>\Parms]
    "BusNumber"=dword:<busnumber>
    "BusType"=dword:<bustype>
<other parameters as needed by the miniport driver, such as IRQ, IOAddr, TcpIP, etc.>
```

A specific example that demonstrates it well is the registry entry settings for any NE2000 compatible adapter. Listing 10-15 is an excerpt from common.reg.

Listing 10-15. *Registry information for a NE2000 network adaptor*

```
[HKEY_LOCAL_MACHINE\Comm\NE20001]
;LOC_FRIENDLYNE2000COMPAT
    "DisplayName"=mui_sz:"netmui.dll,#9001"
    "Group"="NDIS"
    "ImagePath"="ne2000.dll"

[HKEY_LOCAL_MACHINE\Comm\NE20001\Parms]
    "BusNumber"=dword:0
    "BusType"=dword:8
    "InterruptNumber"=dword:03
    "IoBaseAddress"=dword:0300
    "Transceiver"=dword:3
    "CardType"=dword:1

[HKEY_LOCAL_MACHINE\Comm\NE20001\Parms\Tcpip]
    "EnableWINS"=dword:1
```

If the NE2000 adapter is a PCI bus adapter then it must have registry information entry under the HKLM\Drivers\BuiltIn\PCI\Template node. The following listing (10-16) is of a NE2000 PCI NIC:

Listing 10-16. *Registry information for a NE2000 compatible PCI adapter*

```
[HKEY_LOCAL_MACHINE\Drivers\BuiltIn\PCI\Template\NE2000]
    "Dll"="NDIS.dll"
    "Class"=dword:02
    "SubClass"=dword:00
    "ProgIF"=dword:0
    "VendorID"=multi_sz:"10ec","1050"
    "DeviceID"=multi_sz:"8029","0940"
;   "Entry"="NdisPCIBusDeviceInit"
    "Prefix"="NDS"
    ; Flags==2 is DEVFLAGS_LOADLIBRARY
    "Flags"=dword:2
    "Transceiver"=dword:3
```

It is worthwhile to remember that the NE2000 does not use the generic ISR in giisr.dll and loads its own ISR in NE2000ISR.dll to handle interrupts.

Chapter Summary

This chapter was devoted to network drivers with the focus on drivers for the network adapter card. As such, more emphasis was given to NIC miniport drivers than to protocol drivers or intermediate drivers. NIC miniport drivers are responsible for interfacing to the hardware using the API the NDIS framework provides the developers to handle high performance network hardware. It provides the driver developer functions to receive and send large data amounts using scatter/gather DMA, to perform either memory mapped I/O or port mapped I/O operations. It provides functions to handle hardware information, housekeeping, and interrupts and synchronization. All of these APIs make for portable device drivers across operating systems and lower the effort to develop network adapter drivers. One last note regarding NIC device drivers, is that you cannot use NDIS drivers for boot loaders, since NDIS is not part of boot loaders. This means that network device drivers that support boot loaders must implement all the hardware interface within the driver's code.

CHAPTER 11

Debugging Device Drivers

Can you name a developer that can develop a bug-free software unit excluding "Hello World" program? I thought not. The main reason that the development cycle of software is such a lengthy process is errors in the code implementation, better known as "bugs" (with "debugging" becoming the word to describe the process of sieving these bugs out of the software). The end result of the existence of bugs in software is that the executable will fail at one time or another. The complexity of developing software that manages hardware is directly accountable for bugs that are manifold more complex and hard to fix. The most difficult bugs to fix are bugs that occur infrequently and cannot be easily reproduced. These are usually the logical bugs rather than the coding bugs. Kernel mode device drivers present the added danger of crashing the system if failure occurs in their code.

In this chapter

- Overview of the available tools
- Using the simplest tools
- Debug zones
- Kernel debugger
- Hardware assisted debugging
- Post mortem debugging

Overview of Debugging Tools and Techniques

Writing robust code is the key to catching and fixing bugs. Adding error handling code whenever there is a possibility of an error occurring is not just good coding practice but is a must while writing device driver code. Whenever you call an API check the return values and handle error recovery. The same applies to code that manipulates memory and memory pointers, as well as arithmetic computations that may fail, like the divide by zero classic. Having said that, a variety of debugging tools are available to debug device drivers because either coding bugs or logical bugs will still be in the code (at least in my code there are).

Debugging Techniques

The simplest of all debugging techniques is outputting debug messages to a debug shell. This technique is extremely valuable for debugging software such as device drivers. This technique is least intrusive as it does not stop the execution and flow of the device driver. All Windows CE versions including Windows Embedded Compact 7 provide an extremely helpful tool to output conditionally debug messages using debug zones. This is helpful because it curbs the barrage of messages that are displayed and therefore allowing you to view messages related only to a specific area of code you are debugging. So for example if you are debugging a device driver's IST, you can limit the debug messages to just the ones that are triggered in the IST code so you don't get hundreds of messages from every function in the device driver.

The other techniques involve software and hardware debuggers. While software debuggers such as kernel debugger is very useful when debugging initialization, opening a device driver instance and de-initializing and closing device driver instances, it may be quite insufficiently capable to debug device driver code that handles I/O data transactions. This would require hardware debuggers that take advantage of chip debugging capabilities.

Debugging Tools

The tools range from tools provided with Platform Builder such as

- Debug Zones
- kernel debugger
- Target control

Lauterbach's TRACE32, is the third-party tool that interfaces with the debugging capabilities built in the CPU hardware.

- TRACE32 debugger
- eXDI hardware debugging driver by Lauterbach

Simple and Effective Debugging Techniques

As mentioned above, there are quite a few debugging techniques; however, to be effective and efficient it is wise to match the technique to the specific code that we debug. Device drivers are especially sensitive to debugging techniques because of the tight interaction with the hardware and timing sensitivity may not always comply with stopping the flow of execution using break points and examine the code trying to isolate bugs.

While it is fair to assume that initialization and de-initialization code should present no problem using a software debugger such as kernel debugger and set breakpoints within functions such as the *XXX_Init* entry point, it may very well be an issue if we have to debug the device driver's IST. To debug timing sensitive code and code that directly addresses hardware registers we may prefer to resort to less obtrusive techniques such as debug messages or hardware tracing techniques.

While debugging device drivers, it is best to load the device driver manually. This means that instead of allowing Device Manager to load the device driver while the system is booting, and forcing you to perform the debugging when the system loads the device driver, you want to control loading when you are ready to debug. To do this, simply create a small application that will call *ActivateDeviceEx* which loads the device driver.

Debug Messages

Debug messages are the least invasive method to get meaningful information while a unit of execution is executing. Debug messages are not halting execution and depending on how these are formatted can provide a wealth of information. Formatted appropriately, debug messages are useful for other developers unfamiliar with your code implementation details. Some of the following guidelines should help you format debug messages well for the task at hand.

- Specify the source of the message

- Write meaningful messages.

  - Debug messages should be easily understood by someone such as testers who is unfamiliar with the implementation code

- Highlight significant types of messages with consistent symbols that help identify them

- Use debug zones to filter output

You may add the source file name and line where the message originates to help find it swiftly.

```
DEBUGMSG(ZONE_INIT, (_T("DMO!Error Getting window
        information\r\n"),
        _T(__FILE__), _T(__LINE__)));
```

You can identify the component for example a device driver by its prefix as just demonstrated in the message by adding "DMO!" to the output string. You can open from <Target> menu of the Platform Builder IDE the "Debug Message Options" dialog box to include time stamp, process ID, and thread ID information in the message. See Figure 11-1.

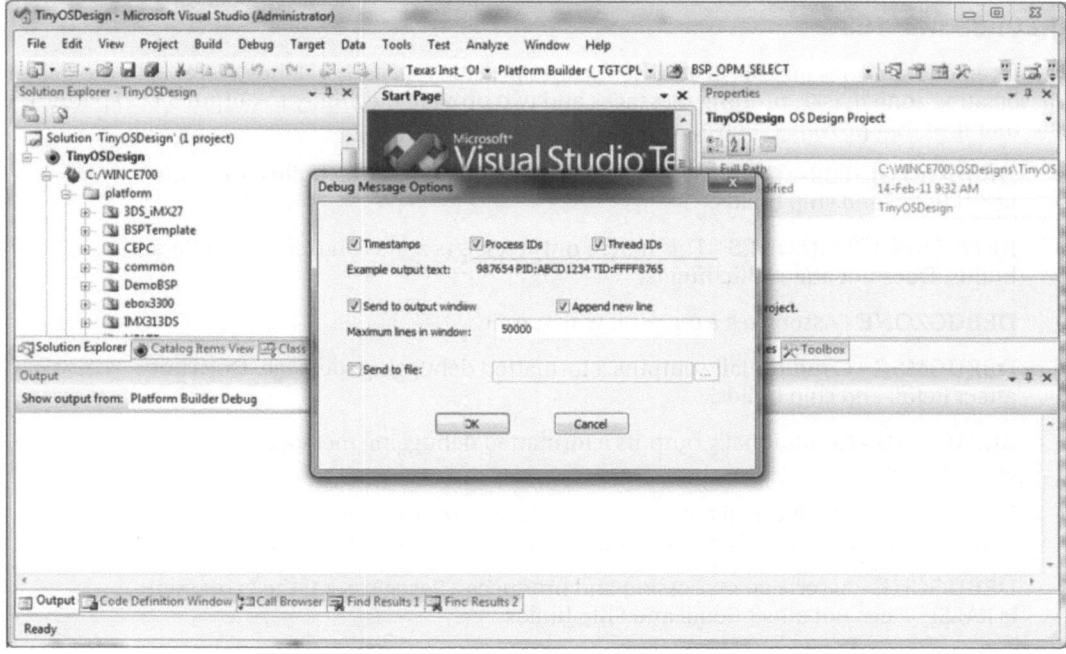

Figure 11-1. *Debug Message Options setting*

The explanation string should clarify what the message is designed to convey for example indicating an ISR handler named so and so was installed for a specific IRQ.

```
DEBUGMSG(ZONE_INIT, (_T("DMO!ISR handler installed ,
        Dll: '%s', Handler: '%s', Irq: %d\r\n"),
        IsrInfo.szIsrDll, IsrInfo.szIsrHandler,
        IsrInfo.dwIrq));
```

For example you may highlight the entry to a function and exit from a function by adding '+' and '-' signs to precede the name of the function.

```
DEBUGMSG(ZONE_INIT, (_T("DMO!+DMO_Init\r\n")));
```

And to be able to filter out and suppress the onslaught of messages that can cloud perception of the problem that you or another developer or tester try to solve use debug zones.

Debug Zones

Debug zones are a mechanism provided to filter debug messages and suppress excessive message chatter. This mechanism supplies the developer with a set of macros that can be embedded in the code to output conditionally controlled debug messages. These macros boil down to calling *NKOutputDebugString* which is an efficient kernel function for printing debug messages.

Debug Zones Macros

There are eleven debug zones macros in all. These zones provide registering debug zones with the debug system, associating zone masks, printing messages and two provide the ability to output a LED pattern in the case that the OEM provides such an interface.

- **DEBUGREGISTER** - This macro only registers zones on Debug builds. Does not affect Retail and ship builds.

- **RETAILREGISTERZONES** - This macro only registers zones on Debug and Retail builds. Does not affect Ship builds.

- **DEBUGZONE** - Associates a mask bit with a zone.

- **DEBUGMSG** - Conditionally outputs a formatted debugging message. Does not affect Retail and ship builds.

- **RETAILMSG** - Conditionally outputs a formatted debugging message. Does not affect ship builds.

- **ERRORMSG** - Conditionally outputs a formatted error message, adding the file name and line number where the error occurred. Does not affect ship builds.

- **DEBUGCHK** - Asserts an expression and produces a `DebugBreak` if the expression is FALSE. Does not affect Retail and Ship builds.

- **ASSERT** - Asserts an expression and produces a `DebugBreak` if the expression is FALSE.

- **ASSERTMSG** - Asserts an expression, and if the expression is FALSE, produces an error message. Does not affect Retail and Ship builds.

- **DEBUGLED** - Conditionally outputs a LED pattern. Does not affect Retail and Ship builds. Not an option on boards without LED hardware. Production boards are not likely to provide LED hardware.

- **RETAILLED** - Conditionally outputs a LED pattern. Does not affect Ship builds.

Terminology in Windows CE is sometimes confusing; note that there are RETAILMSG and DEBUGMSG. The DEBUGMSG macro is used in debug builds only. So, if a module is compiled as retail, that is compiled with WINCEDEBUG=RETAIL set in the build environment it will not output any DEBUGMSG statements. RETAILMSG, on the other hand, outputs messages in both retail and debug builds. If the build is compiled as a "ship build" that is WINCESHIP=1 set in the build environment, no messages will be outputted. Why is the terminology confusing? Because the term "retail" does not mean "ship" as would be expected by the English language.

Registering Debug Zones

Before debug zones can be used in your module these zones have to be registered with the debug system. There are a few preparation steps you have to take. First is to define your debug zones. One thing to remember is that you can define at most sixteen zones per module. Listing 11-1 shows a sample of code defining five zones.

Listing 11-1. Defining module specific debug zones

```
#ifdef DEBUG

#define      ZONE_INIT             DEBUGZONE(0)
#define      ZONE_OPEN             DEBUGZONE(1)
#define      ZONE_IOCTL            DEBUGZONE(2)
#define      ZONE_DEINIT           DEBUGZONE(3)
#define      ZONE_ERROR            DEBUGZONE(15)

#endif //DEBUG
```

Next you have to associate a bitmask to a zone ID. Listing 11-2 presents a way of doing it. This mask is needed to set the `ulZoneMask` field in the `DBGPARAM` structure to indicate which zones are enabled.

Listing 11-2. Associating a bitmask to a zone ID

```
#define      DEBUGMASK(bit)             (1 << (bit))

#define      MASK_INIT             DEBUGMASK(0)
#define      MASK_OPEN             DEBUGMASK(1)
#define      MASK_IOCTL            DEBUGMASK(2)
#define      MASK_DEINIT           DEBUGMASK(3)
#define      MASK_ERROR            DEBUGMASK(15)
```

Before you can register you have to declare a `DBGPARAM` structure that is private for the specific module. Because this structure actually associates your zone IDs to your module and when registered the debug system is able to manage your module's specific zones. Listing 11-3 shows an example of declaring this structure. Note, however, that the assigned variable has to always be named `dpCurSettings`.

Listing 11-3. Declaring DBGPARAM

```
DBGPARAM dpCurSettings = {
        _T("Demodrvr"),
        {
                _T("Init"),  _T("Open"), _T("Ioctl"), _T("DeInit"),
                _T(""),  _T(""),  _T(""),  _T(""),
                _T(""),_T(""),_T(""),_T(""),
                _T(""),_T(""),_T(""),_T("Error")
        },
        MASK_INIT | MASK_DEINIT
};
```

Two things to note about this structure, the first is the name of the module is assigned in the first field of the structure, the last field, `ulZoneMask` indicates which zones are enabled.

```
typedef struct _DBGPARAM {
    WCHAR   lpszName[32];
    WCHAR   rglpszZones[16][32];
    ULONG   ulZoneMask;
} DBGPARAM, *LPDBGPARAM;
```

Next you must register your debug zones with the debug system. Since device drivers must be implemented within DLLs the registration must take place in the *DllEntry* function. Listing 11-4 is a sample code of registering the device driver's debug zones. Notice the call to DisableThreadLibraryCalls that effectively disables DLL_THREAD_ATTACH and DLL_THREAD_DETACH notifications. This helps reduce the initialization code of the device drivers' DLL.

Listing 11-4. *Registering the device driver's debug zones*

```
BOOL WINAPI DllEntry(HANDLE hinstDLL, DWORD dwReason, LPVOID lpvReserved)
{
    switch(dwReason)
    {
        case DLL_PROCESS_ATTACH:
        {
            g_hInstance = hinstDLL;
            DEBUGREGISTER((HINSTANCE)hinstDLL);
            DEBUGMSG(ZONE_INIT,(_T("DMO!PROCESS_ATTACH: Process:
                                    0x%x, ID: 0x%x \r\n"),
            GetCurrentProcess(), GetCurrentProcessId()));
            DisableThreadLibraryCalls ((HMODULE)hinstDLL);
            return TRUE;
        }
        case DLL_PROCESS_DETACH:
        {
            DEBUGMSG(ZONE_INIT,(_T("DMO!PROCESS_DETACH: Process:
                                    0x%x, ID: 0x%x \r\n"),
            GetCurrentProcess(), GetCurrentProcessId()));
        }
        break;
    }
    return TRUE;
}
```

Changing Debug Zones

Following the code samples just presented means that you can debug code in the device driver that you assigned to initialization and de-initialization. What about debugging for example the *DMO_Open* function? In this function debug messages will be output only if ZONE_OPEN zone is enabled. What if you want to change the initial debug zones that you created in code? One way would be to edit the code rebuild and place it in the image. This really is a time-consuming and wasteful procedure. You may use the IDE to launch the Debug Zones dialog box during the debugging session and select your device driver module and check the debug zones you want enabled. Figure 11-2 shows how to enable the ZONE_OPEN zone.

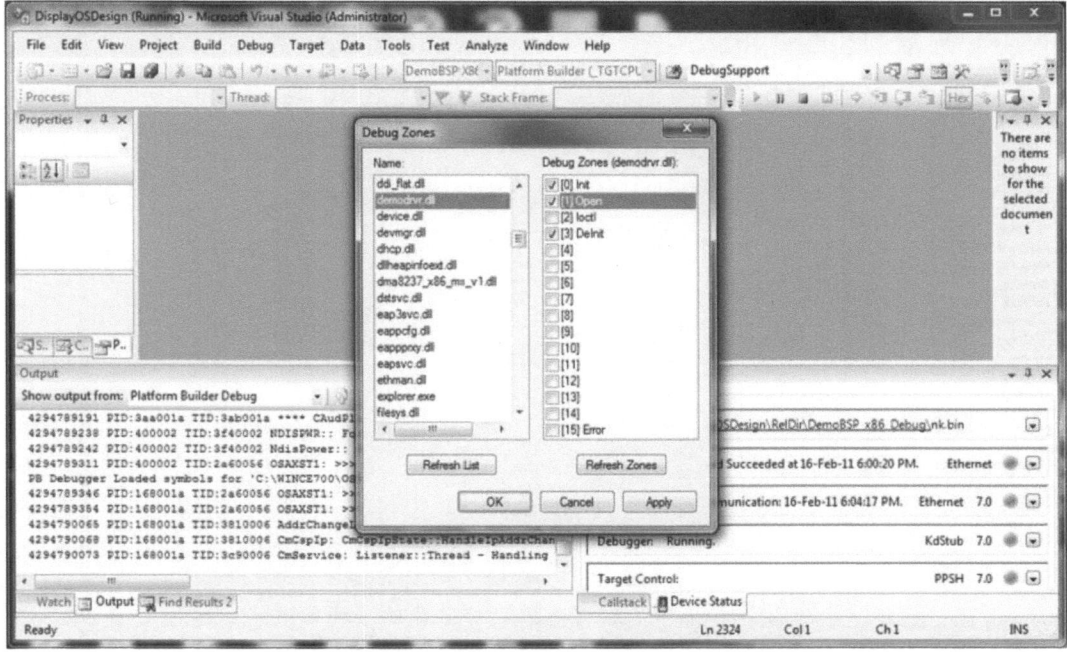

Figure 11-2. *Enabling the* ZONE_OPEN *zone during OS runtime*

Another way of enabling zones without disturbing code or OS image is to edit the registry key
HKEY_CURRENT_USER\Pegasus\Zones on the development workstation. To demonstrate this I reset the
DBGPARAM structure (see Listing 11-5), in the Demodrvr module and rebuilt it.

Listing 11-5. *ulZoneMask set to 0 so no zone is enabled*

```
DBGPARAM dpCurSettings = {
        _T("Demodrvr"),
        {
                _T("Init"), _T("Open"), _T("Ioctl"), _T("DeInit"),
                _T(""), _T(""), _T(""), _T(""),
                _T(""),_T(""),_T(""),_T(""),
                _T(""),_T(""),_T(""),_T("Error")
        },
        0
};
```

Next I created an entry on my development workstation for Demodrvr and set the mask to 1. See
Figure 11-3.

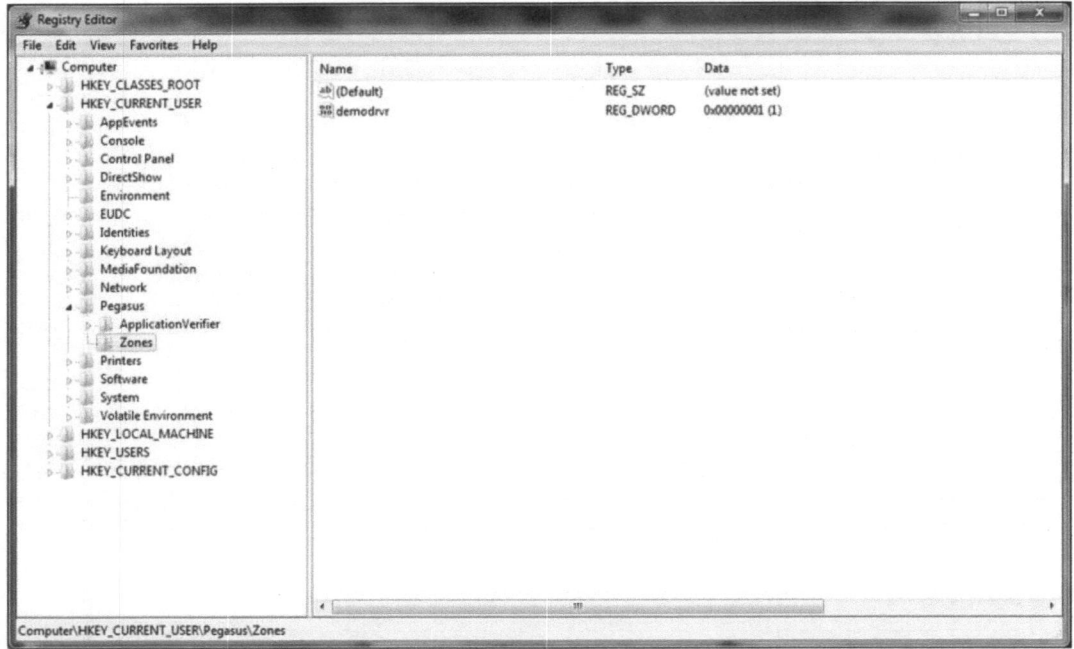

Figure 11-3. *HKEY_CURRENT_USER\Pegasus\Zones DWORD value named demodrvr set to 1*

If I hadn't done that Demodrvr would not output any debug messages. However, editing the development workstation registry enabled the ZONE_INIT zone. Figure 11-4 demonstrates how messages from the Init zone were output to the output pane in Visual Studio and the Debug Zones dialog box shows the Init zone checked.

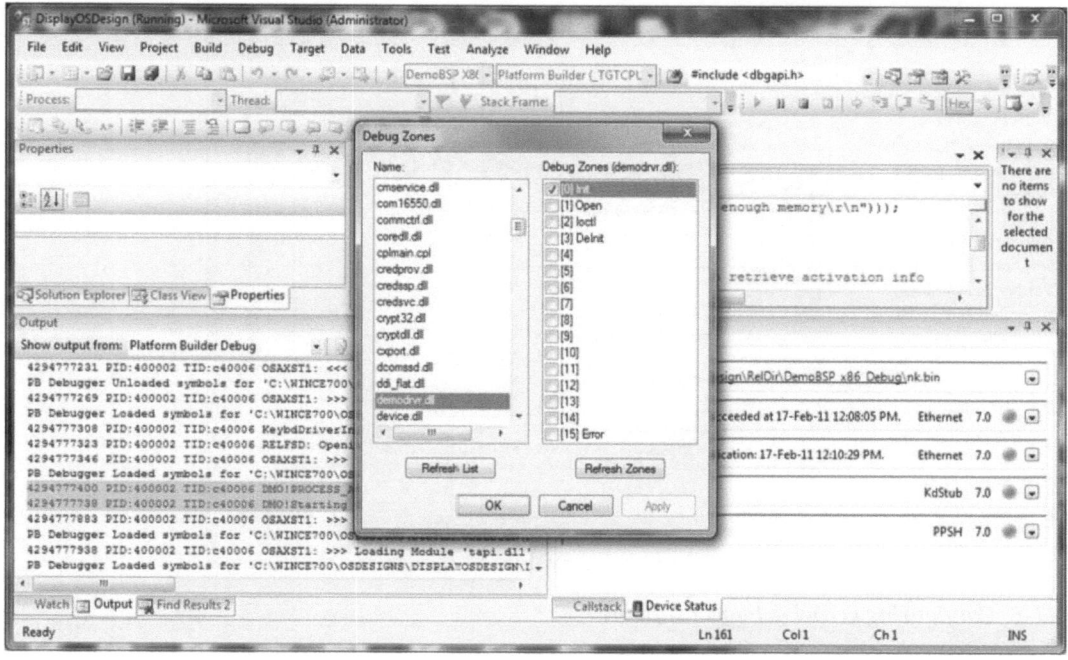

Figure 11-4. *Showing ZONE_INIT checked and in the output pane Demodrvr messages output*

Kernel Debugger

Kernel debugger is part of platform builder. If kernel debugging is enabled for the OS image build kernel debugger runs as a service using the Core Connectivity infrastructure. To be able kernel debugger to perform a debugging stub, KdStub has to be included in the runtime image. Note the device status pane (row 4) in Figure 11-4 showing KdStub running.

To enable kernel debugging all you have to do is open the OS design property pages dialog from the Project menu and select Build Options node and set to "Yes" the "Enable kernel debugger" field, you want to enable KITL while you do that just as well. Using kernel debugger is very similar to using WinDbg or the desktop debugger integrated in Visual Studio, so I'll leave out operational details on how to work with kernel debugger since this can be found in the product documentation. Figure 11-6 demonstrates a debugging session for the Demodrvr driver with a breakpoint set on line 70 indicated by the brown (it least to me it looks brown) bullet and the yellow arrow shows the next statement to be executed. In the Watch pane to the right the **pDevContext** structure contents is shown, while on the left the Callstack pane shows within which function the next statement for execution is located and the stack of function calls that led to this point.

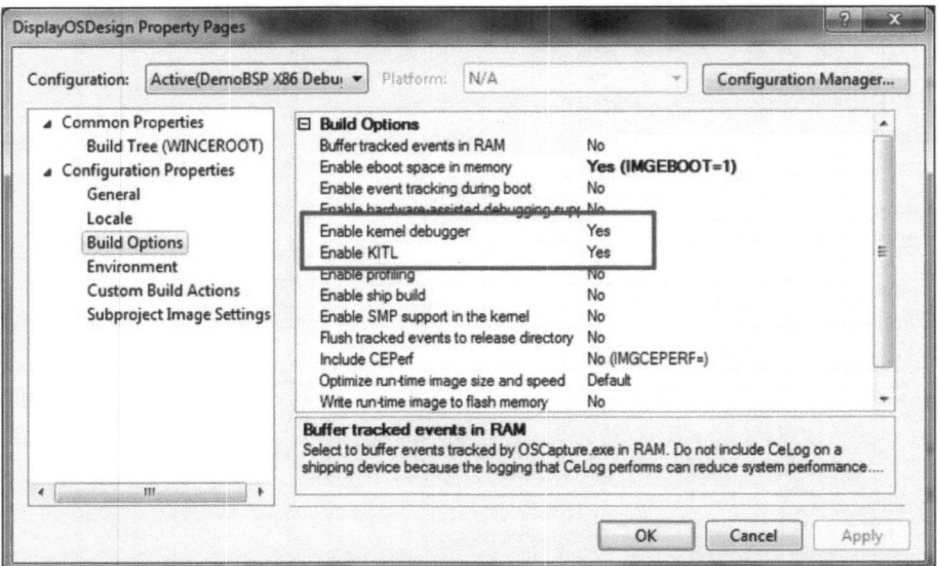

Figure 11-5. *Configuring kernel debugger support*

■ **Note** Ship Build Warning: You do not want to enable kernel debugger in a Ship Build image. If you do that, KdStub will wait for kernel debugger to connect, because a device that runs a ship build usually is not connected to a development workstation running kernel debugger the device will take a very long time to boot.

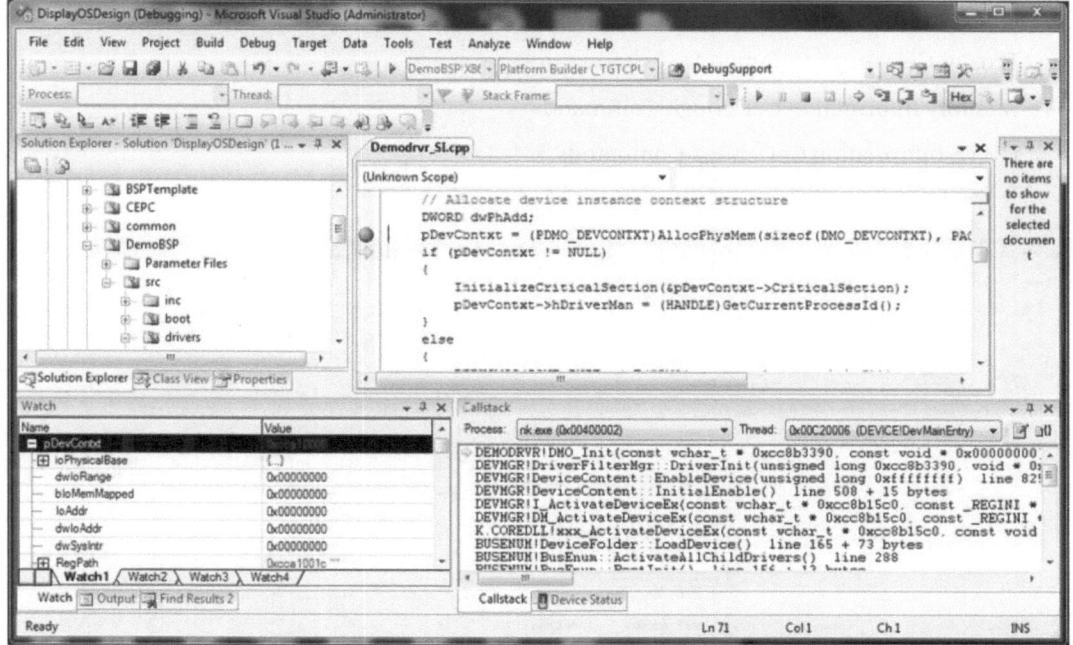

Figure 11-6. *Using Kernel Debugger to break on line 70 of Demodrvr_SI.cpp file*

CeDebugX

CeDebugX is an extension to the kernel debugger. It provides detailed information about the state of the system at break state and attempts to diagnose crashes, hangs, and deadlocks. Target control must be supported in the image and the debugger must be in a break state to be able to use CeDebugX commands. More about Target control later in this chapter. To incorporate target control in your image find Core OS>>Core OS Services>>Kernel Functionality>>Target Control Support(Shell.exe) in the Catalog and check it. Figure 11-7 shows information obtained about Demodrvr using the !module command during a break.

```
!module demodrvr.dll
```

For a list of commands consult the documentation. The commands are grouped in ten groups of related commands:

- Diagnostic CeDebugX Commands

- Extension Help and Control CeDebugX Commands

- General System Information CeDebugX Commands

- Thread Information CeDebugX Commands

- Process Information CeDebugX Commands

- Module Information CeDebugX Commands

- Handles CeDebugX Commands

- Proxies CeDebugX Commands

- Memory Information CeDebugX Commands

- GWES Information CeDebugX Commands

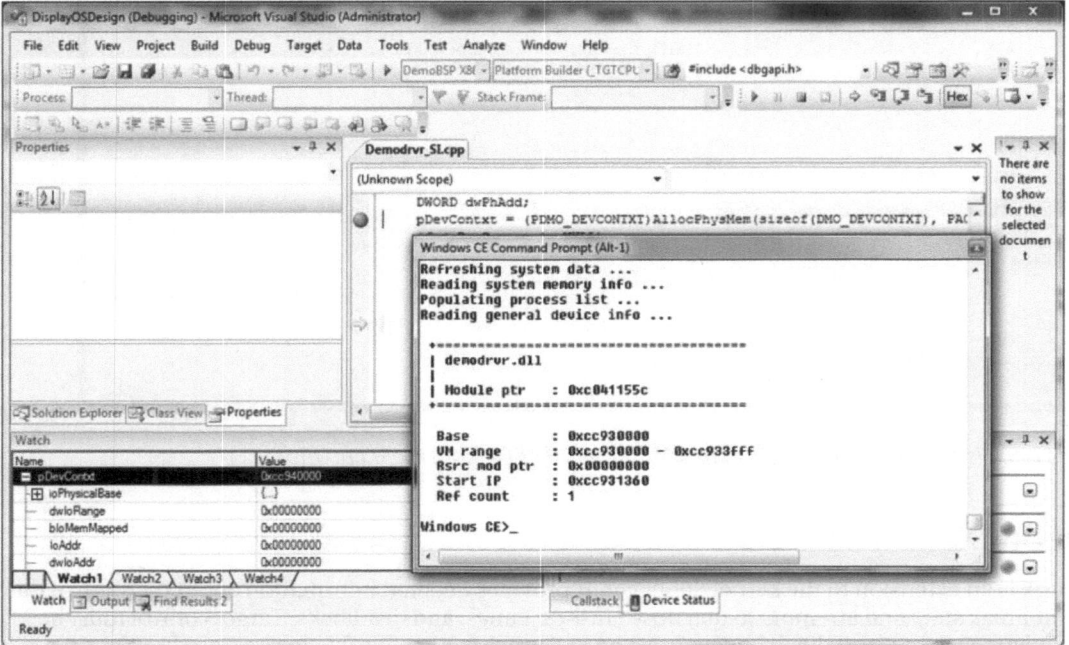

Figure 11-7. *Module information using CeDebugX*

Hardware Assisted Debugging

The advantages that can be gained using hardware assisted debuggers are manifold. The first and most important is when you just start out and you don't even have a bootloader, never mind an operating system. What does it really mean hardware assisted debugger? Most CPUs provide on-chip debug support. The ARM Debug Architecture for example uses the existing JTAG interface as a method of accessing the core.

The scan chains that are around the core for production test are reused in debug state to capture information from the databus and to insert new information into the core or the memory. There are two scan chains around the core:

- A scan chain around the whole periphery of the core

- A subset of the first scan chain, covering only the databus and breakpoint

The shorter scan chain on the databus allows instructions and data to be inserted into the core without the overhead of clocking the data around the entire periphery of the ARM processor core. For more information lookup the debug architecture reference books relevant to your CPU. The on-chip debug system will provide four basic features:

- Read and write memory

- Read and write the CPU registers

- Single step and real time execution

- Hardware breakpoints and trigger features

■ **Note** JTAG (Joint Test Action Group) is the common name for the IEEE 1149.1 Standard Test Access Port and Boundary-Scan Architecture. Initially devised for testing printed circuit boards using boundary scan and is still used for this application.

Today JTAG is used for IC debug ports. In the embedded processor market, practically all modern processors support JTAG. Embedded systems development relies on debuggers talking to chips with JTAG to perform operations like single stepping and setting breakpoints.

TRACE 32

TRACE32 is a good example of a hardware-assisted debugging tool. It provides a JTAG interface to the target device, namely the In Circuit Debugger (TRACE32 ICD), and an IDE on the development workstation to control the device and perform debugging procedures. It provides debugging using high-level language code, assembler and mixed disassembled code. It provides on chip breakpoints and triggers. Of course it allows flash programming, and provides RTOS awareness, the latest support for Windows Embedded Compact 7 including the ability to debug multicore systems. For the device driver developer it provides display of internal and external peripheral on a logical level.

To help make the debugging process automatic, a script language allows scripting a sequence of commands to run the debug session up to the point where you want to start your debugging.

Hardware assisted debugging is invaluable when developing the BSP. Without it is practically impossible to debug a boot loader for example. "Give me a place to stand on, and I will move the Earth" Archimedes is said to have observed of the lever. Well, hardware assisted debugging is this lever.

When it comes to device drivers, it is extremely helpful to have the ability to logically view the hardware, represented by its registers (ports). Debugging Ethernet device drivers for the bootloader can be performed only using tools like TRACE32, because the boot loader does not provide NDIS support and you have to implement the NIC interface from scratch.

Automating the Debugging Procedure

While it is possible to use the TRACE32 IDE to set commands individually using the command interface which is located at the bottom of the window as seen in Figure 11-8. However it is far more efficient to create a scripted batch file that is run by the IDE to perform all of these required commands in sequence without the need to enter each command individually. The bottom part of the main window has four rows; the top row is a command line, the net is a message bar, below that are soft keys that act like shortcut buttons for commands that are entered into the command line, and the bottom one is a status bar.

So for example if we need to set CPU type you would enter the command, in this case TRACE32 provides a list of reference CPUs it supports.

```
SYStem.CPU DM3730
```

And then go on to set other commands in order to initialize the debugger you could write a batch file with the file extension CMM to run them in sequence. Listing 11-6 is a sample batch file I modified from a sample batch file I received from Lauterbach to handle the specific board I was using. Truthfully, without TRACE32 I would never have been able to migrate the WinCE 6.0 BSP created by Adeneo for the OMAP3530 to Windows Embedded Compact 7 for the Variscite board. It is well commented and it can be used as a reference for creating similar batch files.

Listing 11-6. Wince74SOM37.cmm ICD script file

```
;-------------------------------------------------------------------------
;
;     Windows Embedded Compact 7 Demo for TRACE32 RTOS Debugger
;
;     This batch file demonstrates the use of the RTOS Debugger for CE7
;     The example is generated for an OMAP37xx Variscite board using an ICD.
;     It will NOT run on any other board, but may be used as a template for others.
;     The Windows CE image is downloaded via the ICD.
;
;-------------------------------------------------------------------------

; Starting WinCE example with TRACE32:
; - Start TRACE32
; - Power on the board
; - TRACE32: "do wince"
; - Start "application1.exe" on target via CMD

; For debugging with TRACE32 we recommend to disable demand paging
; by setting bit one of ROMFLAGS in PLATFORM\VAR_SOM37_EVM\FILES\config.bib

&winceroot="C:\WINCE700"     ; typically C:\WINCE700
&reldir="&winceroot\OSDesigns\TinyOSDesign\TinyOSDesign\RelDir\VARSOM37_EVM__ARMv7_Debug"

; Debugger Reset
 winpage.reset
 area.reset
 WINPOS 55. 5. 120. 30.
 area
```

```
  print "resetting..."
  RESet

; Initializing Debugger
  print "initializing..."
  SYStem.CPU DM3730
  SYStem.JtagClock 5MHZ              ; hardware dependent (see manual)
  SYStem.Option DACR ON             ; give Debugger global write permissions
  TrOnchip.Set DABORT OFF           ; used by OS for page miss!
  TrOnchip.Set PABORT OFF           ; used by OS for page miss!
  TrOnchip.Set UNDEF OFF            ; my be used by OS for FPU detection
  SYStem.Option MMUSPACES ON        ; enable space ids to virtual addresses

SYStem.Up
  SETUP.IMASKASM ON                 ; lock interrupts while single stepping
; start u-boot to initialize the board
  Go
  print "target setup..."
  wait 1.s
Break

; load eboot
; for physical load address run viewbin -r ebootnand.bin to get everything you need
; see ROMOFFSET for offset to flash load address
; then load eboot to <phys. addr.> - <flash addr.>
  Register.RESet
  print "loading eboot..."
  Data.LOAD.EXE "&reldir\EBOOTNAND.bin" 0x87E00000-0x87E00000
  Register.Set PC 0x87E00000

; let eboot initialize everything
  Go
  print "running eboot..."
  wait 3.s
  Break

; Load the Windows CE image
 ; Use the next lines only to load the image into RAM using the debugger.

  print "loading Windows CE image..."
; Prepare for direct download: disable MMU!
  PER.Set C15:0x1   %Long data.long(c15:1)&~1        ; switch off MMU
  Register.Reset
```

```
; Download the image to physical address.
 Data.LOAD.EXE &reldir\nk.bin
; set PC to physical start address
; see config.bib NK RAMIMAGE or better still run viewbin -r nk.bin to get everything you need
 Register.Set pc 0x8C000000

; We'd like to see something, open a code window.
 WINPOS 0. 0. 77. 22.
 Data.List

; Declare the MMU format to the debugger
 ; table format is "WINCE6"
 ; skip root table (0)
 ; declare default translation for kernel
 MMU.FORMAT WINCE6 0 0x80000000--0x8fffffff 0x80000000
```

Following are a few figures to demonstrate the debugging process initialized by this batch file. Figure 11-8 shows the flow of this batch file executing.

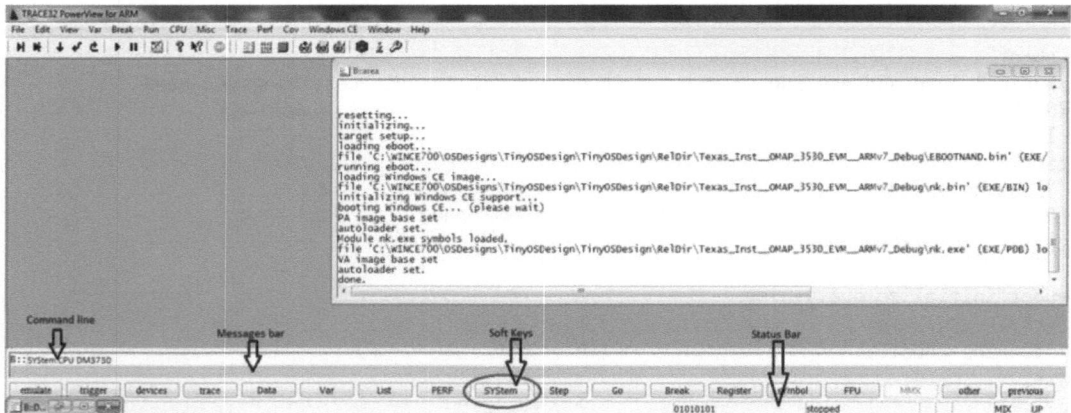

Figure 11-8. *The area window displays the flow of execution of the batch file in Listing 11-6*

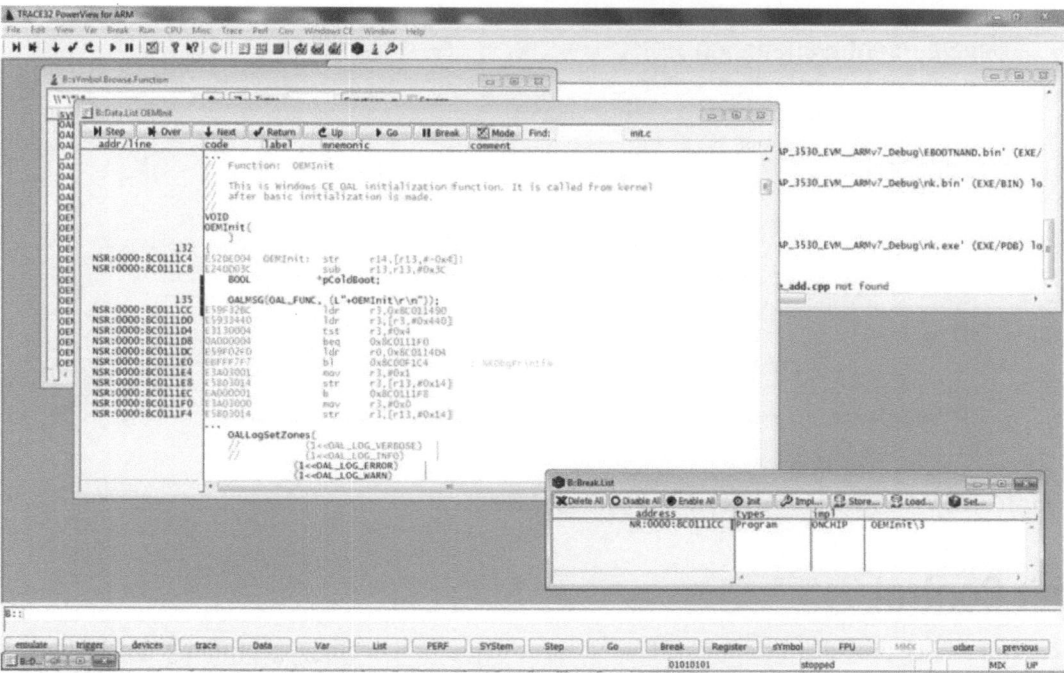

Figure 11-9. *Window showing mixed code listing for OEMInit and breakpoints list*

eXDI

eXDI stands for Extended Debugging Interface. It allows Platform Builder to monitor and control activity of the target device via an In Circuit Debugger such as TRACE32. It is essentially an adaptation layer between Platform Builder and the In Circuit Debugger. eXDI is implemented as a core connectivity service which cooperates with OS access service to provide debugging services to Platform Builder. OS access provides OS awareness to the debugger. It acts as a mediator between the eXDI service and Platform Builder. This allows third-party solution providers to provide debugging tools that are aware of Windows Embedded Compact 7. Figure 11-10 shows how Platform Builder uses the Lauterbach eXDI2 driver to interface between the TRACE32 ICD connected to the target device using the JTAG connection for hardware assisted debugging.

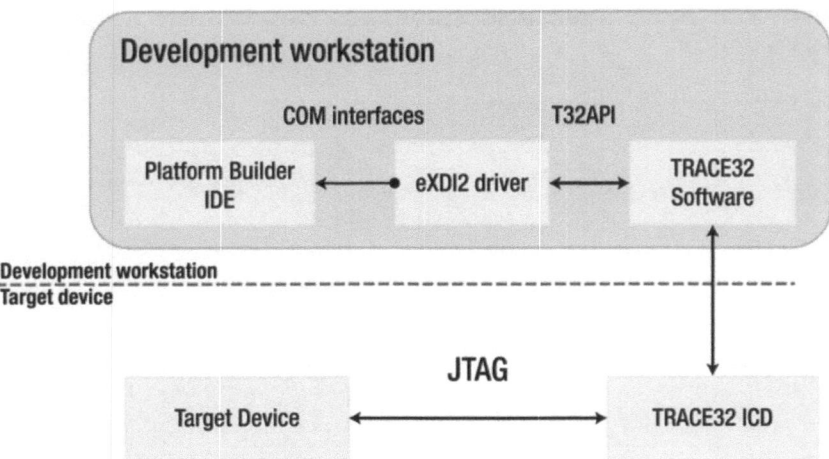

Figure 11-10. eXDI Architecture used to debug without KITL

Target Control

Target control service provides a command line interface to perform debugging, profiling, and logging. Target control commands allow you to execute processes and kill them, dump memory, get information, and so on. However the most interesting capability of target control service is to execute commands for a debugger extension DLL. Microsoft provides such a debugger extension module CeDebugX which we discussed under the kernel debugger section. More than that you can create your own debugging commands customized to your needs.

Creating Debug Extensions

What Microsoft can do, you can do. If you want to customize specific commands it is quite straight forward to create your own debugger extension. While the documentation is very helpful guiding you through this process of creating a Win32 DLL that runs on your development station, there are a few points to remember. Platform Builder is a 32 bit program, it is installed within the < InstallationDisk\Program Files (x86)\Microsoft Platform Builder> directory, so the DLL you create is a 32 bit DLL. You should configure the additional include directories to contain < \Program Files (x86)\Microsoft Platform Builder\7.00\cepb\SDK\Include>, this is where WDbgExts_CE.h is located. You should add the /FORCE:MULTIPLE to the linker command line. This is to avoid a build error that is related to multiple definitions for a symbol when you link your DLL. Add a module definition file to export the extension library functions. Listing 11-8 shows a sample module definition file. When you connect Platform Builder to the device in debug mode and download the OS image you launch Windows CE Debugger Extensions dialog box from the Debug menu. This is a common Open File dialog box that allows you to locate your extension DLL and load it. Once it is loaded you can use your extension commands. Listing 11-7 show the minimum code you need for an extension DLL. Figure 11-11 shows calling the !demo command in Target Control.

Listing 11-7. *Demonstration code of an implementation of an extension DLL*

```
#include <intsafe.h>
#include <wdbgexts_ce.h>

WINDBG_EXTENSION_APIS ExtensionApis = {0};
USHORT g_SavedMajorVersion;
USHORT g_SavedMinorVersion;
EXT_API_VERSION g_ApiVersion = { 3, 5, EXT_API_VERSION_NUMBER32, 0 };

void WDBGAPI WinDbgExtensionDllInit(
                PWINDBG_EXTENSION_APIS lpExtensionApis,
                USHORT MajorVersion, USHORT MinorVersion)
{
    // Copy lpExtensionApis to ExtensionAPIs so that extension
    // functions can access the Platform Builder Debugger
    // Extension API.

        ExtensionApis = *lpExtensionApis;

      g_SavedMajorVersion = MajorVersion;
      g_SavedMinorVersion = MinorVersion;
}
void WDBGAPI WinDbgExtensionDllShutdown()
{

}

LPEXT_API_VERSION ExtensionApiVersion()
{
    return &g_ApiVersion;
}

DECLARE_API(demo)
{
    static ULONG  Frames = 0;
    WCHAR MyString[24] = {0};
        EXTSTACKTRACE stcktr[2];

        Frames = StackTrace(0, 0, 0, stcktr, 2);

    dprintf("Stack frames \n");

        for (int i = 0; i < 2; i++)
        {
                dprintf("Stack frame pointer %08x \n",
                        stcktr[i].FramePointer);
                dprintf("Stack frame instruction pointer %08x \n",
                        stcktr[i].ProgramCounter);
```

```
        dprintf("Return address %08x \n",
                    stcktr[i].ReturnAddress);
    }
}
```

Listing 11-8. *Sample module definition file for the same extension DLL*

```
LIBRARY    "DemoDbgExt"

EXPORTS
    WinDbgExtensionDllInit
    WinDbgExtensionDllShutdown
    ExtensionApiVersion
    demo
```

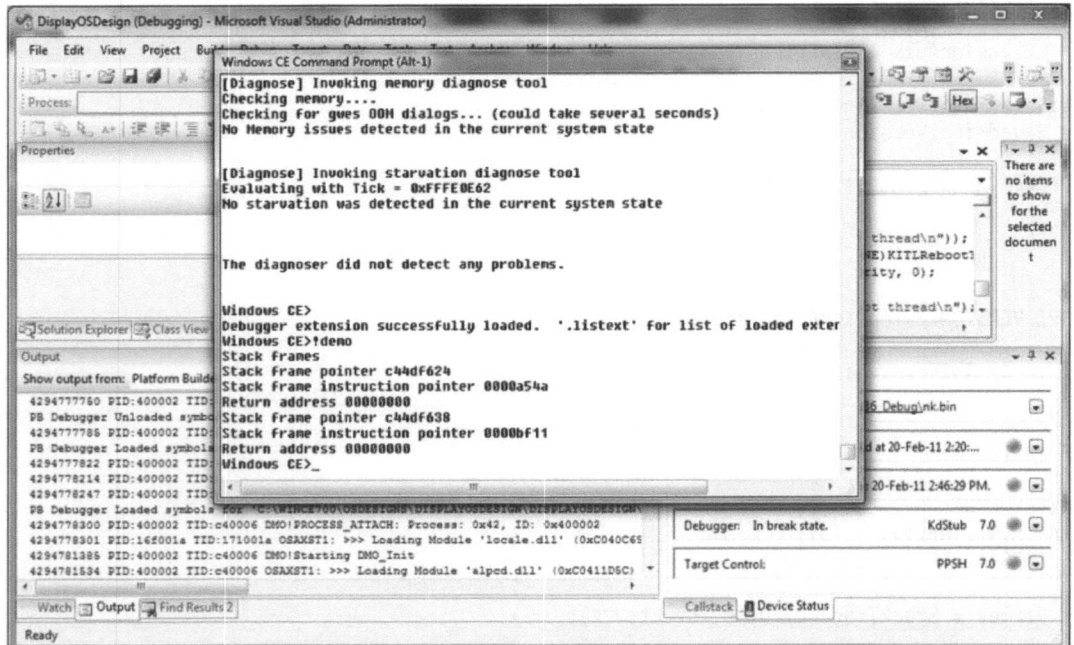

Figure 11-11. *Calling !demo extension command*

Remote Tools

The remote tools that are installed with Platform Builder 7 are based on the Remote Tools Framework which is a .NET Class Library (DLL). The interesting feature, apart from the remote tools that Microsoft provides with Platform Builder, is that you can use the framework to design and develop plug-ins and remote tools customized for your specific needs. This section is dedicated to how to use the Remote

Tools Framework to create a simple remote tool that displays all the active device drivers on the device. The Remote Tools Framework establishes communications with the device over the Core Connectivity infrastructure.

To create your own remote tool you can use Visual Studio 2008 Remote Tools Framework Plug-In Wizard that is located under <New Project\Other Languages\Visual C#\Remote Tools Framework> as you can see in Figure 11-12.

From there, if you select to create a managed device side remote tool it could not be easier. All you have to do is implement the device side tool's functionality and the display on the desktop's shell.

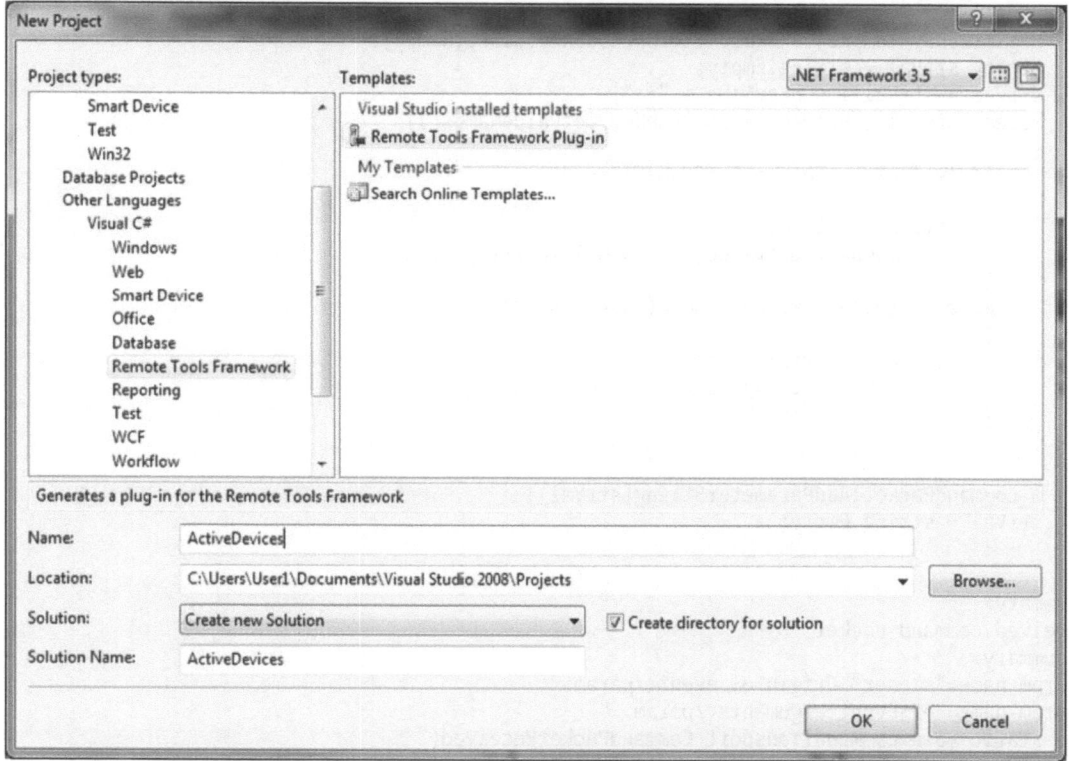

Figure 11-12. *Creating a new remote tool project*

The remote tool example here returns a list of all current active device drivers on the target device.

Device Side Implementation

The wizard created a file named sync.cs which contains a sample that retrieves the current time of the device and sends it back to the desktop. This means that there is very little infrastructure code to implement. Listing 11-9 demonstrates the code for a function, which implements the retrieving of the active device drivers, and using it to send back this information.

Listing 11-9. *Device side remote tool functionality example*

```
static private void DispatchActiveDrivers()
{
    RegistryKey rk = Registry.LocalMachine;
    RegistryKey rkDrvActv = rk.OpenSubKey("Drivers\\Active");

    uint nCount = (uint)rkDrvActv.SubKeyCount;
    m_commandPacket.AddParameterDWORD(nCount);
    foreach (string subKeyName in rkDrvActv.GetSubKeyNames())
    {
        RegistryKey tempKey = rkDrvActv.OpenSubKey(subKeyName);
        string strVal = string.Empty;
        strVal = strVal + subKeyName + "::";
        foreach (string valueName in tempKey.GetValueNames())
        {
            if (valueName.CompareTo("Name") == 0)
            {
                strVal = strVal + ";" +
                    tempKey.GetValue(valueName).ToString();
            }
            else if (valueName.CompareTo("Key") == 0)
            {
                strVal = strVal + ";" +
                    tempKey.GetValue(valueName).ToString();
            }
        }

        m_commandPacket.AddParameterString(strVal);
        strVal = string.Empty;
    }
}
/// <summary>
/// Received command packet
/// </summary>
/// <param name="sender">Origin of event</param>
/// <param name="e">Event arguments</param>
private static void CommandTransport_CommandPacketReceived(
    object sender,
    CommandPacketEventArgs e)
{
    // TODO: Add additional commands
    switch (e.CommandPacketIn.CommandId)
    {
        case 1:

            // The command packet does not come with any
            // parameters.
            m_commandPacket = new CommandPacket();
```

```
        m_commandPacket.CommandId = 1;
        DispatchActiveDrivers();
        e.CommandPacketOut = m_commandPacket;
        break;
    }
}
```

Desktop Remote Tool Plug-In Implementation

The wizard creates three classes: the plug-in class, the data class, and a view class. These classes have all the infrastructure code that is needed to communicate with the device. You need to implement just retrieving the data that has been sent back from the device, and you do this in the data class. Next you have to implement the code that will display the data the way you want in the view class. Listing 11-10 shows how to retrieve the data within the data class with the modified code in bold. Listing 11-11 shows how to implement the display of the data in the view class with the modified code in bold.

Listing 11-10. Retrieving data from the device and storing them in a string array

```
public class MyData : PluginData
{
    /// Array of strings to represent the data.
    private ArrayList strings;

    /// Constructor: Build the empty string array
    /// <param name="host">Plugin owning this data</param>
    /// <param name="guid">Guid of the node owning this data</param>
    public MyData(
        PluginComponent host,
        string guid)
        : base(host, guid)
    {
        this.InitDataAtViewTime = false;
        this.strings = new ArrayList();
    }

    /// Returns the array of strings representing the data
    public ArrayList Strings
    {
        get { return this.strings; }
        set { this.strings = value; }
    }

    /// Store data items coming in from the serializer
    /// <param name="description">Description of the data item</param>
    /// <param name="value">Value of the data item</param>
    protected override void OnAddVirtualDataItem(
        string description,
        string value)
    {
```

```csharp
        this.strings.Add(value);
    }

    /// Retrieve data from the device and store it in the data
    /// items.
    protected override void OnGetData()
    {
        CommandPacket sendCommand = new CommandPacket();

        // Populate the command object (command value of 1)
        sendCommand.CommandId = 1;

        // Process the command
        ProcessCommandExData pcexData = new
                    ProcessCommandExData(sendCommand, this);
        pcexData.CommandReceived += new
                    EventHandler(pcexData_CommandReceived);

        CommandTransport.ProcessCommandEx(pcexData);
    }

    /// Render this object's data items in a generic fashion.
    /// <param name="dataAcceptor">Data acceptor to render data
    /// items to
    protected override void OnRenderGeneric(
                            GenericDataAcceptor dataAcceptor)
    {
        string category = "My category";

        for (int index = 0; index < this.strings.Count; index++)
        {
            dataAcceptor.AddItem(
                category,
                "String #" + index.ToString(),
                this.strings[index].ToString());
        }
    }

    /// Retrieve data from the received command and update the UI
    /// <param name="sender">Origin of event</param>
    /// <param name="eventArgs">Event arguments</param>
    private void pcexData_CommandReceived(object sender,
                                    EventArgs eventArgs)
    {
        // The device side app builds and returns a packet
        // with a WORD, a DWORD, a string, and some bytes.
```

```
        // Take these values and convert to strings and place
        // in our array.
        ProcessCommandExData pcexData =
                            (ProcessCommandExData)sender;
        CommandPacket receivedCommand = pcexData.CommandOut;


        // Take the values from the device and put in a string
        // array
        UInt32 NumOfIter =
                    receivedCommand.GetParameterDWORD();

        try
        {
            for (int i = 0; i < NumOfIter; i++)
            {
                string sActive =
                    receivedCommand.GetParameterString();
                strings.Add(sActive);
            }
        }
        catch
        {
        }

        // By setting Initialized to true, the view panel(s)
        // hooked up to this data object will refresh.
        this.Initialized = true;

        // Unregister from the pcexData event handler so that the
        // object can be garbage collected
        pcexData.CommandReceived -= new
                EventHandler(pcexData_CommandReceived);
    }
}
```

Listing 11-11. Implementation of the view displaying the active device drivers

```
public class MyView : PluginDataView
{
    private ListView listView1;
    private ColumnHeader Handles;
    private ColumnHeader DName;
    private ColumnHeader Key;
    private ListView listView2;

    /// List of string data
    private ListBox listboxStrings;
```

```csharp
        /// Construct a view. This object is created on the primary
        /// UI thread.
        /// <param name="data">Plugin data object</param>
        public MyView(
            MyData data)
            : base(data)
        {
        }


        /// Initialize view controls
        /// This method is called right before the view is
        /// to be rendered for the first time. It is guaranteed
        /// to be running on the primary UI thread, so you do not
        /// need to Invoke.
        ///
        /// You may also use the designer to layout your controls. If
        /// you move the call to InitializeComponent() to this
        /// method, you can improve plugin load-time, as the child
        /// controls will not get created until they are needed.
        /// </remarks>
        protected override void OnBuildControls()
        {
            this.listboxStrings = new System.Windows.Forms.ListBox();
            this.listboxStrings.Dock =
System.Windows.Forms.DockStyle.Fill;
            this.Controls.Add(this.listboxStrings);
        }


        /// Fill in control data
        /// <param name="hint">Additional information for
        /// controls</param>
        /// This method is called on the primary UI thread whenever
        /// the Remote Tool Framework needs to refresh the view to
        /// reflect data changes. The hint parameter is set to null
        /// if the Remote Tools Framework generated this method call.
        /// The data objects can also call their RenderViews method,
        /// which will cause this method to be called on all views
        /// that are hooked up to the data. RenderViews can set the
        /// hint parameter to whatever you like.
        protected override void OnPopulateControls(object hint)
        {
            MyData data = (MyData)this.Data;

            this.listboxStrings.Items.Clear();

            for (int index = 0; index < data.Strings.Count; index++)
            {
                this.listboxStrings.Items.Add(data.Strings[index]);
            }
        }
```

```csharp
private void AddLine(string _strDesc)
{
    string strItem = string.Empty;
    int indx = _strDesc.IndexOf("|");
    string strTemp = _strDesc.Substring(0, indx);
    ListViewItem listItem = new ListViewItem(strTemp);
    int indx2 = _strDesc.LastIndexOf("|");
    int length = _strDesc.Length - indx2;
    strItem = _strDesc.Substring(indx + 2, 5);
    listItem.SubItems.Add(strItem);
    strItem = _strDesc.Substring(indx2 + 2);
    listItem.SubItems.Add(strItem);
    this.listView1.Items.Add(listItem);
}

private void InitializeComponent()
{
    this.listView1 =
                new System.Windows.Forms.ListView();
    this.Handles =
            new System.Windows.Forms.ColumnHeader();
    this.DName =
            new System.Windows.Forms.ColumnHeader();
    this.Key = new System.Windows.Forms.ColumnHeader();
    this.SuspendLayout();
    //
    // listView1
    //
    this.listView1.BackColor =
                System.Drawing.Color.FromArgb(((int)(((byte)(255)))), ↵
((int)(((byte)(255)))), ((int)(((byte)(128)))));
    this.listView1.Columns.AddRange(
            new System.Windows.Forms.ColumnHeader[] {
                                    this.Handles,
                                    this.DName,
                                    this.Key});
    this.listView1.Dock =
            System.Windows.Forms.DockStyle.Fill;
    this.listView1.Location =
                new System.Drawing.Point(0, 0);
    this.listView1.Name = "listView1";
    this.listView1.Size =
                new System.Drawing.Size(262, 196);
    this.listView1.TabIndex = 1;
    this.listView1.UseCompatibleStateImageBehavior =
                                    false;
    this.listView1.View =
                System.Windows.Forms.View.Details;
    //
    // Handles
    //
```

```
        this.Handles.Text = "Handle";
        //
        // DName
        //
        this.DName.Text = "Driver Name";
        //
        // Key
        //
        this.Key.Text = "Key";
        this.Key.Width = 180;
        //
        // MyView
        //
        this.Controls.Add(this.listView1);
        this.Name = "MyView";
        this.Size = new System.Drawing.Size(262, 196);
        this.ResumeLayout(false);

    }
}
```

After you build the project the result is located in a directory <project>\ Bundle\Release and named in this case ActiveDrivers.cetool. Double-clicking on it will open the remote framework shell as seen in Figure 11-13. And when connected to the device it downloads and launches the device side tool and retrives the results as seen in Figure 11-14.

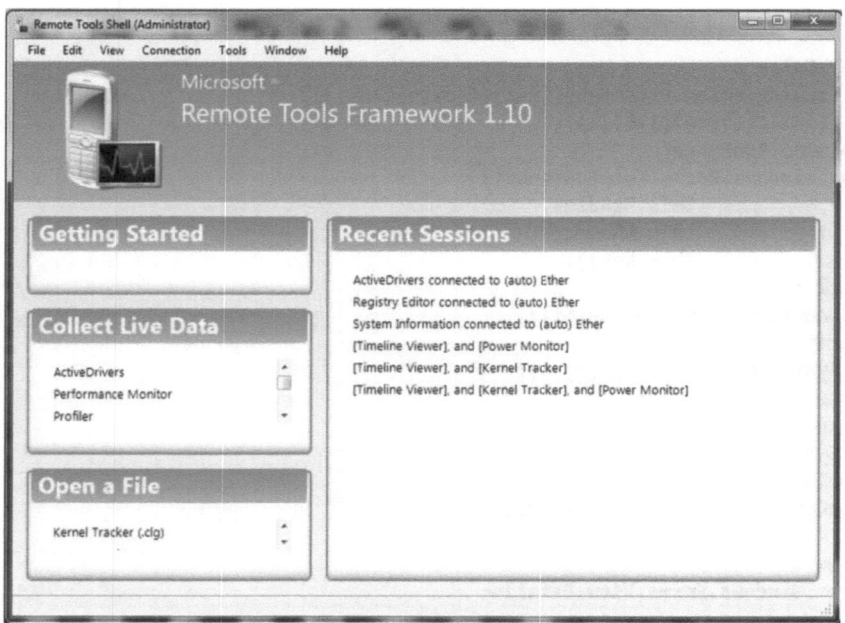

Figure 11-13. Remote Tool Shell

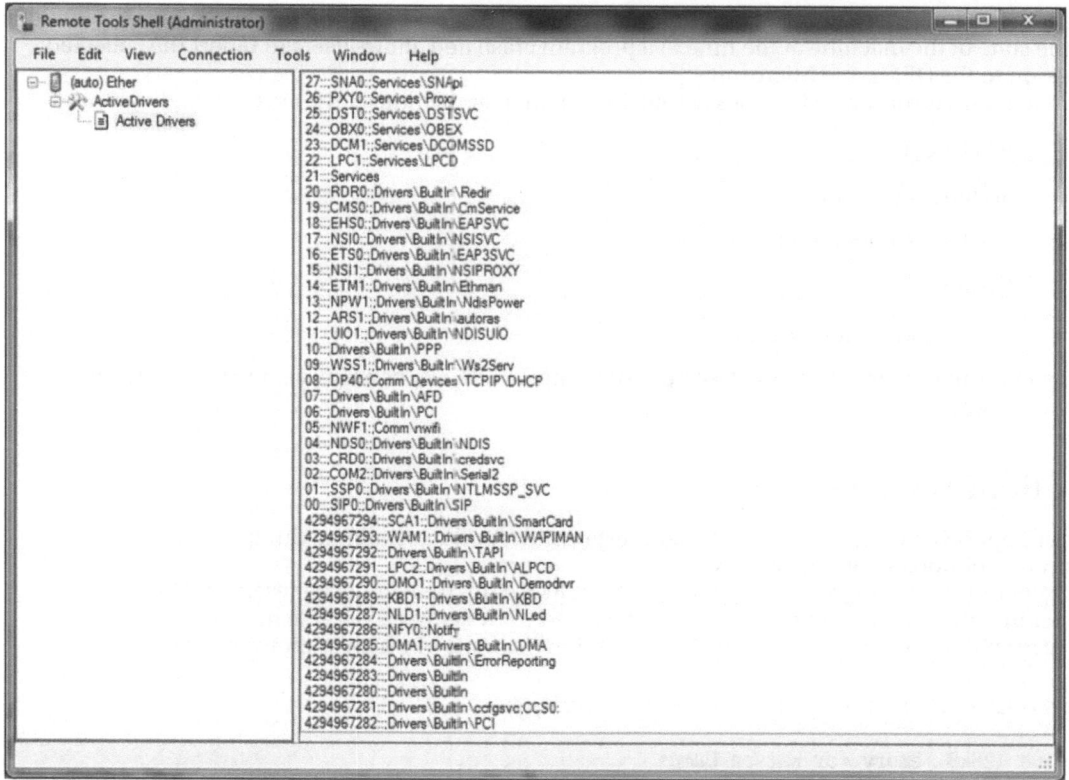

Figure 11-14. *Active device driverslist on the connected device*

■ **Implementation Note**   While it is possible to develop native device side remote tool, the Visual Studio 2008 wizard that creates the remote tool project is restricted to outdated SDKs. Therefore you will have to tweak the device side projects properties to be able to build the executable. Note that you will have to add the rtfhlp10.lib appropriate to the device's processor which is located under <installation disk>\Program Files (x86)\Microsoft Remote Framework Tools\1.10\lib\wce700. Note also that this path is on a 64-bit desktop.

Postmortem Debugging and Dr. Watson

Human beings aren't perfect, nor are their products. Device driver developers are no exception. The development cycle goes from designing the hardware and software that is the device driver, on to implementing, debugging, and testing. Once the cycle is completed the product is out of the door and is being used. Nevertheless from time to time unforeseen problems occur. To solve these problems intelligently, postmortem diagnosing and debugging methods have been developed.

Windows Embedded Compact provides for this purpose a set of tools that captures key information about the state of the machine at the time of a program crash and allows users to report the collected information to the OEMs and Microsoft.

The standard error report includes helpful information at the time of the crash, including:

- Stack details

- System information

- A list of loaded modules

- Exception type

- Global and local variables

Crash information is compressed into a CAB file and, with user consent, sent to the Microsoft Watson web site.

Error Report Generator

The Error Report Generator is the component responsible for the creation of dump files using the configuration options set in the registry.

To generate an error report dump file, at least 128KB of memory must be reserved. The OAL developer initializes the size of the memory to be reserved by setting a variable named *dwNKDrWatsonSize*. This is done in the *OEMInit* function a sample of which is shown in Listing 11-12.

Listing 11-12. *Initializing memory for error report dump file*

```
// Reserve 128kB memory for Watson Dumps
dwNKDrWatsonSize = 0;
if (dwOEMDrWatsonSize != DR_WATSON_SIZE_NOT_FIXEDUP)
{
    dwNKDrWatsonSize = dwOEMDrWatsonSize;
}
```

The kernel will use this size to reserve a block of memory at the end of the main memory. The Sysgen variable SYSGEN_WATSON_DMPGEN must be set to include the Error Report Generator in the image. The [HKLM\System\ErrorReporting\DumpSettings] registry key holds the registry values for error report generation. Listing 11-13 is a sample of such registry setting.

Listing 11-13. *Registry settings for error reporting for a specific OS design*

```
;--------------------------- start WATSON ----------------------
;
; @CESYSGEN IF WCESHELLFE_MODULES_DWXFER
;
[HKEY_LOCAL_MACHINE\Drivers\BuiltIn\ErrorReporting]
    "Dll"="DwXfer.dll"
    "FriendlyName" = "Dump File Transfer"
    "PollInterval"=dword:493E0
; @CESYSGEN IF WCESHELLFE_MODULES_DDXPROBE
; @CESYSGEN ELSE
```

```
    "PollPriority256"=dword:F9
; @CESYSGEN ENDIF WCESHELLFE_MODULES_DDXPROBE
    "Index"=dword:1
    "Order"=dword:0
    "Flags"=dword:2

[HKEY_LOCAL_MACHINE\System\ErrorReporting\DumpSettings]
    "DumpDirectory"="\\Windows\\DumpFiles"
    "ExtraFilesDirectory"="\\Windows\\ExtraDumpFiles"
    "CabDirectory"="\\Windows\\DumpFiles\\CabFiles"
    "UploadClient"="\\Windows\\Dw.exe'
    "MaxDiskUsage"=dword:80000
    "DumpEnabled"= dword:1
    "DumpType"= dword:2
;
; @CESYSGEN ENDIF WCESHELLFE_MODULES_DWXFER
; @CESYSGEN IF WCESHELLFE_MODULES_DDXPROBE
; @CESYSGEN ELSE
[HKEY_LOCAL_MACHINE\System\ErrorReporting\DDxSettings]
    "DDxEnabled"=dword:0
;
; @CESYSGEN ENDIF WCESHELLFE_MODULES_DDXPROBE
;
;------------------------- end WATSON ----------------------
```

The Error Report Transfer Driver transfers registry setting values to the aforementioned reserved memory. The Error Report Generator then retrieves these settings from memory, in order to generate the appropriate dump file. These inform the Error Report Generator where to generate the dump file and what type of dump to create; in this case it's the system dump, and the maximum disk size to use is four times the size of the reserved memory.

While developing an OS design, the developer sets the type of crash dump to be generated, note the value for DumpType key in the registry settings in Listing 11-10. Each type of dump follows the same file format, three of which can be generated:

- Context dumps, 4 KB to 64 KB

  - Information about the crashing system

  - The exception that initiated the crash

  - The context record of the faulting thread

  - A module list, limited to the faulting threads of the owner process

  - A thread list, limited to the faulting threads of the owner process

  - The call stack of the faulting thread

  - 64 bytes of memory above and below the instruction pointer of the faulting thread

  - Stack memory dump of the faulting thread, truncated to fit a 64 KB limit

- System dumps, 64 KB—several MB

  - All information in a Context dump

  - Calls tacks and context records for all threads

  - Complete module, process, and thread lists for the entire device

  - 2048 bytes of memory above and below the instruction pointer of the faulting thread

  - Global variables for the process that was current at the time of the crash

- Complete dumps, including all physical memory plus at least 64 KB

  - All information in a context dump

  - A complete dump of all used memory

Error Report Transfer Driver

The Error Report Transfer Driver moves the registry values (needed by the Error Report Generator) from the registry to the reserved memory block, and moves the generated files from reserved memory into persistent files.

After transferring a dump file to persistent storage, the Error Report Transfer Driver launches the Report Upload Client specified in the registry.

The Sysgen variable "`SYSGEN_WATSON_XFER`" must be set to include the Error Report Transfer Driver in the image. The [`HKLM\Drivers\BuiltIn\ErrorReporting`] registry key holds the registry values for Error Report Transfer Driver. Listing 11-10 shows a sample of such a registry setting, in which the time interval for transfer polling is set to 5 minutes and the poll priority is set to 249.

Error Report Control Panel

The Error Reporting Control Panel allows the user of a display-based device to configure options for dump file generation by way of a Control Panel applet. The options available to the user are:

- Enable/disable error reporting—on a display-based device, error reporting is enabled by default. On a headless device, error reporting is disabled by default.

- Control the amount of storage space allocated for dump files—the control panel dialog box contains a set of radio buttons that allow the user to select the amount of storage space for storing dump files, as can be seen in Figure 11-15.

- Enable user notification dialogs

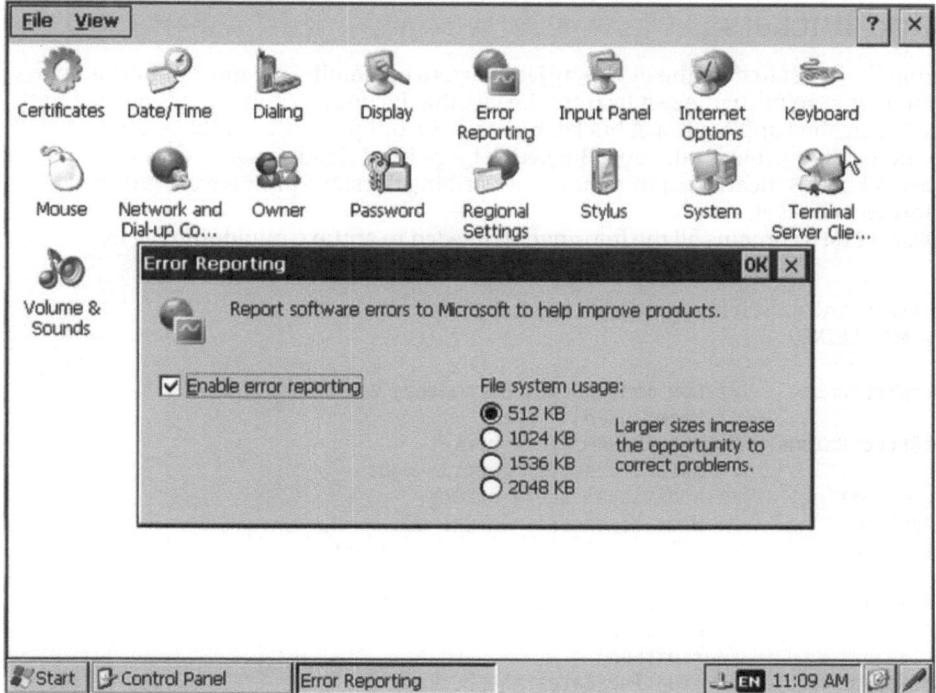

Figure 11-15. *Display based device's error reporting control panel applet*

The Sysgen variable "SYSGEN_WATSON_CTLPNL" must be set to include the Error Reporting Control Panel in the image. The registry settings contained in the [HKLM\System\ErrorReporting\DumpSettings] registry key and in the [HKLM\System\ErrorReporting\UploadSettings] registry key are used by the Error Reporting Control Panel to set the initial values in the control panel dialog.

Report Upload Client

The upload client is responsible for uploading the generated and created dump file to the watson.microsoft.com error reporting web site. It is, however, possible to upload this file to another web site—but that involves code changes, for example to the function FValidBucketResponseURL, so it validates a different website than the above mentioned and implemented in (_PUBLICROOT)\WCESHELLFE\OAK\WATSON\DWUI\ DWUIDLGS.CPP.

Another file you want to look at is (_PUBLICROOT)\COMMON\OAK\INC\DWPUBLIC.H. Here, you can define a valid response server (VALID_RESPONSE_SERVER) for your server, and, of course, you need to create an upload website capable getting bucket parameters, grouping minidumps into buckets, and responding to the upload client. While all this is possible, it might not be worth the trouble.

Minidumps and Buckets

A minidump is a dump file generated on the device by Dr. Watson, containing the most important parts of a crashed application. It's "mini" name results from the fact that it contains only what is needed to identify and analyze the crashed application. A bucket represents a unique bug or problem and identifies the component responsible for the bug. Bucketing helps the upload server to organize uploaded minidumps. All of this means that minidumps describing the same problem are grouped together in what is termed a bucket.

The structure DMPFILEINFO contains all the information needed to group a minidump file in a bucket:

```
// Structure to contain information regarding the dump file
typedef struct tagDMPFILEINFO
{
    WORD        wBucketParams;      // how many bucket parameters are
                                    // being used
    LPWSTR      rgwzBucketParams[MAX_BUCKETPARAMS]; // bucket
                                    // parameters for  generic mode
    LPWSTR      pwzQueryString;     // additional query string
    LPWSTR      pwzAppName;         // Name to display in the UI.
    LPWSTR      pwzFilesToKeep;     // files to include in log but not
                                    // delete
    LPWSTR      pwzFilesToDelete;   // files to include in log but
                                    // delete when
                                    // finished
    BOOL        fGenericParams;     // True indicates the bucket
                                    // parameters are
                                    // generic parameters
} DMPFILEINFO, *PDMPFILEINFO;
```

Chapter Summary

The debugging process is the lengthiest and maybe even the most important facet of the development cycle of a device driver as is of any piece of software. Platform Builder provides an array of tools that are invaluable to the debugging process. Nevertheless all these debugging tools are software tools. From kernel debugger and target control that is also host to calling debug extensions. Platform Builder provides a comprehensive debugging extension DLL named CeDebugX to help diagnose problems efficiently.

Sometimes, however, software debugging tools are not enough, especially when hardware is related to the debugged software. This calls for hardware assisted debugging that in modern processors is supported on chip. Tools like the TRACE32 ICD from Lauterbach provide an interface and an IDE to assist the developer. It provides on chip information and real-time trace capabilities.

CHAPTER 12

Using CTK to Develop Test Code

Testing is the final phase of the development cycle before being able to release any product, software or hardware. The aim of testing is to assure the finished product is of the highest quality. Quality software products are a must in the twenty-first century when reliance on high-quality software has bearing on almost any facet in our lives. Developers seem to sneer at this process and QA people are often regarded as second rate to the designers and coders. However the ISO standards of software development force software vendors and OEMs to take notice and enforce strict testing for quality assurance.

In this chapter

- Windows Embedded Compact Test Kit
- Designing tests
- TUX Test harness
- Viewing results
- Performance testing

Windows Embedded Compact Test Kit

The Windows Embedded Compact Test Kit provided with Platform Builder 7 enables developers and quality assurance engineers to test for failure the functionality and performance of device drivers and related hardware for a Windows Embedded Compact device. The features provided by the CTK offer feedback on the failure or success of functionality of tested device drivers, and provide verification of BSPs.

Overview

The Windows Embedded Compact Test Kit provides considerable improvements to the user interface and the overall feature set compared to the previous tool known as Windows Embedded CE Test Kit (CETK). CTK is a new application with the following major features:

- Improved user interface

- Ability to group user-selected test cases into test passes

- Improved test results viewer lets you store and review test results per test pass

- Upon connection to a device, detection of peripherals and drivers needed for tests

- Integration with the new Graph Tool to graph performance test results

- Users can add custom Tux test harness (TUX)-based tests to the CTK

- Support for x86, MIPSII, MIPSII_FP, ARMv5, ARMv6, ARMv7 processors

User Interface

The graphical user interface is reminiscent of the Visual Studio GUI. It has a Start Page tab for rudimentary getting started options. On the upper right is the Test Case Explorer window containing three tabs:

- The **Test Case Explorer tab** displays the master test catalog in a tree view. It contains the Windows Embedded test catalog by default. You can add your own custom test case. Other catalogs may be added in the future.

- The **Test Pass Template View tab** displays the user-created and built-in test pass templates.

- The **Connection View tab** displays the device the CTK is connected to.

The **Properties** window on the lower right is similar to the Properties windows in Visual Studio. It displays the properties of the currently selected test case, test pass, template, or connection. The **Connection Output** window on the lower left displays debug messages from the CTK and from a test case as it runs. Figure 12-1 shows CTK open without connection.

Otherwise the menus and toolbar are in the tradition of Windows GUI application. They are straight forward and easy to manipulate, with tooltips showing what the toolbar buttons signify.

The Windows Embedded CTK introduces the concept of a **test pass** as a collection of tests which is executed on a device and whose results can be viewed and saved. The tests in a test pass can be run all together in one pass or run selectively.

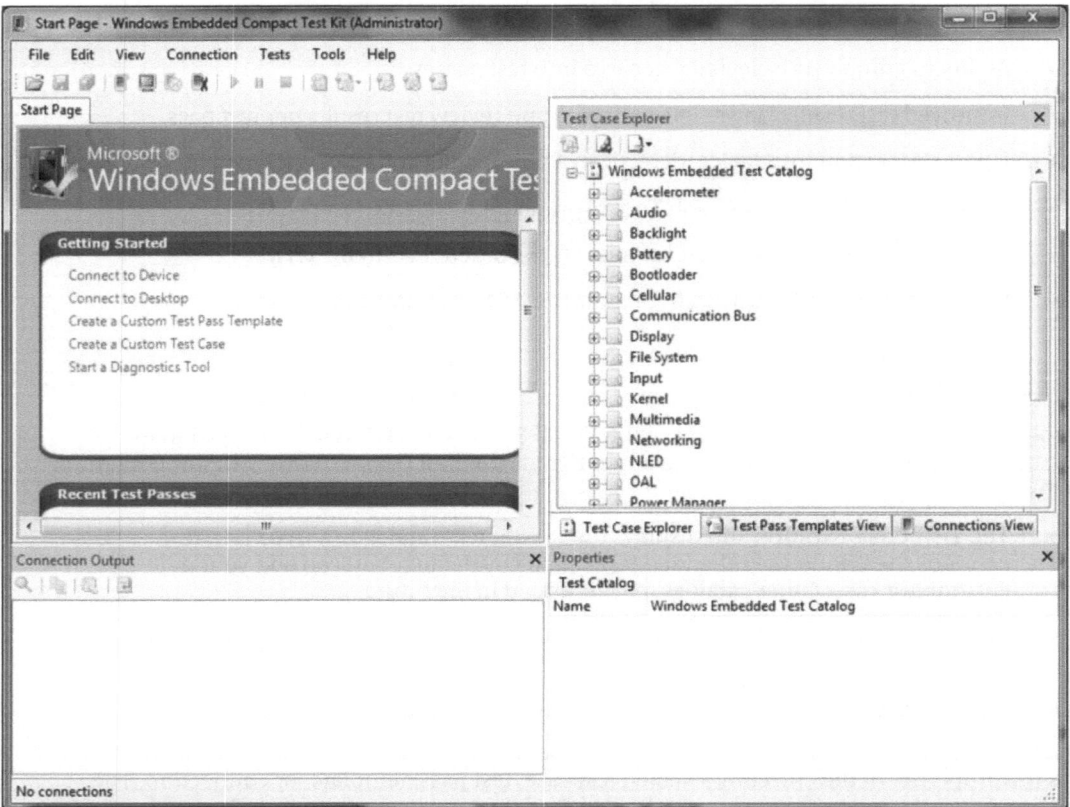

Figure 12-1. CTK GUI

The terminology used by CTK.

TestCatalog - A collection of tests associated with a particular product

TestCategory - A logical grouping of tests inside a TestCatalog, most often based on a particular technology area

TestCase - A test that is executed for a pass/fail result on a device/desktop

TestCaseRun - An instance of a test case being executed on a device/desktop

TestPass - A collection of tests which is executed on a device and whose results can be viewed and saved

TestPassTemplate - A collection of tests which serve as a template for creating a TestPass that is executed on a device

Creating a Test Pass

Before you create a test pass, you must create a template on which to base your test pass. This section explains how to create a test pass template and how to create a test pass from this template.

Creating a Test Pass Template

The easiest way to launch the Test Manager is clicking the "Create a Custom Test Pass Template" option on the start page. The Test Manager is the tool to manage the creation, editing, and removal of test cases. Figure 12-2 shows the Test Manager dialog box and a new template ready to be named.

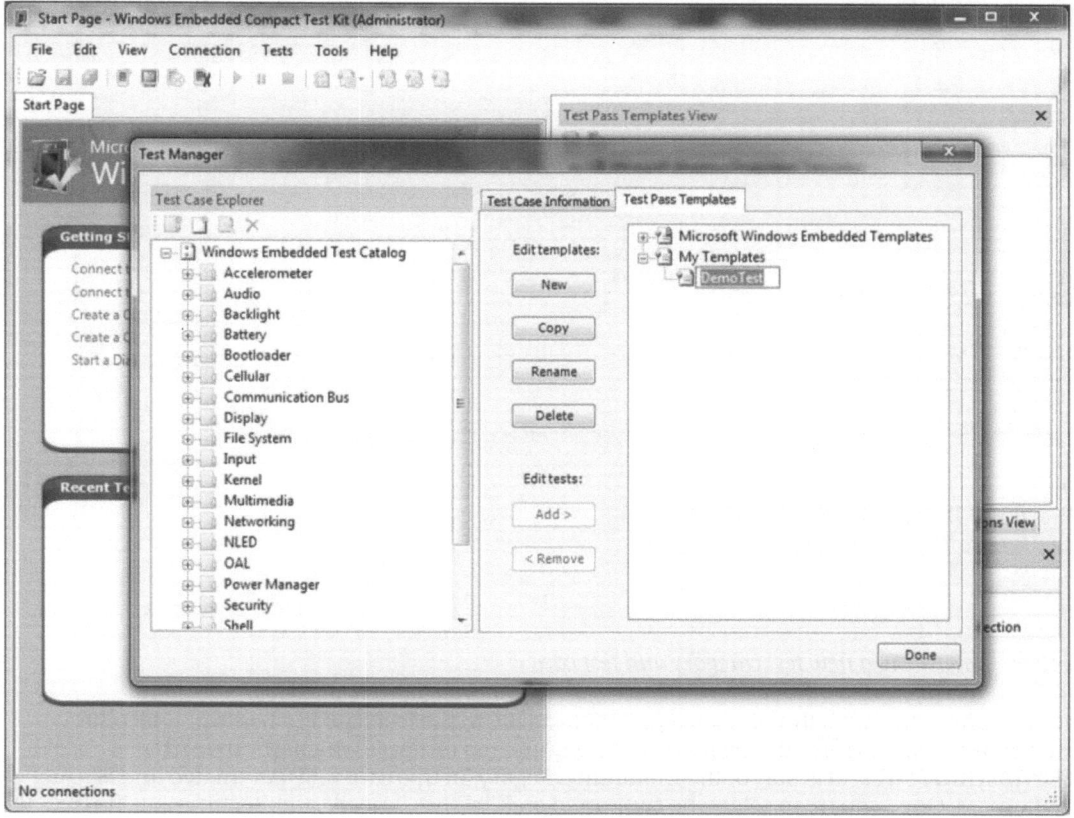

Figure 12-2. Test Manager after the "New" button was clicked

Creating a Test Case

Creating a test case is relating a TUX test DLL that you develop to test your device driver. To bind the test case to a test pass you have to bind this test case to the test pass template you have created. Using the test pass template "DemoTest" just created, select it and switch to the "Test Case Information" tab. Create a new category in the "Windows Embedded Test Catalog." In this example I kept on the Demo theme and named it DemoCat. In the "Test Case Information" tab click on the "New" button and setup the new test case. Figure 12-3 is indicative of this process.

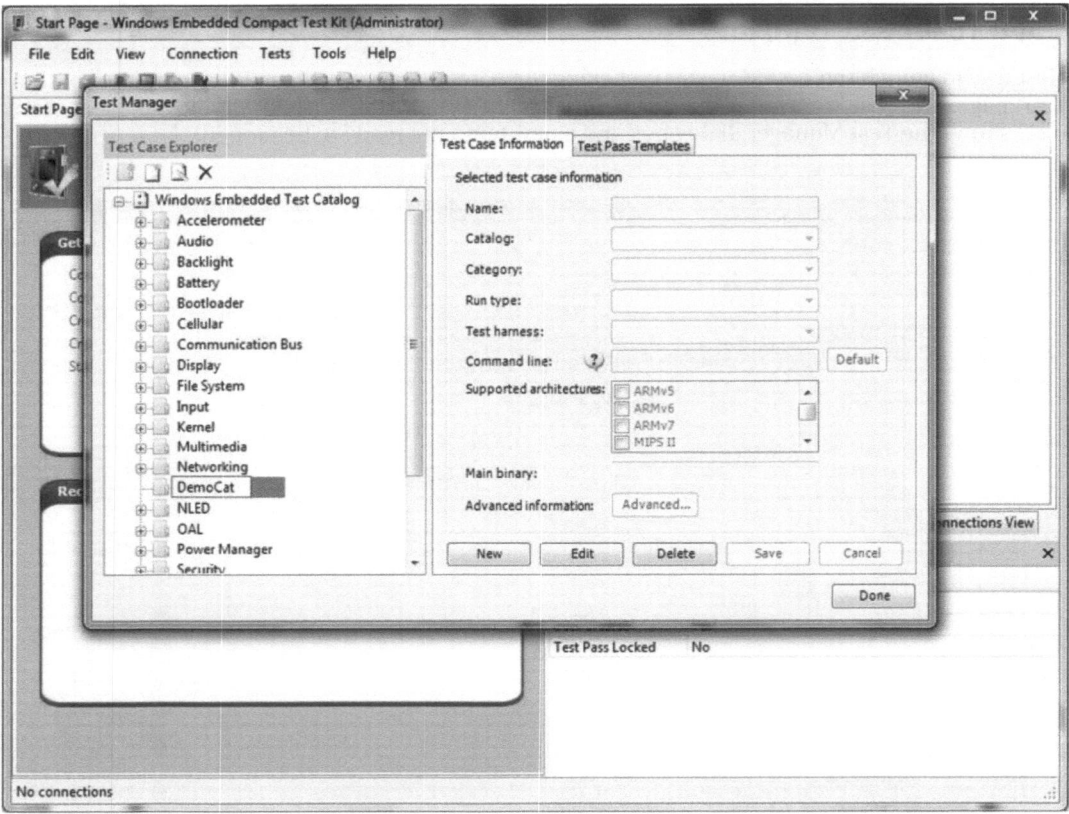

Figure 12-3. *Generating a new test category and test case*

The step where you actually connect your TUX test DLL to the test case is when you select the supported architecture. Figure 12-4 displays the newly created test case which was named "DemoDrvrAsynIOTest" and is part of the DemoCat category, in this case fully automated and is using TUX test harness. Once you try to select the supported architecture it needs architecture specific files. In this case it is a x86 architecture based device, so note that the main binary is the TUX test DLL Demodrvrtest.dll which is located in:

`WINCEROOT\OSDesigns\DemoOSDesign\DemoOSDesign\RelDir\DemoBSP_x86_Debug`

Of course if you are going to develop a CPU agnostic device driver that you'd locate under the PUBLIC tree, you would create a specific folder hierarchy that would hold a set of CPU dependent TUX test DLLs under CPU specific folders and reference these DLLs for each CPU architecture that you test.

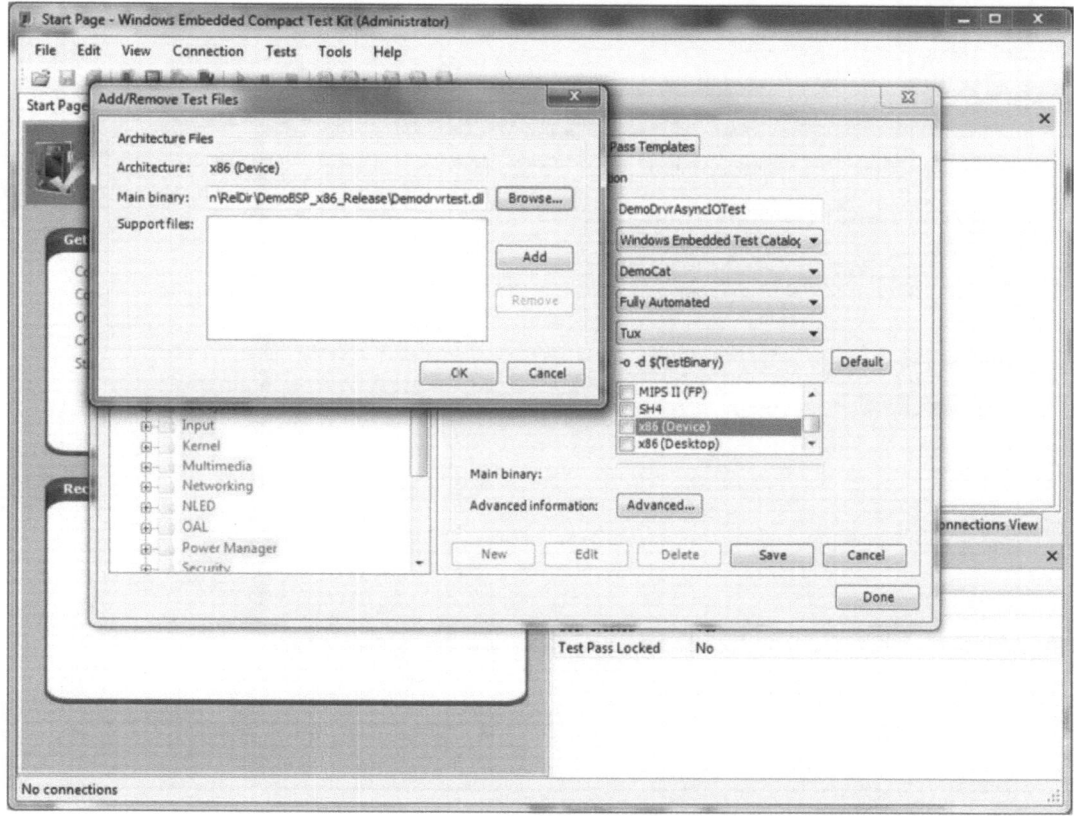

Figure 12-4. *Creating a new test case and linking the architecture specific TUX test DLL files*

Creating a Test Pass from a Template

At this juncture you have a new test "DemoDrvrAsynIOTest" that is contained in the new test category "DemoCat". This allows you to give meaning to the test pass template "DemoTest". Switch back to the "Test Pass Template" tab and add (selecting the test case and clicking the "Add" button) the newly created test case to the "DemoTest" pass template. You can actually use this procedure to add as many test cases form the Test Case Explorer as you wish for a test pass.

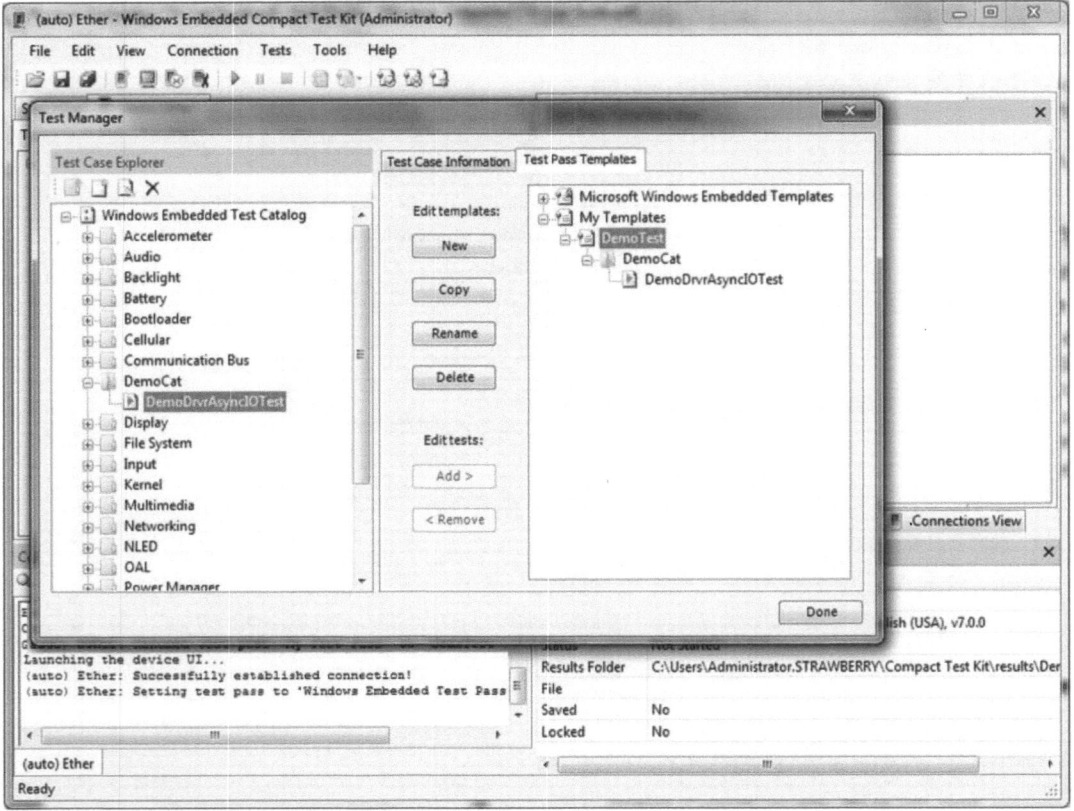

***Figure 12-5.** Adding a test case to a test pass*

So why go to all that trouble of creating a test pass template? Basically to manage your testing sessions for efficiency, time, and size of log files. In the described example the testing is confined to just the asynchronous IO support of the device driver. This demonstrated that you can create a test pass for just a single device driver. This allowed to cut the time of testing instead of going through all tests in the catalog and most importantly manageable size log files as you can see in Listing 12-2. In Figure 12-6 you can observe a test pass display of just the "DemoTest" pass.

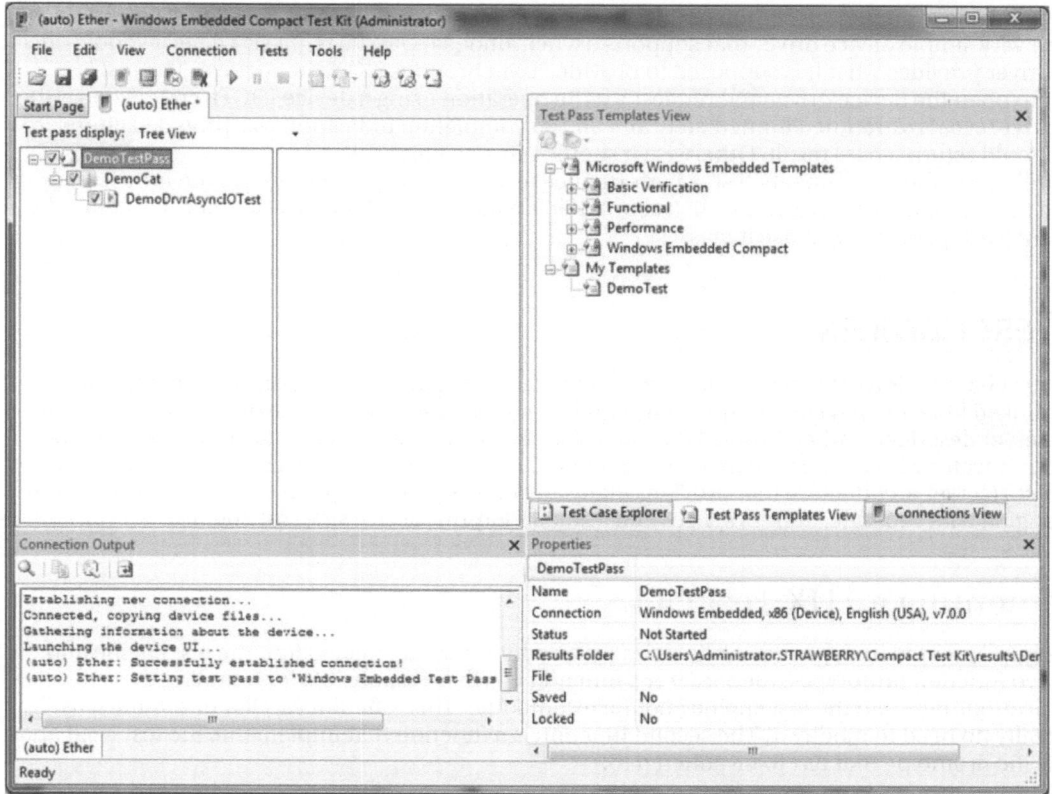

Figure 12-6. Running the DemoTest pass

Designing Test

Designing tests sounds a bit pompous, but it is way simpler than it sounds. The purpose of testing a device driver is to make sure that it is robust and does not fail when erroneous input comes its way. Since it is impossible to test for every possible input, there is a need to identify the most vulnerable areas in the object of the test and provide testing procedures to best evaluate its vulnerability.

Quality assurance and testing have a defined set of metrics that need to be measured. These metrics need to be qualified to pass the tests. Device drivers for embedded devices need a relatively small set of quality metrics because embedded devices, unlike general purpose computers and device drivers for embedded devices in particular, do not need testing for such cases as install ability, availability, and documentation. What embedded device drivers need to be tested for is reliability and performance.

Both reliability and performance are derived from the functionality of the device driver. Before testing a device driver you need to be absolutely clear of the device driver's functionality. The design requirements for the device driver are a good place to start.

So what are quality metrics? Let's define a metric first. A metric is a verifiable measure stated in either quantitative or qualitative terms. It captures performance in terms of how something is being done relative to a standard.

The following example will demonstrate in a very simplified manner what this all means. For this example a very simple device driver that supports asynchronous I/O write request. The test should check that the driver provides what it is supposed to provide, asynchronous I/O write request. The test is designed to open the device driver and request a write operation using a device IOCTL code. Then if the call to **DeviceIoControl** retuned immediately and an I/O completion indication was provided afterwards the test should return a pass result. Otherwise it should return a fail result.

In addition to the functionality test, a performance test is added and it compares the time it takes to complete the I/O request to a reference tick count. If it is equal or less than the reference tick count the performance test passes; otherwise it fails.

TUX Test Harness

The TUX test harness is a device-side client executable that loads device-side tests implemented as dynamic linked libraries and can perform tests either in standalone mode on the device or triggered by the CTK server described earlier. Tux.exe is an architecture-related device-side executable test engine that communicates with the development workstation CTK test server via core connectivity. This is a typical client/server architecture that provides many advantages, including the separation of GUI from the test engine with separate address spaces and a small footprint device side test engine.

Implementing a TUX Test DLL

Tests are implemented in dynamic link libraries test modules that are loaded into the test engine and provide two function prototypes, the *ShellProc* function which is responsible for handling the communications between the test engine and the test module. This function was left unmodified as there is really no need to modify it. The second function is a function that implements the test itself and has a specific prototype that has to be adhered to:

```
TESTPROCAPI TestProc(UINT uMsg, TPPARAM tpParam, LPFUNCTION_TABLE_ENTRY lpFTE)
```

You can implement as many test functions in a module as you designed for. Platform Builder provides an application wizard to create a skeleton TUX test DLL implementation that can be regarded as a jumpstart implementation for your test module. The Device Driver Wizard provides a similar capability but it renames the module name and customizes the initial TUX function table. Figure 12-7 shows the Device Driver Wizard's CTK support panel.

The implementation of a test is really an implementation that you would develop for an application that opens the device driver and requests the driver to perform an action. The example in Listing 12-1 does just this. The device driver being tested provides support for asynchronous write request just like in the example in Chapter 7. The test function code is very similar to the example demonstration application that was described in Chapter 7. The **TestProc** function simply calls another function that implements the test code and returns a Boolean indicating success or failure and logs results using Kato and returns test status to CTK.

Listing 12-1. *Implementation of a test procedure (test.cpp)*

```
#include "main.h"
#include "globals.h"
#include "..\SDK\DemodrvrSDK.h"
```

```
HANDLE g_hDevice;
#define WRITE_TEST_STRING_SIZE 65536
TCHAR szBuf[WRITE_TEST_STRING_SIZE];

BOOL TestAsynchWrite()
{
    BOOL bRc = FALSE;
    DEVMGR_DEVICE_INFORMATION ddiDemo;
    TCHAR strDrvrName[5] = {'D', 'M', 'O', '*', 0};
    volatile OVERLAPPED ovlpd;
    HANDLE hCompltEvent = NULL;
    DWORD dwWaitRet = WAIT_FAILED, dwBytes = 0;

    memset(&ddiDemo, 0, sizeof(DEVMGR_DEVICE_INFORMATION));
    ddiDemo.dwSize = sizeof(DEVMGR_DEVICE_INFORMATION);

    g_hDevice = FindFirstDevice(DeviceSearchByLegacyName,
                                &strDrvrName, &ddiDemo);
    if (g_hDevice == INVALID_HANDLE_VALUE)
    {
        return bRc;
    }
    else
    {
        g_hDevice = CreateFile(L"DMO1:", 0, 0, NULL, 0, 0, NULL);
        if (g_hDevice == INVALID_HANDLE_VALUE)
        {
            return bRc;
        }
        bRc = TRUE;
    }
    // Create a completion event for IOControl IO operation
    ovlpd.hEvent = CreateEvent(NULL, TRUE, FALSE, NULL);
    if (!ovlpd.hEvent)
    {
        return FALSE;
    }
    for (int i = 0; i <  WRITE_TEST_STRING_SIZE; i++)
    {
        szBuf[i] = i;
    }

    memset((void*)&ovlpd, 0, sizeof(ovlpd));

    bRc = DeviceIoControl(g_hDevice,IOCTL_DEMODRVR_ASYNC_WRITE,
                          szBuf, WRITE_TEST_STRING_SIZE, NULL,
                          0,NULL,(LPOVERLAPPED)&ovlpd);
    while (!bRc)        // I/O is not done yet
    {
        bRc = GetOverlappedResult(g_hDevice,
                                  (LPOVERLAPPED)&ovlpd,
                                  &dwBytes, FALSE);
```

```
    }
    CloseHandle(ovlpd.hEvent);
    CloseHandle(g_hDevice);
    return bRc;
}

//////////////////////////////////////////////////////////////////////
// TestProc
//  Executes one test.
//
// Parameters:
// uMsg             Message code.
// tpParam          Additional message-dependent data.
// lpFTE            Function table entry that generated this call.
//
// Return value:
// TPR_PASS if the test passed, TPR_FAIL if the test fails, or possibly
// other special conditions.

TESTPROCAPI TestProc(UINT uMsg, TPPARAM tpParam,
                     LPFUNCTION_TABLE_ENTRY lpFTE)
{
    INT TP_Status = TPR_FAIL;

    // The shell doesn't necessarily want us to execute the test.
    // Make sure first.
    if(uMsg != TPM_EXECUTE)
    {
        return TPR_NOT_HANDLED;
    }

    // TODO: Replace the following line with your own test code
    // here. Also,change the return value from TPR_SKIP to the
    // appropriate code.

    if(TestAsynchWrite())
    {
        TP_Status = TPR_PASS;
        g_pKato->Log(LOG_COMMENT, TEXT("This test passed."));
    }
    else
    {
        g_pKato->Log(LOG_COMMENT, TEXT("This test failed."));
    }

    return TP_Status;
}

//////////////////////////////////////////////////////////////////////
```

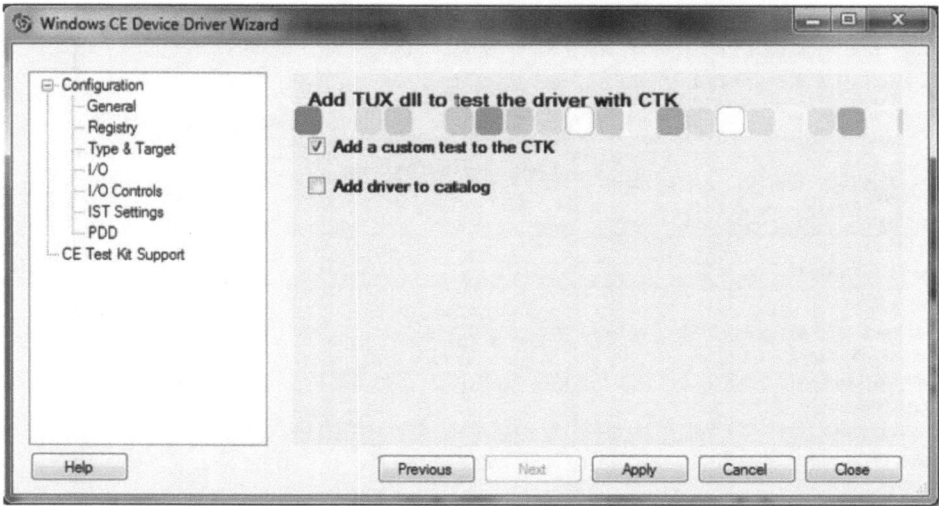

Figure 12-7. Adding a skeleton TUX test module to the device driver directory hierarchy

Running the Test

Once a TUX test DLL is developed and the various test procedures have been implemented to perform designed tests you can run the TUX device side console application, and use the command line to load test DLLs and run tests in a standalone fashion or run CTK server on the development workstation to trigger the tests. In Figure 12-8 we use the test pass template as our default test pass simply run the specific test.

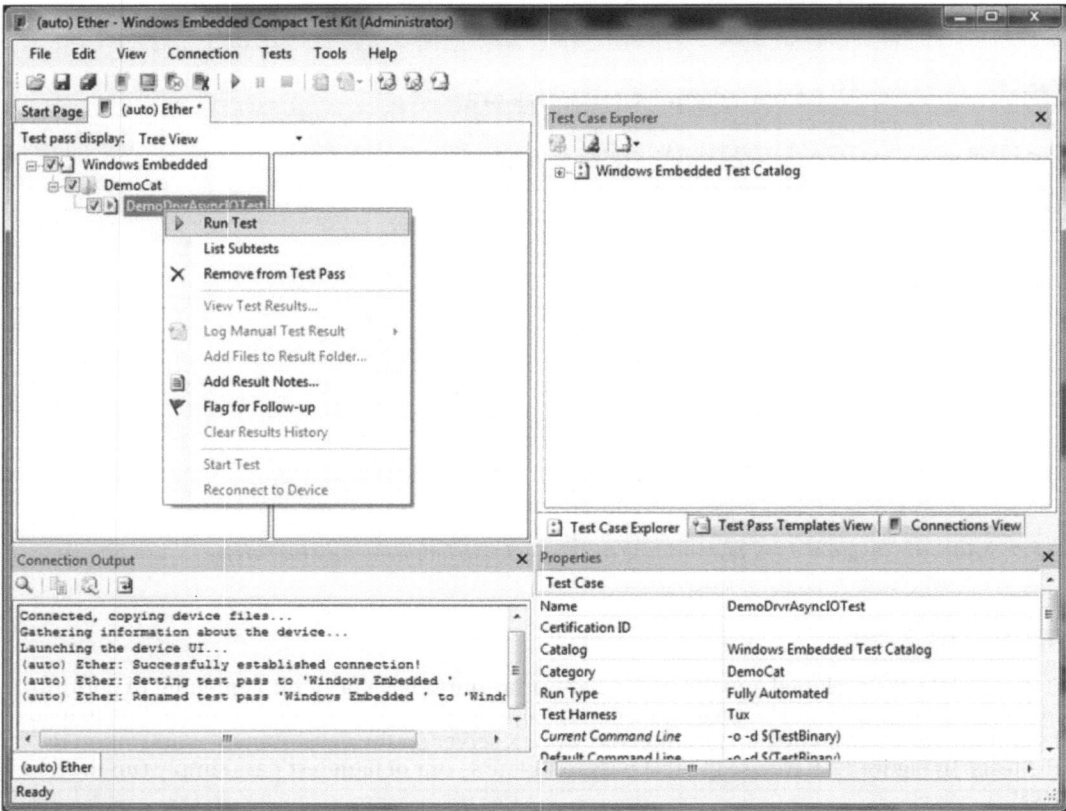

Figure 12-8. *Running a test from the Windows Embedded Compact Test Kit*

Once the request to run a test has been issued TUX loads the Demodrvrtest.dll module runs the **ShellProc** function which registers the test procedure with TUX so it can be run. Just a reminder, that more than one test procedure can be implemented in a test DLL. Once the test is run a log file is written and can be accessed using the results tab on the left as is described in Figure 12-10. Double-clicking on a log file icon will open this file in notepad. When the test has completed it will show a concise results output in the connection output on the lower left corner as you can see in Figure| 12-9.

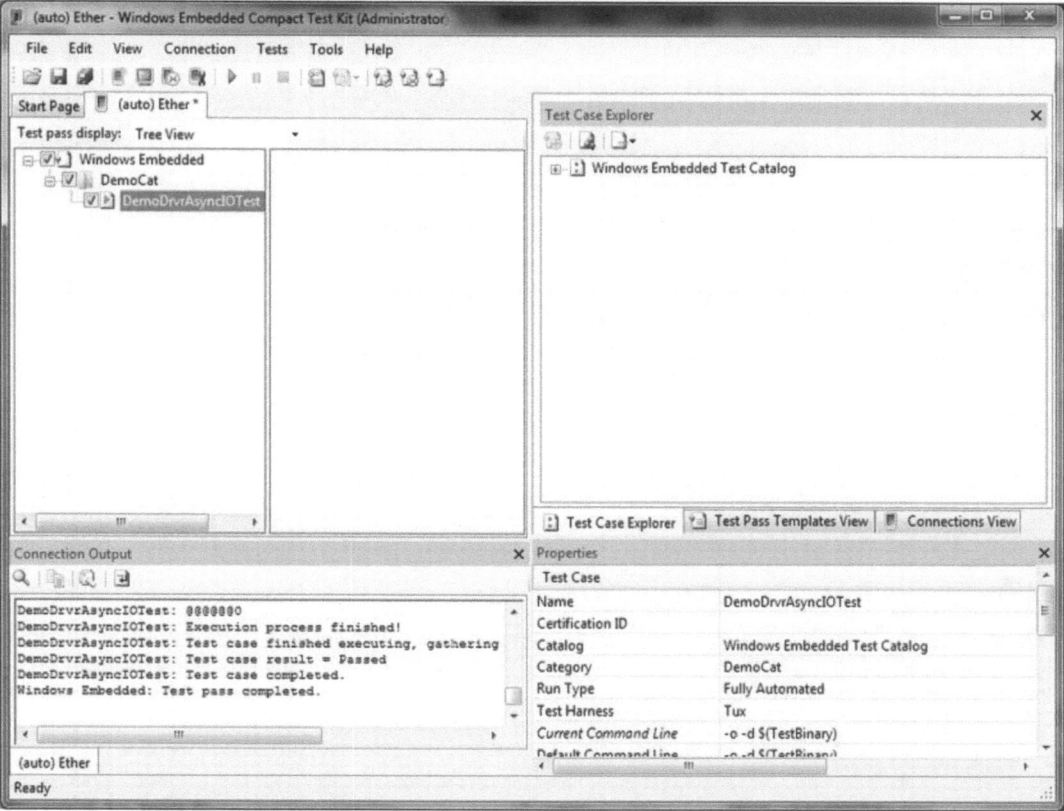

Figure 12-9. Connection output after test has been run

Viewing and Analyzing Test results

The brief results output gives an immediate indication if test passed or failed. If the test passed then most likely you would conclude the session. You may want to create more elaborate tests that automatically repeat the test so many times and maybe different parameters or retry the test a few times, which is really a very inefficient testing procedure. However if the test failed you certainly may wish to have a more detailed examination of the results. If you use the results tab as described in Figure 12-10, you will open the log file for the test and be able to scan the log for possible problems. Listing 12-2 demonstrates the test result log of the "DemoDrvrAsynIOTest" test.

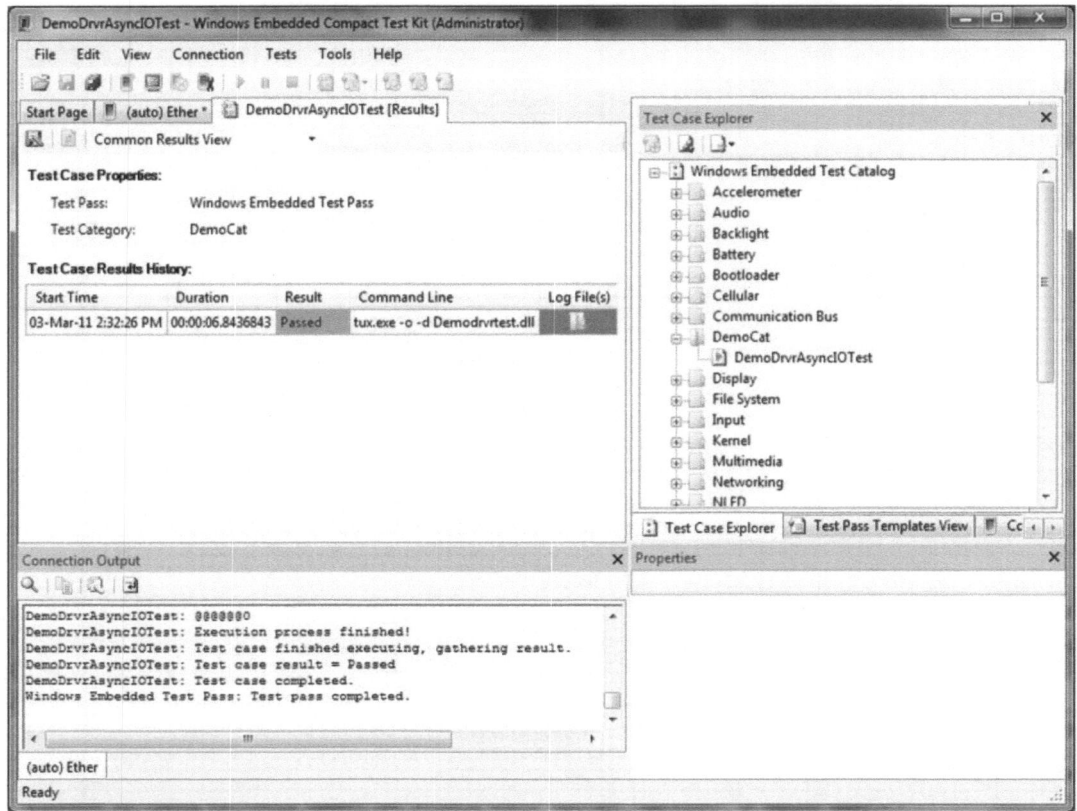

Figure 12-10. *Using the test case results history of a test to open the test log file*

The initial section of the log file provides memory and storage status information. The next section describes the test cases and results of each test. It is grouped under the TUX test DLL and separated by test case IDs. The next section provides memory and storage status information after the test has been conducted. This may very well indicate possible memory leaks, both in the test suite and/or the tested object. At the end is a section that describes the test suite summary.

Listing 12-2. *contents of results.log*

```
***
*** Memory Total:      330,600,448 bytes
*** Memory Used:        11,542,528 bytes
*** Memory Free:       319,057,920 bytes
***
*** Kernel Used:          471,040 bytes
*** Water Mark:            77,895 pages
***
*** Store Total:       133,971,968 bytes
*** Store Used:            999,424 bytes
```

```
*** Store Free:      132,972,544 bytes
*** ===================================================================

BEGIN GROUP: Demodrvrtest.DLL
   <TESTCASE ID=1>
   *** vvvvvvvvvvvvvvvvvvvvvvvvvvvvvvvvvvvvvvvvvvvvvvvvvvvvvvvvvvvvvvv
   *** TEST STARTING
   ***
   *** Test Name:      Demodrvr test
   *** Test ID:        1
   *** Library Path:   \release\demodrvrtest.dll
   *** Command Line:
   *** Kernel Mode:    No
   *** Random Seed:    5511
   *** Thread Count:   0
   *** vvvvvvvvvvvvvvvvvvvvvvvvvvvvvvvvvvvvvvvvvvvvvvvvvvvvvvvvvvvvvvv
   BEGIN TEST: "Demodrvr test", Threads=0, Seed=5511
      This test passed.
   END TEST: "Demodrvr test", PASSED, Time=0.050
   *** ^^^^^^^^^^^^^^^^^^^^^^^^^^^^^^^^^^^^^^^^^^^^^^^^^^^^^^^^^^^^^^^
   *** TEST COMPLETED
   ***
   *** Test Name:      Demodrvr test
   *** Test ID:        1
   *** Library Path:   \release\demodrvrtest.dll
   *** Command Line:
   *** Kernel Mode:    No
   *** Result:         Passed
   *** Random Seed:    5511
   *** Thread Count:   1
   *** Execution Time: 0:00:00.050
   *** ^^^^^^^^^^^^^^^^^^^^^^^^^^^^^^^^^^^^^^^^^^^^^^^^^^^^^^^^^^^^^^^

   </TESTCASE RESULT="PASSED">
END GROUP: Demodrvrtest.DLL
*** ===================================================================
*** MEMORY INFO
***
*** Memory Total:   330,600,448 bytes
*** Memory Used:     11,751,424 bytes
*** Memory Free:   318,849,024 bytes
***
*** Kernel Used:       471,040 bytes
*** Water Mark:         77,844 pages
***
*** Store Total:   133,971,968 bytes
*** Store Used:        999,424 bytes
*** Store Free:    132,972,544 bytes
*** ===================================================================

*** ===================================================================
*** SUITE SUMMARY
```

```
***
*** Passed:          1
*** Failed:          0
*** Skipped:         0
*** Aborted:         0
*** -------- ---------
*** Total:           1
***
*** Cumulative Test Execution Time: 0:00:00.050
*** Total Tux Suite Execution Time: 0:00:00.070
*** CPU Idle Time:                  0:00:00.000
*** ================================================================
</TESTGROUP>
@@@@@@0
```

Performance testing

Testing for performance is really evaluating a reference yardstick to which results are compared. If the comparison result is better or equal to this reference then the test passes; if it is inferior to the reference value then the test fails. The functionality test returns a pass result if the device drivers provides asynchronous I/O write request. Extending the test to measure the duration of this request and comparing it to a specific reference tick count provides the testers a performance test.

Adding a Second Test Procedure

Adding a second test procedure to Demodrvrtest TUX test DLL means that a second test procedure is added to the code. Listing 12-3 shows how test.cpp was modified to provide two tests and Listing 12-4 demonstrates how the second function was added to the TUX function table so that it can be registered by the *ShellProc* function. This implementation is a simplistic example and it uses the same helper function to perform the actual test and determine the results. This function adds tick count measurements and then compares the tick count duration to a specific reference tick count value to provide a pass or fail result, while the functionality test remains basically the same. An argument passed to this function determines which test to perform. The second test procedure is named *PerfomanceTestProc* and must adhere to the TESTPROCAPI declaration.

Listing 12-3. *Implementation of two test procedures (test.cpp)*

```cpp
#include "main.h"
#include "globals.h"
#include "..\SDK\DemodrvrSDK.h"

HANDLE g_hDevice;
#define WRITE_TEST_STRING_SIZE 65536
TCHAR szBuf[WRITE_TEST_STRING_SIZE];
```

```
BOOL TestAsynchWrite(int nTest)
{
    BOOL bRc = FALSE;
    DEVMGR_DEVICE_INFORMATION ddiDemo;
    TCHAR strDrvrName[5] = {'D', 'M', 'O', '*', 0};
    volatile OVERLAPPED ovlpd;
    HANDLE hCompltEvent = NULL;
    DWORD dwWaitRet = WAIT_FAILED, dwBytes = 0;
    DWORD dwOldTime = 0, dwTimeElapsed = 0;

    memset(&ddiDemo, 0, sizeof(DEVMGR_DEVICE_INFORMATION));
    ddiDemo.dwSize = sizeof(DEVMGR_DEVICE_INFORMATION);

    g_hDevice = FindFirstDevice(DeviceSearchByLegacyName,
                                &strDrvrName,
                                &ddiDemo);
    if (g_hDevice == INVALID_HANDLE_VALUE)
    {
        return bRc;
    }
    else
    {
        g_hDevice = CreateFile(L"DMO1:", 0, 0, NULL, 0, 0, NULL);
        if (g_hDevice == INVALID_HANDLE_VALUE)
        {
            return bRc;
        }
        bRc = TRUE;
    }
    // Create a completion event for IOControl IO operation
    ovlpd.hEvent = CreateEvent(NULL, TRUE, FALSE, NULL);
    if (!ovlpd.hEvent)
    {
        return FALSE;
    }
    for (int i = 0; i <  WRITE_TEST_STRING_SIZE; i++)
    {
        szBuf[i] = i;
    }

    memset((void*)&ovlpd, 0, sizeof(ovlpd));

    dwOldTime = GetTickCount();
    bRc = DeviceIoControl(g_hDevice,IOCTL_DEMODRVR_ASYNC_WRITE, szBuf,
                          WRITE_TEST_STRING_SIZE, NULL,
                          0,NULL,(LPOVERLAPPED)&ovlpd);
```

```
    while (!bRc)          // I/O is not done yet
    {
        bRc = GetOverlappedResult(g_hDevice,
                                  (LPOVERLAPPED)&ovlpd,
                                  &dwBytes, FALSE);
        if (!!bRc)
        {
            g_pKato->Log(LOG_COMMENT,
                        TEXT("Asynch IO pending and %d bytes written\r\n"),
ovlpd.InternalHigh);
        }
    }
    dwTimeElapsed = GetTickCount() - dwOldTime;

    CloseHandle(ovlpd.hEvent);
    CloseHandle(g_hDevice);
    switch (nTest)
    {
    case 1:
        if (dwBytes < WRITE_TEST_STRING_SIZE)
        {
            bRc = FALSE;
        }
        else if (dwBytes == WRITE_TEST_STRING_SIZE)
        {
            bRc = TRUE;
        }
        break;
    case 2:
        if (dwTimeElapsed > 250)
        {
            bRc = FALSE;
        }
        else
        {
            bRc = TRUE;
        }
        break;
    }
    return bRc;
}
```

```
/////////////////////////////////////////////////////////////////
// TestProc
//  Executes one test.
//
// Parameters:
//  uMsg                Message code.
//  tpParam             Additional message-dependent data.
//  lpFTE               Function table entry that generated this
//                          call.
// Return value:
//  TPR_PASS if the test passed, TPR_FAIL if the test fails, or
//  possibly other special conditions.

TESTPROCAPI TestProc(UINT uMsg, TPPARAM tpParam,
                      LPFUNCTION_TABLE_ENTRY lpFTE)
{
    INT TP_Status = TPR_FAIL;

      // The shell doesn't necessarily want us to execute the
    // test. Make sure first.
    if(uMsg != TPM_EXECUTE)
    {
        return TPR_NOT_HANDLED;
    }

    // TODO: Replace the following line with your own test code
    // here. Also,change the return value from TPR_SKIP to the
    // appropriate code.

    if(TestAsynchWrite(1))
    {
        TP_Status = TPR_PASS;
            g_pKato->Log(LOG_COMMENT, TEXT("This test passed."));
    }
      else
      {
            g_pKato->Log(LOG_COMMENT, TEXT("This test failed."));
      }

    return TP_Status;
}
```

```
///////////////////////////////////////////////////////////////////
// PerfomanceTestProc
//   Executes one test.
//
// Parameters:
//   uMsg              Message code.
//   tpParam           Additional message-dependent data.
//   lpFTE             Function table entry that generated this
//                      call.
//
// Return value:
//   TPR_PASS if the test passed, TPR_FAIL if the test fails, or
//   possibly other special conditions.

TESTPROCAPI PerfomanceTestProc(UINT uMsg, TPPARAM tpParam,
                                LPFUNCTION_TABLE_ENTRY lpFTE)
{
    INT TP_Status = TPR_FAIL;

      // The shell doesn't necessarily want us to execute the
    // test. Make sure first.
    if(uMsg != TPM_EXECUTE)
    {
        return TPR_NOT_HANDLED;
    }

    // TODO: Replace the following line with your own test code
    // here. Also,change the return value from TPR_SKIP to the
    // appropriate code.

    if(TestAsynchWrite(2))
    {
        TP_Status = TPR_PASS;
        g_pKato->Log(LOG_COMMENT, TEXT("This test passed."));
    }
    else
    {
        g_pKato->Log(LOG_COMMENT, TEXT("This test failed."));
    }

    return TP_Status;
}
```

Listing 12-4. *Updated TUX function table (ft.h)*

```
BEGIN_FTE
    FTH(0, "Demodrvr test cases")
    FTE(1,      "Demodrvr test", 1, 0, TestProc)
    FTE(2,      "Demodrvr perfomace test", 2, 0, PerfomanceTestProc)
END_FTE
```

Adding this new test to the test pass and running the tests is straightforward, as you can see in Figure 12-11 and viewing the results is just the same as before as you can see in Figure 12-12. Listing 12-5 shows the results log file for both tests.

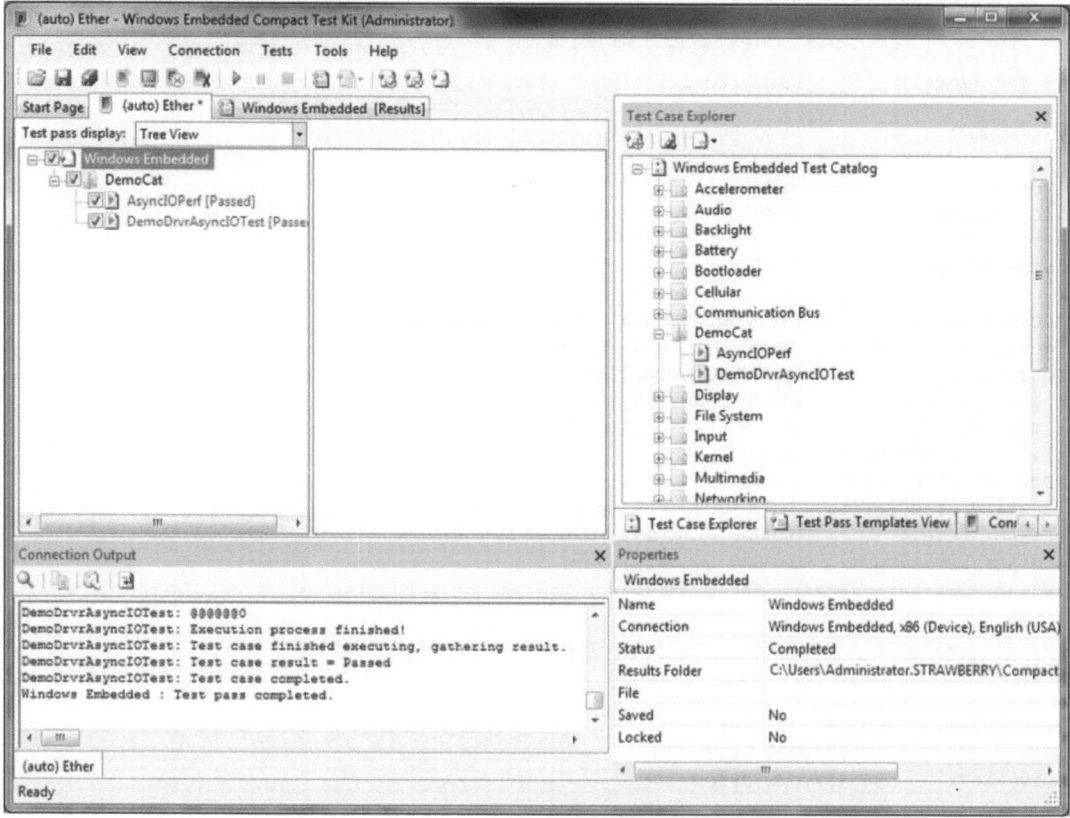

Figure 12-11. *Running the added test in the test pass*

Listing 12-5. *Results log file for both tests*

```
<TESTGROUP>

*** ================================================================
*** SUITE INFORMATION
***
*** Suite Name:          N/A (built on the fly)
*** Suite Description: N/A
*** Number of Tests:   2
*** ================================================================

*** ================================================================
*** SYSTEM INFORMATION
***
*** Date and Time:          03/08/2011 11:19 AM (Tuesday)
***
*** Device Name:            PC-009909210147
***
*** OS Version:             7.00
*** Build Number:           1486
*** Platform ID:            3 "Windows CE"
*** Version String:         ""
***
*** Processor Type:         0x000002AE (686) "Intel Pentium II"
*** Processor Architecture: 0x0000     (0) "Intel"
*** Page Size:              0x00001000 (4,096)
*** Minimum App Address:    0x00010000 (65,536)
*** Maximum App Address:    0x7FFFFFFF (2,147,483,647)
*** Active Processor Mask:  0x00000001
*** Number Of Processors:   1
*** Allocation Granularity: 0x00010000 (65,536)
*** Processor Level:        0x000F      (15)
*** Processor Revision:     0x000D      (13)
*** ================================================================

*** ================================================================
*** MEMORY INFO
***
*** Memory Total:   366,153,728 bytes
*** Memory Used:     11,771,904 bytes
*** Memory Free:    354,381,824 bytes
***
*** Kernel Used:        491,520 bytes
*** Water Mark:          86,484 pages
***
*** Store Total:    133,971,968 bytes
*** Store Used:         999,424 bytes
*** Store Free:     132,972,544 bytes
*** ================================================================
```

```
BEGIN GROUP: Demodrvrtest.DLL
    <TESTCASE ID=1>
    *** vvvvvvvvvvvvvvvvvvvvvvvvvvvvvvvvvvvvvvvvvvvvvvvvvvvvvvvvvvvvvvvvv
    *** TEST STARTING
    ***
    *** Test Name:      Demodrvr test
    *** Test ID:        1
    *** Library Path:   \release\demodrvrtest.dll
    *** Command Line:
    *** Kernel Mode:    No
    *** Random Seed:    26007
    *** Thread Count:   0
    *** vvvvvvvvvvvvvvvvvvvvvvvvvvvvvvvvvvvvvvvvvvvvvvvvvvvvvvvvvvvvvvvvv
    BEGIN TEST: "Demodrvr test", Threads=0, Seed=26007
       Asynch IO pending and 65536 bytes written
       This test passed.
    END TEST: "Demodrvr test", PASSED, Time=0.163
    *** ^^^^^^^^^^^^^^^^^^^^^^^^^^^^^^^^^^^^^^^^^^^^^^^^^^^^^^^^^^^^^^^^^
    *** TEST COMPLETED
    ***
    *** Test Name:      Demodrvr test
    *** Test ID:        1
    *** Library Path:   \release\demodrvrtest.dll
    *** Command Line:
    *** Kernel Mode:    No
    *** Result:         Passed
    *** Random Seed:    26007
    *** Thread Count:   1
    *** Execution Time: 0:00:00.163
    *** ^^^^^^^^^^^^^^^^^^^^^^^^^^^^^^^^^^^^^^^^^^^^^^^^^^^^^^^^^^^^^^^^^

    </TESTCASE RESULT="PASSED">
    <TESTCASE ID=2>
    *** vvvvvvvvvvvvvvvvvvvvvvvvvvvvvvvvvvvvvvvvvvvvvvvvvvvvvvvvvvvvvvvvv
    *** TEST STARTING
    ***
    *** Test Name:      Demodrvr perfomace test
    *** Test ID:        2
    *** Library Path:   \release\demodrvrtest.dll
    *** Command Line:
    *** Kernel Mode:    No
    *** Random Seed:    19430
    *** Thread Count:   0
    *** vvvvvvvvvvvvvvvvvvvvvvvvvvvvvvvvvvvvvvvvvvvvvvvvvvvvvvvvvvvvvvvvv
```

```
    BEGIN TEST: "Demodrvr perfomace test", Threads=0, Seed=19430
        Asynch IO pending and 65536 bytes written
        This test passed.
    END TEST: "Demodrvr perfomace test", PASSED, Time=0.139
    *** ^^^^^^^^^^^^^^^^^^^^^^^^^^^^^^^^^^^^^^^^^^^^^^^^^^^^^^^^^^^^^^^^^^^
    *** TEST COMPLETED
    ***
    *** Test Name:      Demodrvr perfomace test
    *** Test ID:        2
    *** Library Path:   \release\demodrvrtest.dll
    *** Command Line:
    *** Kernel Mode:    No
    *** Result:         Passed
    *** Random Seed:    19430
    *** Thread Count:   1
    *** Execution Time: 0:00:00.139
    *** ^^^^^^^^^^^^^^^^^^^^^^^^^^^^^^^^^^^^^^^^^^^^^^^^^^^^^^^^^^^^^^^^^^^

    </TESTCASE RESULT="PASSED">
    END GROUP: Demodrvrtest.DLL
    *** =================================================================
    *** MEMORY INFO
    ***
    *** Memory Total:   366,153,728 bytes
    *** Memory Used:     11,980,800 bytes
    *** Memory Free:    354,172,928 bytes
    ***
    *** Kernel Used:        491,520 bytes
    *** Water Mark:          86,451 pages
    ***
    *** Store Total:    133,971,968 bytes
    *** Store Used:       1,003,520 bytes
    *** Store Free:     132,968,448 bytes
    *** =================================================================


    *** =================================================================
    *** SUITE SUMMARY
    ***
    *** Passed:      2
    *** Failed:      0
    *** Skipped:     0
    *** Aborted:     0
    *** -------- ---------
    *** Total:       2
    ***
```

```
*** Cumulative Test Execution Time: 0:00:00.302
*** Total Tux Suite Execution Time: 0:00:00.329
*** CPU Idle Time:                   0:00:00.003
*** ================================================================
</TESTGROUP>
@@@@@@0
```

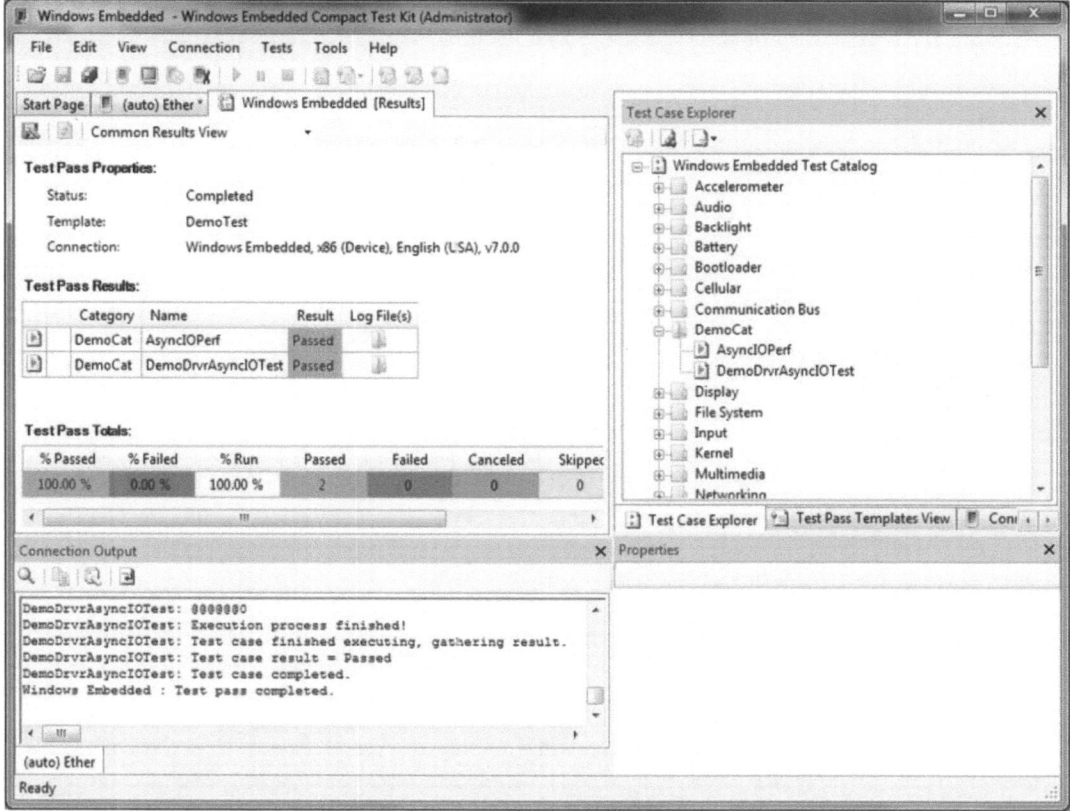

Figure 12-12. *Viewing the test results*

Chapter Summary

Testing is a crucial part of development that is now a required practice by most vendors. You cannot receive ISO 9000 certification if you do not test your device drivers and verify them. Microsoft requires tests to verify and certify device drivers for Windows Embedded Compact 7.

Testing device drivers in Windows Embedded Compact 7 is available through the TUX harness. You are not limited to using TUX but it is available and it combines well to operate with the Windows Embedded Compact Test Kit (CTK) server. It provides extensive capabilities and comprehensive graphic user interface. You develop test cases in TUX and test DLLs using a code skeleton DLL as a jumpstart for development. Analyzing results is aided by log files created by CTK for supplying more reliable and better performing device drivers.

Index

Numbers & Symbols

!demo command, 209

!module command, 202

A

access checking, 111–112

ACKNAK, 58–59

ActivateDeviceEx, 72, 85, 94–95, 102, 115, 121

Active key, 16–17, 74

AdvertiseInterface, 84–85

advertising interfaces, 85

ALD (Arbitration Loss Detected), 58

AllocPhysMem, 95, 122

Arbitration Loss Detected (ALD), 58

architectures, of embedded operating systems

microkernel, 2–3

monolithic, 3–4

overview, 1

Windows CE and I/O handling, 5–12

ASSERT, 195

ASSERTMSG, 195

B

BAD (Bus Error Detected), 59

BAT file, 32

batch files, command line build, 37–38

Board Support Packages (BSPs), 23, 47

BSP driver, 47

BSP Environment Variables, 33

BSP_NO Environment Variables, 33

BSPs (Board Support Packages), 23, 47

buckets, minidumps and, 225

Build Options node, 200

build system, 30–38

command line build, 32

environment variables, 33

Master Build Tool, 33–34

overview, 30–31

preparing development environment, 34–38

Build.exe tool, 34–35

command line build batch files, 37–38

DIRS files, 35

SOURCES file, 35–36

SOURCES.cmn file, 36–37

255